100 SMART Board™ LESSONS

TERMS AND CONDITIONS

IMPORTANT – PERMITTED USE AND WARNINGS – READ CAREFULLY BEFORE USING

Copyright in the Control software contained on this CD-ROM and in its accompanying material belongs to Scholastic Ltd. All rights reserved. © 2007, Scholastic Ltd.

Notebook™, including the Notebook™ artwork (contained within the Gallery), incorporated on this CD-ROM is the exclusive property of SMART Technologies Inc. Copyright © 2007 SMART Technologies Inc. All rights reserved. SMART Board is a registered trademark of SMART Technologies Inc in the UK.

The material contained on this CD-ROM may only be used in the context for which it was intended in *100 SMART Board™ Lessons*. Scholastic Ltd accepts no liability for any adaptation of Scholastic or SMART copyrighted material. School site use is permitted only within the school of the purchaser of the book and CD-ROM. Any further use of the material contravenes Scholastic Ltd's copyright and that of other rights holders.

Save for these purposes, or as expressly authorised in the accompanying materials, the software including artwork or images may not be copied, reproduced, used, sold, licensed, transferred, exchanged, hired, or exported in whole or in part or in any manner or form without the prior written consent of Scholastic Ltd. Any such unauthorised use or activities are prohibited and may give rise to civil liabilities and criminal prosecutions.

This CD-ROM has been tested for viruses at all stages of its production. However, we recommend that you run virus-checking software on your computer systems at all times. Scholastic Ltd cannot accept any responsibility for any loss, disruption or damage to your data or your computer system that may occur as a result of using either the CD-ROM, software, website links or the data held on it.

Due to the nature of the web, the publisher cannot guarantee the content or links of any websites referred to. It is the responsibility of the user to assess the suitability of websites.

IF YOU ACCEPT THE ABOVE CONDITIONS YOU MAY PROCEED TO USE THIS CD-ROM.

Minimum specification:
- PC/Mac with a CD-ROM drive and at least 128 MB RAM
- Microsoft Office 2000 or higher
- Adobe® Reader®
- Interactive whiteboard
- Notebook™ software
- Facilities for printing and sound (optional)

PC:
- Pentium II 450 MHz processor
- Microsoft Windows 2000 SP4 or higher

Mac:
- 700 MHz processor (1 GHz or faster recommended)
- Mac OS X.4 or higher

For all technical support queries, please phone Scholastic Customer Services on 0845 6039091.

YEAR 4

Scottish Primary 5

CREDITS

Authors
Jon Audain (foundation subjects and science), Rhona Dick (history), Eileen Jones (English), Ann Montague-Smith (mathematics), Alan Rodgers and Angella Streluk (geography)

Development Editor
Niamh O'Carroll

Editor
Nicola Morgan

Assistant Editors
Kim Vernon and Margaret Eaton

Illustrators
Jim Peacock (book and Notebook file illustrations), William Gray, Theresa Tibbetts (additional Notebook file illustrations)

Series Designer
Joy Monkhouse

Designers
Rebecca Male, Allison Parry, Andrea Lewis and Melissa Leeke

CD-ROM developed in association with
Q & D Multimedia

ACKNOWLEDGEMENTS

SMART Board™ and Notebook™ are registered trademarks of SMART Technologies Inc in Canada, the United States, the European Union and other countries.

Microsoft Office, Word and Excel are either registered trademarks or trademarks of Microsoft Corporation in the United States and/or other countries.

With grateful thanks for advice, help and expertise to Angus McGarry (Trainer) and Fiona Ford (Education Development Consultant) at Steljes Ltd.

All Flash activities designed and developed by Q & D Multimedia.

Interactive Teaching Programs (developed by the Primary National Strategy) © Crown copyright.

With thanks to Mike Longden for the use of various photographs.

The publishers gratefully acknowledge:
The Chicken House for the use of the publicity blurb for *The Conch-Bearer* by Chitra Banerjee Divakaruni from the website www.doublecluck.com © 2005, The Chicken House.
Scholastic Children's Books for the use of publicity blurbs for *Buster Bayliss: Night of the Living Veg* by Philip Reeve (2005, Scholastic) and *The Stunning Science of Everything* by Nick Arnold (2005, Scholastic).

Every effort has been made to trace copyright holders for the works reproduced in this book, and the publishers apologise for any inadvertent omissions.

Designed using Adobe InDesign.

Made with Macromedia is a trademark of Macromedia, Inc. Director ® Copyright © 1984-2000 Macromedia, Inc.

Published by Scholastic Ltd
Villiers House
Clarendon Avenue
Leamington Spa
Warwickshire CV32 5PR
www.scholastic.co.uk

Printed by Bell and Bain Ltd, Glasgow

123456789   7890123456

Text © 2007 Jon Audain (foundation subjects and science), Rhona Dick (history), Eileen Jones (English), Ann Montague-Smith (mathematics), Alan Rodgers and Angella Streluk (geography)

© 2007 Scholastic Ltd

British Library Cataloguing-in-Publication Data
A catalogue record for this book is available from the British Library.

ISBN 978-0439-94540-0

The rights of the authors of this work have been asserted by them in accordance with the Copyright, Designs and Patents Act 1988.

Extracts from the Primary National Strategy's *Primary Framework for literacy and mathematics* (2006) www.standards.dfes.gov.uk/primaryframework © Crown copyright. Reproduced under the terms of the Click Use Licence.

Extracts from The National Literacy Strategy and The National Numeracy Strategy © Crown copyright. Material from the National Curriculum © The Queen's Printer and Controller of HMSO. Reproduced under the terms of HMSO Guidance Note 8.

Extracts from the QCA Scheme of Work © Qualifications and Curriculum Authority.

All rights reserved. This book is sold subject to the condition that it shall not, by way of trade or otherwise, be lent, hired out or otherwise circulated without the publisher's prior consent in any form of binding or cover other than that in which it is published and without a similar condition, including this condition, being imposed upon the subsequent purchaser.

No part of this publication may be reproduced, stored in a retrieval system, or transmitted, in any form or by any means, electronic, mechanical, photocopying, recording or otherwise, other than for the purposes described in the lessons in this book, without the prior permission of the publisher. This book remains copyright, although permission is granted to copy pages where indicated for classroom distribution and use only in the school which has purchased the book, or by the teacher who has purchased the book, and in accordance with the CLA licensing agreement. Photocopying permission is given only for purchasers and not for borrowers of books from any lending service.

Due to the nature of the web, the publisher cannot guarantee the content or links of any of the websites referred to in this book. It is the responsibility of the reader to assess the suitability of websites. Ensure you read and abide by the terms and conditions of websites when you use material from website links.

CONTENTS

4 INTRODUCTION
6 HOW TO USE THE CD-ROM

CHAPTER 1: ENGLISH

8 OVERVIEW GRID
11 LESSONS
41 PHOTOCOPIABLES

CHAPTER 2: MATHEMATICS

56 OVERVIEW GRID
59 LESSONS
89 PHOTOCOPIABLES

CHAPTER 3: SCIENCE

105 OVERVIEW GRID
108 LESSONS
128 PHOTOCOPIABLES

CHAPTER 4: FOUNDATION

138 OVERVIEW GRID
141 LESSONS
141 History
145 Geography
149 Design and technology
152 Art and design
156 Music
159 Religious education
161 PHOTOCOPIABLES

170 GENERAL PHOTOCOPIABLES
172 USING YOUR SMART BOARD™
174 USING NOTEBOOK™ SOFTWARE
175 TOOLS GLOSSARY

100 SMART Board™ LESSONS • YEAR 4

Introduction

100 SMART BOARD™ LESSONS

Interactive whiteboards are fast becoming the must-have resource in today's classroom as they allow teachers to facilitate children's learning in ways that were inconceivable a few years ago. The appropriate use of interactive whiteboards, whether used daily in the classroom or once a week in the ICT suite, will encourage active participation in lessons and should increase learners' determination to succeed. Interactive whiteboards make it easier for teachers to bring subjects across the curriculum to life in new and exciting ways.

'There is a whiteboard revolution in UK schools.'
(Primary National Strategy)

What can an interactive whiteboard offer?
For the **teacher**, an interactive whiteboard offers the same facilities as an ordinary whiteboard, such as drawing, writing and erasing. However, the interactive whiteboard also offers many other possibilities to:
- save any work created during a lesson
- prepare as many pages as necessary
- display any page within the Notebook™ file to review teaching and learning
- add scanned examples of the children's work to a Notebook file
- change colours of shapes and backgrounds instantly
- use simple templates and grids
- link Notebook files to spreadsheets, websites and presentations.

Using an interactive whiteboard in the simple ways outlined above can enrich teaching and learning in a classroom, but that is only the beginning of the whiteboard's potential to educate and inspire. a

For the **learner**, the interactive whiteboard provides the opportunity to share learning experiences, as lessons can be delivered with sound, still and moving images, and websites. Interactive whiteboards can be used to cater for the needs of all learning styles:
- kinaesthetic learners benefit from being able to physically manipulate images
- visual learners benefit from being able to watch videos, look at photographs and see images being manipulated
- auditory learners benefit from being able to access audio resources such as voice recordings and sound effects.

With a little preparation all of these resource types could be integrated in one lesson, a feat that would have been almost impossible before the advent of the interactive whiteboard!

Access to an interactive whiteboard
In schools where learners have limited access to an interactive whiteboard the teacher must carefully plan lessons in which the children will derive most benefit from using it. As teachers become familiar with the whiteboard they will learn when to use it and, importantly, when not to use it!

Where permanent access to an interactive whiteboard is available, it is important that the teacher plans the use of the board effectively. It should be used only in ways that will enhance or extend teaching and learning. Children still need to gain practical first-hand experience of many things. Some experiences cannot be recreated on an interactive whiteboard but others cannot be had without it. *100 SMART Board™ Lessons* offers both teachers and learners the most accessible and creative uses of this most valuable resource.

About the series
100 SMART Board™ Lessons is designed to reflect best practice in using interactive whiteboards. It is also designed to support all teachers in using this valuable tool by providing lessons and other resources that can be used on a whiteboard with little or no preparation. These inspirational lessons cover all National Curriculum subjects. They are perfect for all levels of experience and are an essential for any SMART Board users.

Safety note: Avoid looking directly at the projector beam as it is potentially damaging to eye s, and never leave the children unsupervised when using the interactive whiteboard.

Introduction

About the book
This book is divided into four chapters. Each chapter contains lessons and photocopiable activity sheets covering:
- English
- Mathematics
- Science
- Foundation subjects.

At the beginning of each chapter a **planning grid** identifies the title, the objectives covered and any relevant cross-curricular links in each lesson. Objectives are taken from the relevant Primary National Strategy, National Curriculum Programmes of Study (PoS), or the QCA Schemes of Work. All of the lessons should therefore fit into your existing medium-term plans. The planning grids have been provided in Microsoft Word format on the CD-ROM for this purpose.

Lesson plans
The lessons have a consistent structure with a starter activity, activities for shared and independent work, and a plenary to round up the teaching and learning and identify any assessment opportunities. Crucially, each lesson plan identifies resources required (including photocopiable activity sheets P and Notebook files that are provided on the CD-ROM). Also highlighted are the whiteboard tools that could be used in the lesson.

Photocopiable activity sheets at the end of each chapter support the lessons. These sheets provide opportunities for group or individual work to be completed away from the board, but link to the context of the whiteboard lesson. They also provide opportunities for whole-class plenary sessions in which children discuss and present their work.

Two general record sheets are provided on pages 170 and 171. These are intended to support the teacher in recording ways in which the interactive whiteboard is used, and where and how interactive resources can be integrated into a lesson.

What's on the CD-ROM?
The accompanying CD-ROM provides an extensive bank of Notebook files. These support, and are supported by, the lessons in this book. As well as texts and images, a selection of Notebook files include the following types of files:

- **Embedded Microsoft Office files:** These include Microsoft Word and Excel documents. The embedded files are launched from the Notebook file and will open in their native Microsoft application.
- **Embedded interactive files:** These include specially commissioned interactive files as well as Interactive Teaching Programs (ITPs) from the Primary National Strategy.
- **Printable PDF versions** of the photocopiable activity and record sheets, as well as the answers to the mathematics activities, are also provided on the CD-ROM.
- **'Build your own' file:** This contains a blank Notebook page with a bank of selected images and interactive tools from the Gallery, as well as specially commissioned images. It is supported by lesson plans in the book to help you to build your own Notebook files.

Introduction

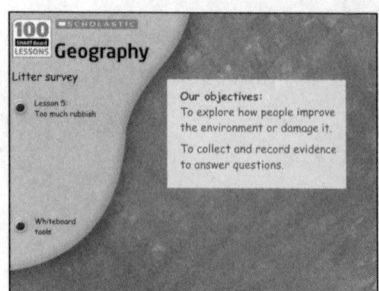
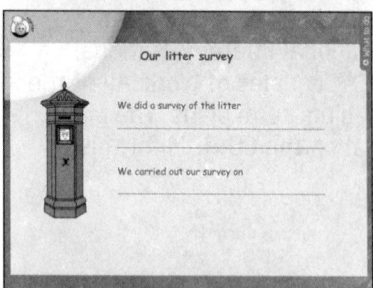

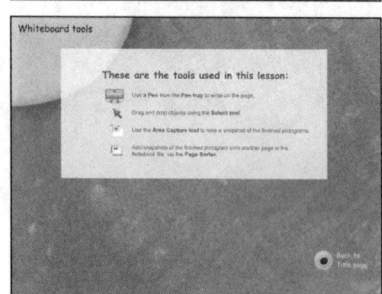

The Notebook files
All of the Notebook files have a consistent structure as follows:

Title and objectives page
Use this page to highlight the focus of the lesson. You might also wish to refer to this page at certain times throughout the lesson or at the end of the lesson to assess whether the learning objective was achieved.

Starter activity
This sets the context to the lesson and usually provides some key questions or learning points that will be addressed through the main activities.

Main activities
These activities offer independent, collaborative group, or whole-class work. The activities draw on the full scope of Notebook software and the associated tools, as well as the SMART Board tools.

What to do boxes are also included in many of the prepared Notebook files. These appear as tabs in the top right-hand corner of the screen. To access these notes, simply pull out the tabs to reveal planning information, additional support and key learning points.

Plenary
A whole-class activity or summary page is designed to review work done both at the board and away from the board. In many lessons, children are encouraged to present their work.

Whiteboard tools page
The whiteboard tools page gives a reminder of the tools used in the lesson and provides instructions on how they are used.

HOW TO USE THE CD-ROM

Setting up your screen for optimal use
It is best to view the Notebook pages at a screen display setting of 1280 × 1024 pixels. To alter the screen display, select Settings, then Control Panel from the Start menu. Next, double-click on the Display icon and then click on the Settings tab. Finally, adjust the Screen area scroll bar to 1280 × 1024 pixels. Click on OK.

If you prefer to use a screen display setting of 800 × 600 pixels, ensure that your Notebook view is set to 'Page Width'. To alter the view, launch Notebook and click on View. Go to Zoom and select the 'Page Width' setting. If you use a screen display setting of 800 x 600 pixels, text in the prepared Notebook files may appear larger when you edit it on screen.

Viewing the printable resources
Adobe® Reader® is required to view the printable resources. All the printable resources are PDF files.

Visit the Adobe® website at **www.adobe.com** to download the latest version of Adobe® Reader®.

Introduction

Getting started

The program should run automatically when you insert the CD-ROM into your CD drive. If it does not, use My Computer to browse to the contents of the CD-ROM and click on the *100 SMART Board™ Lessons* icon.

When the program starts, you are invited to register the product either online or using a PDF registration form. You also have the option to register later. If you select this option, you will be taken, via the Credits screen, to the Main menu.

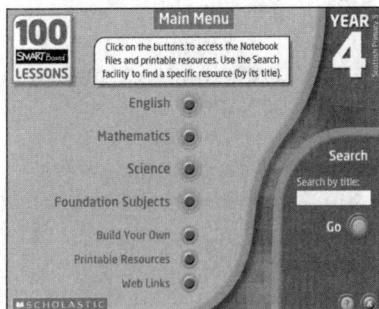

Main menu

The Main menu divides the Notebook files by subject: English, mathematics, science and foundation subjects. Clicking on the appropriate blue button for any of these options will take you to a separate Subject menu (see below for further information). The 'Build your own' file is also accessed through the Main menu (see below). The activity sheets are provided in separate menus. To access these resources, click on Printable resources.

Individual Notebook files or pages can be located using the search facility by keying in words (or part words) from the resource titles in the Search box. Press Go to begin the search. This will bring up a list of the titles that match your search.

The Web Links button takes you to a list of useful web addresses. A help button is included on all menu screens. The Help notes on the CD-ROM provide a range of general background information and technical support for all users.

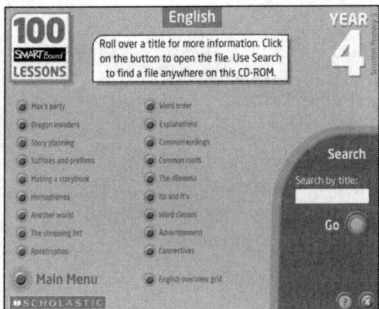

Subject menu

Each Subject menu provides all of the prepared Notebook files for each chapter of the book. Roll over each Notebook file title to reveal a brief description of the contents in a text box at the top of the menu screen; clicking on the blue button will open the Notebook file. Click on Main menu to return to the Main menu screen.

'Build your own' file

Click on this button to open a blank Notebook page and a collection of Gallery objects, which will be saved automatically into the My Content folder in the Gallery. You only need to click on this button the first time you wish to access the 'Build your own' file, as the Gallery objects will remain in the My Content folder on the computer on which the file was opened. To use the facility again, simply open a blank Notebook page and access the images and interactive resources from the same folder under My Content. If you are using the CD-ROM on a different computer you will need to click on the 'Build your own' button again.

Printable resources

The printable PDF activity sheets are also divided by chapter. Click on the subject to find all the activity sheets related to that subject/chapter. The answers to Chapter 2, mathematics, are also provided.

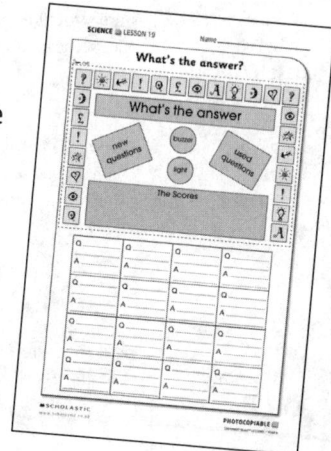

To alternate between the menus on the CD-ROM and other open applications, hold down the Alt key and press the Tab key to switch to the desired application.

English ⬜ Chapter 1

English

The 30 lessons in this chapter match the objectives in the Primary National Strategy's *Primary Framework for literacy*. These objectives are listed in the curriculum grid below, along with the corresponding objectives from the medium-term planning in the National Literacy Strategy. The curriculum grids in this book are also provided on the accompanying CD-ROM, in editable format, to enable you to integrate the lessons into your planning.

The interactive whiteboard offers pace and visual excitement. Words can be made to appear or disappear; text can be manipulated; the children can see sentences being constructed and watch paragraphs and stories emerging.

Be generous with the wonderful powers of the whiteboard and involve the children as much as possible in operating the board's tools. This will bring special benefits to children with dominant visual and kinaesthetic styles of learning. The interactive whiteboard is a stimulating resource for the teaching of English. Its role should always be to support the interaction between you, the children and literacy.

Lesson title	PNS objectives	NLS objectives	Expected prior knowledge	Cross-curricular links
Lesson 1: Verbs and tense	Sentence structure and punctuation Word structure and spelling • Know and apply common spelling rules.	S2 To investigate verb tenses (past, present and future). W7 To spell regular verb endings.	• Know that verbs can be in the present or past.	History QCA Unit 18 'What was it like to live here in the past?'
Lesson 2: Irregular tense changes	Sentence structure and punctuation Word structure and spelling • Know and apply common spelling rules.	W8 To spell irregular tense changes.	• Know that verbs can change spelling.	ICT QCA Unit 4A 'Writing for different audiences'
Lesson 3: Character sketches	Creating and shaping texts • Use characterisation to engage readers' interest.	T11 Write character sketches, focusing on small details to evoke sympathy or dislike. S3 Identify the use of powerful verbs.	• Experience of thinking about fictional characters.	History QCA Unit 6 'Why have people invaded and settled in Britain in the past?'
Lesson 4: Adverbs	Sentence structure and punctuation • Clarify meaning and point of view by using varied sentence structure.	S4 To identify adverbs and understand their functions in sentences.	• Know the function of verbs.	Citizenship QCA Unit 1 'Taking part – developing skills of communication and participation'
Lesson 5: Story planning	Text structure and organisation • Organise text into paragraphs to distinguish between different information, events or processes.	T4 To explore narrative order: identify and map out the main stages of the story. T15 To use paragraphs in story writing to organise and sequence the narrative.	• Know that text is divided into paragraphs.	History QCA Unit 9 'What was it like for children in the Second World War?'
Lesson 6: Collecting and classifying words	Word structure and spelling • Know and apply common spelling rules.	W9 To recognise and spell suffixes.	• Know that word beginnings may be grouped.	History QCA Unit 6A 'Why have people invaded and settled in Britain in the past?'
Lesson 7: Written instructions	Text structure and organisation • Organise text to distinguish between different information, events or processes.	T22 To identify features of instructional texts. T26 To improve the cohesion of written instructions and directions through the use of link phrases and organisational devices.	• Know the term *instruction*.	Design and technology QCA Unit 4B 'Storybooks – To design and make a book that has moving parts for a particular purpose' ICT QCA Unit 4A 'Writing for different audiences'
Lesson 8: Alphabetical order	Word structure and spelling • Know and apply common spelling rules.	W12 To use 3rd and 4th place letters to locate and sequence words in alphabetical order.	• Know that lists are often in alphabetical order.	Speaking and listening Objective 39: Group discussion and interaction: To take different roles in groups.

English — Chapter 1

Lesson title	PNS objectives	NLS objectives	Expected prior knowledge	Cross-curricular links
Lesson 9: Newspaper stories	**Understanding and interpreting texts** **Creating and shaping texts** • Summarise and shape material and ideas from different sources to write convincing and informative non-narrative texts.	**T21** To predict newspaper stories from the evidence of headlines, making notes and then checking against the original. **T24** To write newspaper style reports.	• Familiarity with some IT texts.	**Citizenship** QCA Unit 11 'In the media – what's the news?'
Lesson 10: Commas	**Sentence structure and punctuation** • Use commas to mark clauses.	**S5** To practise using commas within sentences; link to work on editing and revising own writing. **T24** To write newspaper style reports, using IT to draft and lay out reports.	• Be aware of common use of a comma.	**Citizenship** QCA Unit 11 'In the media – what's the news?'
Lesson 11: Homophones	**Word structure and spelling** • Distinguish the spelling and meaning of common homophones.	**W6** To distinguish between the spelling and meanings of common homophones.	• Know that different words may sound the same.	**History** QCA Unit 6A 'Why have people invaded and settled in Britain in the past?'
Lesson 12: Adjectives	**Creating and shaping texts** • Show imagination through the language used to create emphasis, humour, atmosphere or suspense.	**S1** To revise and extend work on adjectives from Y3. **T10** To develop use of settings in own writing, making use of work on adjectives and figurative language to describe settings effectively.	• Know that adjectives describe nouns.	**Speaking and listening** Objective 41: To respond appropriately to the contributions of others in the light of alternative viewpoints.
Lesson 13: Spelling patterns	**Word structure and spelling** • Know and apply common spelling rules.	**W5** To investigate what happens to words ending in -f when suffixes are added.	• Know the term *suffix*.	**Speaking and listening** Objective 41: To respond appropriately to the contribution of others in the light of alternative viewpoints.
Lesson 14: Expressive writing	**Creating and shaping texts** • Show imagination through the language used to create emphasis, humour, atmosphere or suspense.	**T13** To write own examples of descriptive, expressive language based on those read. Link to work on adjectives and similes.	• Knowledge of adjectives.	**Speaking and listening** Objective 44: To tell stories using voice effectively.
Lesson 15: Apostrophes	**Sentence structure and punctuation** • Use the apostrophe for possession.	**S2** To use the apostrophe accurately to mark possession. **T11** To write poetry based on the structure and/or style of poems read.	• Know that apostrophes can mark possession.	**Science** QCA Unit 4C 'Keeping warm'
Lesson 16: Word order	**Sentence structure and punctuation** • Clarify meaning and point of view by using varied sentence structure (phrases, clauses and adverbials). • Use commas to mark clauses.	**S3** To understand the significance of word order. **S4** To recognise how commas, connectives and full stops are used to join and separate clauses.	• Know that punctuation aids comprehension.	**History** QCA Unit 7 'Why did Henry VIII marry six times?'
Lesson 17: Explanations	**Text structure and organisation** • Organise texts into paragraphs to distinguish between different information, events or processes. **Creating and shaping texts**	**T19** To identify how and why paragraphs are used to organise and sequence information. **T20** To identify from the examples the key features of explanatory texts. **T25** To write explanations of a process, using conventions identified through reading.	• Experience of non-fiction texts.	**Science** QCA Unit 4D 'Solids, liquids and how they can be separated'
Lesson 18: Common endings	**Word structure and spelling** • Know and apply common spelling rules.	**W6** To spell words with the common endings: *-ight*, and so on.	• Know that spelling does not follow one set of rules.	**Citizenship** QCA Unit 9 'Respect for property'

English — Chapter 1

Lesson title	PNS objectives	NLS objectives	Expected prior knowledge	Cross-curricular links
Lesson 19: Collecting and presenting information	**Understanding and interpreting texts** • Identify and summarise evidence from a text. • Use knowledge of different organisational features of texts to find information effectively.	**T21** To make short notes, for example, by abbreviating ideas, selecting key words, listing or in diagrammatic form.	• Know that information can be abbreviated.	**Science** QCA Unit 4D 'Solids, liquids and how they can be separated'
Lesson 20: Prefixes	**Word structure and spelling** • Know and apply common spelling rules.	**W7** To recognise and spell the prefixes: *-al*, and so on.	• Know the order of the alphabet.	**History** QCA Unit 7 'Why did Henry VIII marry six times?'; Unit 8 'What were the differences between the lives of rich and poor people in Tudor times?'
Lesson 21: Writing poetry	**Creating and shaping texts** • Choose and combine words, images and other features for particular effects.	**T15** To produce polished poetry through revision. **S1** To understand that some words can be changed in particular ways and others cannot.	• Know that editing and rewriting are important. • Know that words belong to different classes.	**Speaking and listening** Objective 44: Identifying the ways presentational features contribute to message and impact.
Lesson 22: Word roots	**Understanding and interpreting texts** • Use knowledge of word structures and origins to develop their understanding of word meanings.	**W7** Collect/classify words with common roots.	• Knowledge of root words.	**History** QCA Unit 6A 'Why have people invaded and settled in Britain in the past?'
Lesson 23: Punctuation	**Sentence structure and punctuation** • Clarify meaning and point of view by using varied sentence structure.	**S2** To identify the common punctuation marks.	• Awareness of punctuation marks in text.	**History** QCA Unit 6A 'Why have people invaded and settled in Britain in the past?'
Lesson 24: Summaries	**Creating and shaping texts** • Choose and combine words, images and other features for particular effects.	**T20** To summarise a sentence or paragraph by identifying the most important elements and rewording them in a limited number of words.	• Be aware that not every word is of equal importance.	**History** QCA Unit 6A 'Why have people invaded and settled in Britain in the past?'
Lesson 25: Its and it's	**Sentence structure and punctuation** • Use the apostrophe for possession.	**W10** To distinguish the two forms: *its* and *it's*.	• Words may sound the same but be spelled and used differently.	**Science** QCA Unit 4B 'Habitats'
Lesson 26: Word endings and classes	**Word structure and spelling** • Know and apply common spelling rules.	**S1** To understand that some words can be changed in particular ways and others cannot.	• Be aware that words are divided into classes.	**Speaking and listening** Objective 44: To tell stories using voice effectively.
Lesson 27: Spelling compound words	**Word structure and spelling** • Use knowledge of phonics, morphology and etymology to spell new and unfamiliar words.	**W11** To investigate compound words and recognise that they can aid spelling even when pronunciation obscures it.	• Be aware that pronunciation does not always help spelling.	**History** QCA Unit 6A 'Why have people invaded and settled in Britain in the past?'
Lesson 28: Sentence types	**Sentence structure and punctuation** • Clarify meaning and point of view by using varied sentence structure.	**S3** To understand how the grammar of a sentence alters when the sentence type is altered.	• Not all sentences are the same type.	**History** QCA Unit 18 'What was it like to live here in the past?'
Lesson 29: Advertisements	**Creating and shaping texts** • Choose and combine words, images and other features for particular effects.	**T19** To evaluate advertisements for their impact, appeal and honesty, focusing in particular on how information about the product is presented. **T25** To design an advertisement.	• Experience of seeing advertisements.	**Science** QCA Unit 4C 'Keeping warm'
Lesson 30: Connectives	**Sentence structure and punctuation** • Clarify meaning and point of view by using varied sentence structure (phrases, clauses and adverbials).	**S4** The use of connectives to structure an argument.	• Know the term *connective*.	**Citizenship** QCA Unit 11 'In the media – what's the news?'

English Lesson 1

Learning objectives
PNS: Sentence structure and punctuation
PNS: Word structure and spelling
- Know and apply common spelling rules.

Resources
'Max's party' Notebook file; exercise books and pens.

Links to other subjects
History
QCA Unit 18 'What was it like to live here in the past?'
- Link the independent writing to this unit. Invite an elderly local resident to talk about local school life when he or she was a child.

Verbs and tense

Starter
Revise the term *verb*. Define a verb as a *doing* or *being* word. It can express an action, a happening, a process or a state. Remind the children that:
- every sentence needs a verb
- a verb can be a chain of words.

Open the Notebook file 'Max's party' and look at the text on page 2. Together, read the passage, identify the verbs and highlight them.

Whole-class shared work
- Go to page 3. The three hyperlinked football buttons lead to the invitation to Max's party, the voiceover Max wrote to go with a video of the day and the entry Max wrote in his diary at the end of the day.
- Press the football button next to *The invitation*. Read it and together identify the verbs. Ask volunteers to highlight them. Reveal the correct answers by pressing the button.
- Move to *Max's voiceover*. Press on the text to hear Max's voiceover. Repeat the process, highlighting the verbs first, and then checking the answers.
- For *Max's diary*, ask the children to drag the verbs into the text before pressing the button to check that they are correct.
- Challenge the children to explain the difference between the verbs in each passage. (They are in different tenses.)
- Revise the word *tense*: the tense of a verb gives information about when the action took place. Identify the tenses of these three pages of information: present, past and future.
- Investigate how the tenses are formed. Focus on the verb endings in each text. Point out the frequent use of *-s, -ing* and *-ed*. Explain that these are some of the regular verb endings. If required, use page 7 to write notes about verb tenses and the different verb endings.
- Look again at the paragraph on page 2. Encourage the children to say what tense has been used here. (The present tense.)

Independent work
- Ask the children to write two more paragraphs in their exercise books to continue the text on page 2. One paragraph should be about education in the past, the other about education in the future.
- The children should use the verbs that they highlighted on page 2, but change their tense.
- Supply opening words for both paragraphs:
  - *When our great-grandparents were children...*
  - *In the future...*
- Provide a framework for the sentences for less confident learners, with a box of verbs for each paragraph.
- As an extra challenge, ask the children to convert other paragraphs in the past tense into the present tense.

Plenary
- Invite the children to share their work. Write examples of their sentences on page 8. Discuss the verb forms used.
- Look for examples of the usual spelling patterns: *-s, -ed* and *-ing*. Identify instances of verbs doubling a consonant (for example, *chats* becomes *chatted*).

Whiteboard tools
 Pen tray
 Highlighter pen
 Select tool
 On-screen Keyboard

English — Lesson 2

Irregular tense changes

Learning objectives
PNS: Sentence structure and punctuation
PNS: Word structure and spelling
- Know and apply common spelling rules.

Resources
Photocopiable page 41 'Now and then' for each child; individual whiteboards and pens. Prepared Notebook file with the following sentences written in separate text boxes:
Tom blinked fast.
Harry shuts his eyes.
Dad went white.
Mum wrote an email.
The neighbours fled.
The baby wept.
The postman runs.
Shaun reads a story.
Stacey raced to the rescue.

Links to other subjects
ICT
QCA Unit 4A 'Writing for different audiences'
- Provide opportunities for the children to use computers to make their poems into appealing texts for a class poetry anthology.

Whiteboard tools
Use the On-screen Keyboard to enter text or use the Pen from the Pen tray. To upload scanned images, select Insert, then Picture File, and browse to where you have saved the image.

 Pen tray

 Highlighter pen

 Select tool

 On-screen Keyboard

Starter
Open your prepared Notebook file (see Resources). Ask the children to identify the verbs and challenge them to sort the sentences into two groups. Give thinking time before you ask a volunteer to demonstrate this on the whiteboard, creating:
- a group in the present tense
- a group in the past tense.

Focus on the second group. Ask: *How can this group be divided again into two groups?* Encourage the children to look carefully at the spelling and construction of the past tense verbs. Highlight the different endings in different colours. Finally, create two groups:
- sentences with verbs ending in *-ed*
- sentences with different verbs.

Whole-class shared work
- Explain that the regular ending for past tense verbs is *-ed*. Irregular past forms show other changes, usually to the medial vowel (*blow* becomes *blew*; *rise* becomes *rose*).
- Point out that the children probably make many of these tense changes without thinking. Play an oral game of 'boasting' to prove this. Make a boastful statement about yourself in the present: *I begin karate this week.*
- Ask the children to better this, making the same boast about themselves in the past: *I began karate last week.*
- Record the tense changes on the whiteboard. Look for verbs that can be grouped together, and group them under headings. For example: *-ing* becomes *-ang* (*sing* – sang, *ring* – rang); *-ind* becomes *-ound* (*find* – found, *wind* – wound); *-ow* becomes *-ew* (*blow* –blew); *-ell* becomes *-old* (*sell* – sold).
- Allow the children time to play a further short session of 'boasting' with a partner. Ask them to keep a record of their verb changes on individual whiteboards.
- Share results by letting the children add examples to the headings on the whiteboard. Create new headings if verbs can be grouped together.
- Point out that some past tenses follow no set pattern. Demonstrate how to use a dictionary to check past tenses.

Independent work
- Ask the children to complete the poem on photocopiable page 41, comparing themselves 'now' in Year 4 to 'then' in babyhood.
- The 'Now' lines use present tense verbs. The children must use these verbs in the past tense in the 'Then' lines.
- Making rough drafts and checking awkward verbs in a dictionary will help the children to produce a polished, final poem.
- Give less confident learners a box of past tense verbs to fit into their lines.
- As an extra challenge, ask the children to write additional pairs of 'Now' and 'Then' lines.

Plenary
- Scan in and view some of the results from the independent work.
- Ask some children to read their poems to the class. Are any unusual tense changes discovered?

English Lesson 3

Character sketches

Learning objective
PNS: Creating and shaping texts
● Use characterisation to engage readers' interest.

Resources
'Dragon invaders' Notebook file; individual whiteboards and pens.

Links to other subjects
History
QCA Unit 6 'Why have people invaded and settled in Britain in the past?'
● Link the text to information about the Viking raiders.

Starter
Display page 2 of the Notebook file. Read the text and discuss it. Find out whether the majority of the children like or dislike Father and Mother by asking them to vote. They could do this by writing *Like* or *Dislike* by each character's name on their individual whiteboards and holding them up. Discuss the results. Highlight parts of the text which could have affected feelings (not wanting to share, not being rich, the word *schemed*).

Whole-class shared work
● Display page 3. Discuss the events of the text (Aled's actions, dragons coming by sea).
● Focus on the character, Aled. Ask: *What sort of person do you think he is? How can you tell? Do you like or dislike him? Why?* Encourage discussion and different viewpoints, emphasising that people respond to writing differently.
● Point out specific details from the passage. Discuss each of the details in turn, asking the children to think about how the words make them feel about Aled. (For example, *He got rid of all signs of his presence* might show that Aled has a careful nature.)
● Ask the children whether the words add information about the character. Does it make them feel more sympathetic towards him? Does one detail make them dislike Aled? Encourage varied viewpoints.
● If required, draw out details from the text by double-pressing on the text, then highlighting the words you want to isolate and dragging them out of the text box. This adds the words to the page as a separate object.
● Focus on the verbs the writer has chosen. Are they good choices? (The verbs are often weak and there is repetition.)
● Make the point that more powerful verbs could improve this passage.
● Highlight some weak verbs in the first two lines.
● Print a copy of the text for every child.

Independent work
● Ask the children to read the text by themselves. Encourage them to highlight at least 15 verbs that need to be replaced. They should then write their replacement, powerful verbs.
● Support less confident learners by focusing on a smaller number of replacements of the weakest verbs. *(put, saw, got)*
● As an extra challenge, ask more confident learners to write the next part of the story, using powerful verbs and small details to evoke more sympathy or dislike of Aled.

Plenary
● A copy of the text is on page 4 of the Notebook file. Let the children use this to demonstrate their replacement verbs.
● Discuss the effect more powerful verbs have on audience reaction. Return to the original version on page 3 so that other children can write alternative verbs.
● There is a text using stronger verbs on page 5 of the Notebook file, but other verbs are, of course, possible.

Whiteboard tools
Double-press on the text to edit existing text. To add words from existing text to the page as a separate object, double-press on the text, highlight the word, then drag it out of the text box.

 Pen tray
 Select tool

English — Lesson 4

Adverbs

Learning objective
PNS: Sentence structure and punctuation
● Clarify meaning and point of view by using varied sentence structure.

Resources
'Dragon invaders' Notebook file; photocopiable page 42 'The meeting' for each child.

Links to other subjects
Citizenship
QCA Unit 1 'Taking part - developing skills of communication and participation'
● During circle time, ask the children to write the adverb that best describes how they feel about a school issue. Share the words, and use them as a starting point for an exchange of views.

Starter
Look at page 6 of the Notebook file. Remind the children that words belong to different classes. A word's class depends on its function in a sentence. Revise familiar word classes: verbs and nouns. Ask the children to highlight the nouns (*Margaret, labels*) and verbs *(held, looked)*. Ask: *What class do the words in red belong to?* Identify them as adverbs. Make a separate list of the adverbs by double-pressing on the text, then highlight each adverb and drag it out of the text box onto the page.

Whole-class shared work
● Display page 7. Explain that an adverb's usual function is to add meaning to a verb.
● Investigate the adverbs used in the Starter text. Point out that most answer the question *How?* (For example, *clearly* explains how the names were written; *shyly* explains how Margaret looked.) Question the children about *wearily, tightly,* and *silently*. (They all answer *How?*)
● Focus on the word *Eventually*. Agree that it answers the question *When?*
● Ask if the children have noticed anything special about the spellings of adverbs. Explain that adverbs commonly (but not always) end in *-ly*.
● Investigate the position of the adverbs. Can the children tell which word the adverb adds meaning to? (The verb.) Which word should it stay near? (The verb.) *Eventually* is an exception in this text.
● Look at page 8 of the Notebook file. Can the children spot an adverb ending in *-ly*? (*Finally*.) Highlight the word.
● Suggest improving the text with eight to ten adverbs. Share ideas and make additions to the whiteboard. Page 9 demonstrates adverbs that could be used in the text.
● Warn against unnecessary adverbs: the verb may already express the meaning of a suggested adverb.
● Adverbs are useful in dialogue passages because they help the reader to 'see' a speaker's face and to 'hear' the tone of voice. (For example: *'I don't know,' John replied glumly.*)
● Encourage the children to suggest more adverbs that could describe how people speak, and write a few of their ideas on page 7. (For example: *loudly, quietly, cheerfully, miserably, happily*.)

Independent work
● Ask the children to complete the dialogue on photocopiable page 42 'The meeting'.
● Explain that each of the speaking verbs needs an adverb to bring the text to life. The spoken words must suit the adverbs chosen.
● Provide less confident learners with a list of adverbs to use.
● As an extra challenge, ask more confident learners to write their own narrative with dialogue, using a different set of adverbs.

Plenary
● Invite the children to share their finished texts. Add examples of their sentences to page 10, highlighting the adverbs used.
● Discuss whether the spoken words suit the adverbs chosen.
● Let the children speak the words in the appropriate voice. This can be recorded using the Windows® Sound Recorder if a microphone is available.

Whiteboard tools
To add words from existing text to the page as a separate object, double-press on the text, highlight a word and then drag it out of the text box. Convert handwritten words to text by selecting them and choosing the Recognise option from the dropdown menu. If a microphone is available, use Windows® Sound Recorder (accessed through Start, then Programs, then Accessories, then Entertainment) to record speech.

 Pen tray
 Select tool
 Highlighter pen

English Lesson 5

Story planning

Learning objective
PNS: Text structure and organisation
- Organise text into paragraphs to distinguish between different information, events or processes.

Resources
'Story planning' Notebook file; photocopiable page 43 'Story planning' for each child; individual whiteboards and pens; exercise books.

Links to other subjects
History
QCA Unit 9 'What was it like for children in the Second World War?'
- Link the story writing to the experiences of child evacuees.

Starter
Display page 2 of the Notebook file. Read the text and ask the children what they notice about it. (The narrative is not in the correct sequence.) Keeping the story in paragraphs, invite children to change the paragraph order. When you have agreed on a correct sequence, use the Eraser from the Pen tray to rub over the circles to reveal the correct order.

Whole-class shared work
- Discuss paragraphs, making notes on page 3. Explain that paragraphs mark different stages in the story: they help writers to organise their thoughts and readers to follow the story line.
- Explain that paragraphs can vary in length: the introduction and the ending to a story are often shorter than other paragraphs.
- Go to page 4 and open the story planning activity. Discuss the picture sequence. Ask: *What do you think is happening? Which events are important? Is there a main character?*
- Ask the children what is wrong with the pictures. (They are in the wrong order.) Challenge them to decide and note on their individual whiteboards what the picture order should be.
- Discuss their answers and agree on an order. Move the frames into the correct sequence. How does it compare with their individual whiteboard suggestions? Were there points the children had not thought about?
- Take a snapshot of the correct story sequence using the Area Capture tool and add it to the Notebook page.
- Suggest that each picture represents a paragraph. Annotate each picture with a planning sentence.
- Write these stage names next to the pictures, discussing each one as you do so:
  1. introduction
  2. build-up
  3. climax
  4. resolution
  5. ending.
- Go to page 5 of the Notebook file. Ask the children to plan another story about the evacuees, using the stages that have been discussed. Write a few subject ideas on page 5 - for example: *Mum's first visit; an adventure with local children; problems at the village school.* Emphasise that the children's own ideas should be better.

Independent work
- The children should plan their stories on photocopiable page 43 and write the opening paragraph in their exercise books.
- Work in a group with less confident learners by explaining each story stage.
- As an extra challenge, suggest that not every story stage has to be the same length: for example, the build-up could have two paragraphs.

Plenary
- Scan in and view some of the children's plans and opening paragraphs.
- Discuss the progression. Use page 6 of the Notebook file to write down the sequence of events in some of the story plans.
- Listen to some of the children read their introductions, and discuss as a class how effective they are.
- Use an extended writing session to finish the story.

Whiteboard tools
Use the Area Capture tool to take a snapshot of the sequencing activity. To upload scanned images, select Insert, then Picture File, and browse to where you have saved the image.

 Pen tray

 Select tool

 Area Capture tool

English Lesson 6

Collecting and classifying words

Learning objective
PNS: Word structure and spelling
● Know and apply common spelling rules.

Resources
'Suffixes and prefixes' Notebook file; individual whiteboards and pens; printed copy of page 5 of the Notebook file for each child.

Links to other subjects
History
QCA Unit 6A 'Why have people invaded and settled in Britain in the past?'
● Provide etymological dictionaries for investigation work. Ask the children to identify the Latin root word and find out the meaning of these words: *centurion, century, centenary, cent, porcupine, pork, porcelain, granary, granite, pomegranate, tractor, distract, attract, terrier, interred, territory, puncture, punctuation, punctual, audition, auditorium, audible.*

Starter
Display page 2 of the Notebook file. Discuss how to sort the words, eventually moving them so that they are grouped like this:
● Group 1: champion, member, owner, neighbour
● Group 2: partnership, childhood, ownership

Explain that the words in Group 1 are root words and the words in Group 2 are made from root words plus additional letters.

Show the children how *owner* with *ownership* make a pair. Ask volunteers to supply the missing word to pair with the root words on the page. (*champion – championship; member – membership; neighbour – neighbourhood; partner – partnership; child – childhood.*)

Whole-class shared work
● Explain that a suffix is a group of letters added to the end of a word. Each root word in the Starter uses a suffix to become another word.
● Focus on the suffix *-ship*. Talk about words ending this way, such as *fellowship* or *partnership*. Write them on to page 3. Ask the children to highlight the root words.
● Discuss how the suffix affects the meaning of the new word. Encourage the class to think about what *-ship* means in these words. Establish that it is a way of living or a skill.
● Display page 4 of the Notebook file. Point to a root word and ask the children to choose a suffix for it, writing *a* or *b* on their individual whiteboards.
● Ask volunteers to drag the words into the correct boxes. Note that *silly* does not work in either, although *silliness* is a valid word. Point out that the addition of a suffix can alter the spelling of the root word: if the root word ends in *y*, the *y* usually changes to *i* when a suffix is added.
● Reverse the activity, looking at the new, extended word and identifying the original, root word.

Independent work
● Print out a copy of page 5 for each child. The children must choose a suffix for each root word, listing the root word and the new word in the correct column.
● Encourage the children to use dictionaries for their investigation.
● Reduce the list of root words and limit the choice of suffixes to two for less confident learners.
● As an extra challenge, ask more confident learners to make their own additions to the columns.

Plenary
● Display page 5 and invite children to drag the words into the table.
● Note the words that do not work because of spelling changes.
● Encourage the children to suggest other words that could be added to the lists. Use page 6 to work together on lists of words for the suffixes *-dom, -ance, -ence, -ology, -ation*.

Whiteboard tools
 Pen tray
 Select tool
 Highlighter pen

English Lesson 7

Written instructions

Learning objective
PNS: Text structure and organisation
• Organise text to distinguish between different information, events or processes.

Resources
'Making a storybook' Notebook file; one computer for each pair of children, if available. (Microsoft Word is required to view the embedded text document in the Notebook file.)

Links to other subjects
Design and technology
QCA Unit 4B 'Storybooks – To design and make a book that has moving parts for a particular purpose'
ICT
QCA Unit 4A 'Writing for different audiences'
• The work in this lesson links well to both of the objectives above.

Whiteboard tools
To upload scanned images, select Insert, then Picture File, and browse to where you have saved the image.

 Pen tray

 Highlighter pen

 Select tool

Starter
Display page 2 of the Notebook file 'Making a storybook'. Discuss the text. Ask the children to explain the process in their own words to a partner. Point out the emphasis on correct sequential order. Ask questions such as: *What has to be done first? What is the final step?* Ask the children to identify words reinforcing this sequence. Highlight these words: *First, Then, Eventually, Finally.* Explain that they are link words.

Whole-class shared work
- Display page 3 and read the text aloud. Can the children identify the text type as instructions?
- Investigate the special features of instruction texts, using this example:
  1. Highlight its different sections:
     - Title: the objective of the text is stated.
     - Requirements: necessary materials are listed.
     - Method: the reader is told what to do.
  2. Highlight some of the verbs (*discuss, display, demonstrate*). Explain that they are *imperative* (command) verbs. Point out their sentence position. (The start of the sentence.) Question the children about the verbs' tense. (The present tense.)
  3. Draw the children's attention to the use of short sentences and the importance of sequential order.
- Encourage the children to recall written instructions that they have used. Are there any in their text books? Investigate examples.
- Ask the class: *Can you think of additional features missing from here?* Agree on important, missing features. Use page 4 of the Notebook file to add them to the list, for example:
  - Dividing the text into sections.
  - Having a subheading for each section.
  - Listing the requirements vertically.
  - Starting a new line for each instruction.
  - Using organisational devices, such as numbers, letters, or bullet points.
  - Including informative illustrations or diagrams.
  - Varying the font to make the information clearer.
  - Using link phrases.

Independent work
- Print out a copy of the story-making instructions on page 3 for each child. Ask the children to work in pairs to plan improvements.
- Suggest that the children have subheadings for these three sections:
  1. What you need
  2. What to do
  3. How to display
- Once planned, let the children produce a new copy of the text, preferably on a computer. (An editable version of the text is available by pressing the blue box on page 3.)
- Support less confident learners by suggesting where to divide the text.
- As an extra challenge, ask the children to write instructions for making a storybook using the computer.

Plenary
- Scan in some of the children's texts, and discuss which organisational features were the most popular. Make a note of the techniques on page 5.
- Look at instructional texts on the classroom walls. Do any need improving? How would the children improve them?

17

100 SMART Board™ LESSONS • YEAR 4

English Lesson 8

Alphabetical order

Learning objective
PNS: Word structure and spelling
● Know and apply common spelling rules.

Resources
'Making a storybook' Notebook file; copy of photocopiable page 44 'Alphabetical order' for each child; individual whiteboards and pens.

Links to other subjects
Speaking and listening
Objective 39: Group discussion and interaction: To take different roles in groups.
● Allow group discussion when children contribute to the whole-class ordering of words.

Starter
Play some oral games to revise alphabetical order. For example, creating an animal alphabet, reciting the alphabet backwards, or starting from a letter and finding the letter before or after it.

Whole-class shared work
● Display page 6 of the Notebook file. Highlight the *p* words.
● Encourage the children to put the words in alphabetical order. Draw the words out from the text by double-pressing on the text, highlighting the relevant word and dragging it to the white box at the side.
● Compare the children's results. Ask: *How did you decide?* Agree on the need to look past the first letter *p*. Underline the second letter in each of the words. Encourage the children to decide which of these is first in the alphabet. Drag this word to the bottom of the screen.
● Repeat this process with the other words, placing them in order. What problem do the children notice? (Two words have *e* as a second letter.) Agree to look at the third letter. Continue until you have: *paper, pens, pencils, pictures*.
● Repeat the exercise with the *d* words. Point out that for *discuss* and *display* you have to move to the fourth letter.
● Display page 7. Give each pair of children a word to write on their individual whiteboards and ask them to underline the second letter. Explain that you will recite the alphabet slowly and when they hear you say the underlined letter they must raise their hands.
● Start reciting, stopping when children raise their hands and allowing them to come to the board and move their words into the vertical list.
● Now review the list. Ask: *Are there problems? Do any words have the same second letter?* Remove those words from the list, placing them to one side.
● The owners of those words should then underline their third letters. Repeat the process of calling out the alphabet. When their letter is reached, the children move to the front and place their words in the line.
● Again look for problems. Do any words have the same third letter? If so, check the fourth letter. Agree on the final list.

Independent work
● Ask the children to complete photocopiable page 44 'Alphabetical order'.
● Support less confident learners by reducing the list.
● As an extra challenge, ask more confident learners to make their own *b* section.

Plenary
● Display page 8 of the Notebook file and ask for volunteers to order the words correctly. Highlight words where third and fourth place letters have to be taken into account.
● Using page 9 of the Notebook file, compile an alphabetically ordered list of first names in the class.

Whiteboard tools
To draw out words from the text before ordering, double-press on the text, highlight the relevant word and drag it to the white box at the side. Use a Pen from the Pen tray or the On-screen Keyboard, accessed through the Pen tray or SMART Board tools menu, to add text to the page.

 Pen tray

 Highlighter pen

 Select tool

 On-screen Keyboard

English Lesson 9

Newspaper stories

Learning objectives
PNS: Understanding and interpreting texts
PNS: Creating and shaping texts
● Summarise and shape material and ideas from different sources to write convincing and informative non-narrative texts.

Resources
Photocopiable page 45 'Story summaries'; example of local newspaper; example of online newspaper such as www.timesonline.co.uk; individual whiteboards and pens.

Links to other subjects
Citizenship
QCA Unit 11 'In the media – what's the news?'
● Select newspaper stories that are of local or national interest.

Starter
Read one of the summaries on photocopiable page 45 to the class, leaving out the book title. Ask the children to propose a title. Choose the one closest to the author's and write it onto a blank Notebook page. Use a different colour to write the real title. Which version do the children think is better? Why? Repeat this with the other story summaries. Play the game with some of the children's stories. Ask: *What does the title say about the plot? Does it make you want to read it?* Discuss what a title should achieve.

Whole-class shared work
● Open an online newspaper or magazine. Explain that stories in a newspaper do not have titles; they have headlines.
● Use the Spotlight tool to focus on one news headline. What do the children think this story will be about? Read some of the story to them. Discuss whether it is what they expected from the headline.
● Return to the front page. Choose another headline. Repeat the process, predicting the content of the story, and then checking to see if the story meets expectations.
● What do the children notice about the headlines? Agree on common features and write them on the whiteboard. For example:
  ● eye-catching
  ● quick to read
  ● arouses interest
  ● uses key words rather than lengthy sentences
  ● encourages the reader to read the story.
● Read some news headlines from a local newspaper. Challenge the children to guess what the story will be about. Read the subheadings and discuss whether these give any more information. Invite the children to make brief notes on their individual whiteboards, predicting a story's content.
● Read parts of the reports to the children. Ask: *Were the headlines helpful? Are subheadings a good device? How well do your notes match the story?*

Independent work
● Type up these headlines onto a blank Notebook page:
  ● Protest over lunch
  ● Swarm stings school!
  ● Why did they win?
  ● School sees sense
● Suggest that the headlines all relate to (imaginary) school news.
● Ask the children to choose a headline and write a newspaper report for the school newspaper. Tell them to write it in their exercise books, as they will be editing it in another lesson.
● Less confident learners could work with a partner.
● As an extra challenge, ask the children to write two reports with different events but the same headline.

Plenary
● Ask some children to read part of their reports, involving as many of them as possible.
● Discuss how much variety there is between different reports. Scan a few reports and display them on the whiteboard.
● Discuss whether headlines predict the reports accurately, and if subheadings are also needed.

Whiteboard tools
Use the Spotlight tool in the SMART Board tools menu to focus on newspaper headlines. Use a Pen from the Pen tray or the On-screen Keyboard, accessed through the Pen tray or the SMART Board tools menu, to enter text.

 Pen tray
 Select tool
 Spotlight tool
 On-screen Keyboard

English ▸ Lesson 10

Commas

Learning objective
PNS: Sentence structure and punctuation
• Use commas to mark clauses.

Resources
Computers for the children to use; individual whiteboards and pens.

Links to other subjects
Citizenship
QCA Unit 11 'In the media - what's the news?'
• Follow up the lesson by asking the children to edit and revise their newspaper reports.
• Provide computers, and help the children to lay out their report in a newspaper column format.

Starter
Put a comma on a blank Notebook page and remind the children of its name. Ask them to count the commas on a page of their last story. Compare totals. Ask: *Why did you use a comma? Was it essential? Why was it the best punctuation mark?* Record their answers on the whiteboard.

Whole-class shared work
- Write: *A comma is a punctuation mark used to help the reader by separating parts of a sentence. It sometimes corresponds to a pause in speech.* Discuss this, and then type the following paragraph:
  The editor was furious. The deadline was four o'clock. It was now five past four. No article had appeared. Where was it? He reached for the phone.
- Invite the children to close their eyes while you read the paragraph aloud to them. Can they 'hear' any commas? (No.) Discuss why. (The sentences are mainly short.)
- Explain that longer spoken sentences can be difficult for a listener to make sense of, so the speaker will make pauses. Commas break up written sentences in the same way, dividing the sentence into meaningful portions.
- Demonstrate this by reading the following sentence aloud: *Wayne Yorke, the youngest reporter, ignored the phone.*
- Ask the children to write, on their individual whiteboards, which words need commas after them. Repeat the sentence, advising the children that two commas are needed. Finally, write the punctuated sentence on the whiteboard.
- With different colour highlighting, split the sentence into three sections:
  Wayne Yorke,   the youngest reporter,   ignored the phone.
  Explain that:
  • Section 1 names someone.
  • Section 2 adds extra information about the person.
  • Section 3 takes action.
- Repeat this exercise with other sentences of a similar construction. For example: *Suki, the receptionist, opened the biscuits.* Each time, read the sentence aloud for the children to 'hear' the commas and decide where to place them. Afterwards, write the punctuated sentence on the whiteboard (or invite a child to add the commas), then highlight the sections.
- Make sure that your intonation helps the children to become confident about identifying the position of the commas.

Independent work
- Ask the children to edit their newspaper report from Lesson 9 by changing, removing and adding words. Encourage them to add three sentences similar to the examples, with two commas in each.
- Support less confident learners by dividing the task into stages:
  1. Create sentences with commas.
  2. Place the sentences in their report.
- As an extra challenge, ask the children to do further editing, combining and changing their short sentences so that commas are needed.

Plenary
- Encourage some children to read their sentences aloud. Can others 'hear' commas?
- Ask some children to write their sentences on the whiteboard and highlight each part.

Whiteboard tools
Add text to the page using a Pen from the Pen tray or the On-screen Keyboard, accessed through the Pen tray or the SMART Board tools menu.

 Pen tray

 Select tool

 Highlighter pen

 On-screen Keyboard

English Lesson 11

Homophones

Learning objective
PNS: Word structure and spelling
• Distinguish the spelling and meaning of common homophones.

Resources
'Homophones' Notebook file; individual whiteboards and pens; copy of photocopiable page 46 'Letter from Britain' for each child.

Links to other subjects
History
QCA Unit 6A 'Why have people invaded and settled in Britain in the past?'
• Link the lesson to work on the Roman invasion of Britain.

Starter
Look at page 2 of the Notebook file. Ask the children what the three words under the pictures have in common. (They are pronounced the same way.) Point out that although they are said the same way, they are spelled differently.
   Explain that you want to sort the words on page 3 into small groups by playing 'Sound snap'. Drag one word into one of the circles, and ask a volunteer to identify another that sounds the same. If the answer is wrong, the turn passes to someone else. If correct, say *Snap* and drag the matching word to the circle. Some of the words are in groups of three. In these cases, highlight a word in a circle for the children to guess the third one of the group. Keep going until all the words are in circles. If the children find the sound matching difficult, play the game more than once.

Whole-class shared work
• Point to the word *Homophone* on page 4. Ask the children what they think it means. Reveal the definition behind the red box.
• Explain that the words they played 'Sound snap' with are homophones.
• Encourage the children to suggest other examples and add them to the page 3 in the remaining three circles.
• Play 'Solve my riddle' by asking the children to tell you which word on page 3 fits the clue. For example:
  • *I am very wet.* (sea)
  • *I get fried in batter.* (plaice)
  • *I am more than one.* (four)
  • *I say baa.* (ewe)
• Allow partner collaboration and thinking time as the children write their answers on individual whiteboards. Highlight words as they are identified. Encourage the children to make up some riddles of their own.
• Discuss whether the children confuse particular homophones. Ask: *How do you remember the correct one?* Share helpful memory tips.
• Display page 5 of the Notebook file. Work together to invent mnemonics (devices to aid memory).

Independent work
• Give each child a copy of photocopiable page 46. Explain that the Roman soldier, writing a letter from Britain, has all the words he needs in the box. The children must decide which word goes where.
• Advise less confident learners which set of homophones to choose from.
• As an extra challenge, encourage more confident learners to compose their own Roman letter containing between 10 and 15 deliberate mistakes. Can someone else spot the mistakes?

Plenary
• Display page 6 of the Notebook file. Discuss possible answers before allowing children to drag the correct words from the homophones box into the text. Delete incorrect words. Pull the screen across the text to reveal the correct answers.

Whiteboard tools
Remove unwanted objects by pressing the Delete button or selecting Delete from the dropdown menu.

 Pen tray
 Highlighter pen
 Select tool
 Delete button

English Lesson 12

Adjectives

Learning objective
PNS: Creating and shaping texts
● Show imagination through the language used to create emphasis, humour, atmosphere or suspense.

Resources
'Another world' Notebook file; exercise books and pens.

Links to other subjects
Speaking and listening
Objective 41: To respond appropriately to the contributions of others in the light of alternative viewpoints.
● Encourage the children to express opinions about the adjectives used.

Starter
Open page 2 of the Notebook file and read the text to the children. Question them about their reactions. Ask: *How does the description make you feel? What mood do the words create?*

Now lower the Screen Shade ▣ to reveal the second paragraph. Read it to the children and repeat the questions. Compare the texts. Ask: *Does the second version make you feel differently when it is read? How? Why?* Note down some comments on the whiteboard. Express the view that the second text arouses expectations, making you want to see what will happen.

Whole-class shared work
● Highlight the additional words and the changed final word in the second extract on page 2.
● Ask the children what class these words belong to. (Adjectives.)
● Define *adjective*: a word describing somebody or something. Investigate which nouns are described by the adjectives.
● Discuss the benefits of adding adjectives to this text. (Tension is built.)
● Play a game in which the children suggest an adjective to describe a given classroom object. Encourage informative or expressive adjectives, rather than bland ones, for example: a *grazed* knee; a *tanned* face; a *modern* computer; a *useless* box; a *confused* expression.
● Display page 3 of the Notebook file, read it to the children and discuss it together. How does it make the children feel?
● Point out the word *afraid*. Does this piece of writing make the children feel afraid? Suggest that well-chosen adjectives could add to the mood.
● Work together, experimenting with adding adjectives. Encourage adjectives of sufficient intensity, avoiding those that are too obvious. (An amended version of the text, showing possible adjectives, appears on page 4.)
● Ask the children to think up an imaginary world. List some of their ideas on page 5 of the Notebook file. Some examples are given below, but encourage the children's own ideas:
  ● A world on the other side of an ordinary doorway.
  ● A place reached by travel.
  ● A world reached through a theme park ride.
  ● A house that changes as night falls.

Independent work
● Ask the children to write a description of their world. They should use well-chosen adjectives to create atmosphere and tension.
● Suggest writing a rough draft, before editing and producing a polished version (computers would be useful).
● Direct less confident learners to the ideas on the whiteboard.
● As an extra challenge, ask the children to describe the same imaginary world but using different adjectives and creating a different atmosphere.

Plenary
● Invite some children to read their descriptions to the class.
● Ask listeners to pick out memorable adjectives and list them on page 5. Discuss the children's reactions to those words.

Whiteboard tools
Lower the Screen Shade to reveal the hidden part of the screen on page 2 of the Notebook file.

 Pen tray

 Highlighter pen

 Screen Shade

 Select tool

22
100 SMART Board™ LESSONS • YEAR 4

English Lesson 13

Spelling patterns

Learning objective
PNS: Word structure and spelling
● Know and apply common spelling rules.

Resources
'The shopping list' Notebook file; photocopiable page 47 'A strange shopping list' for each child; writing books and pens.

Links to other subjects
Speaking and listening
Objective 41: To respond appropriately to the contribution of others in the light of alternative viewpoints.
● Encourage the children to use partner discussion to help them identify plurals that sound correct.

Starter
Display page 2 of the Notebook file and ask the children to write in the plural forms for the first three words. Use the Eraser from the Pen tray to reveal the answers on the right and highlight the suffixes that form the plural. Do the same for the next three words. Then extend the work to plurals where -s is not added by repeating the activity for the next group of words on page 3.

Whole-class shared work
● Go to page 4 of the Notebook file. Group the children in pairs: one partner should read the word in the left-hand column of the table; then the other partner should say its plural form. Ask them to agree on the pronunciation of the plural.
● Discuss the plurals with the class. If there is dispute, let the children say answers in sentences. Can they now hear which sounds correct?
● Invite children to write the plural of each word in the central column. Check the answer is right each time, using the Eraser.
● When the table is complete, ask the children to study the words and to work out a spelling rule for converting these words from singular to plural.
● Share ideas and write a list on the next page:
  1. Words ending in -f, change to -ves in the plural.
  2. Words ending in -ff, add -s in the plural.
  3. Words ending in -fe, change to -ves in the plural.
● Investigate which rule applies to each word in the table on page 4.
● Write the word *chief* under the rules on page 5. Ask: *Which rule should we apply?* (You would expect to use rule 1.) *What will the plural be?* (Chieves.) *Does it sound correct?* (No.)
● Explain that the correct plural is *chiefs*. Spelling rules cannot always be applied. There are many exceptions.
● Demonstrate how a dictionary can help with problem words.

Independent work
● Ask the children to complete photocopiable page 47. (Tell them that a *plum duff* is a plum pudding.)
● Divide the words into groups for less confident learners.
● As an extra challenge, ask the children to add further text, using other -ff, -f and -fe words and their plural forms.

Plenary
● Work through the photocopiable sheet together and compare the children's answers with the answers on pages 6 and 7 of the Notebook file. Invite the children to write the answer you agree upon.
● Show the correct plural forms by deleting the stars on the right-hand side of pages 6 and 7. (Draw attention to *scarf:* the plural can be *scarfs* or *scarves.*)
● Share some of the children's spells from their photocopiable sheets.

Whiteboard tools
Use a Pen from the Pen tray or the On-screen Keyboard to enter text.

 Pen tray
 Highlighter pen
 Select tool

English Lesson 14

Expressive writing

Learning objective
PNS: Creating and shaping texts
● Show imagination through the language used to create emphasis, humour, atmosphere or suspense.

Resources
'Another world' Notebook file; individual whiteboards and pens.

Links to other subjects
Speaking and listening
Objective 44: To tell stories using voice effectively.
● Ask the children to talk about the similes they hear and the images they form from them.

Starter
Display page 6 of the Notebook file and ask: *What is Dean's shirt compared to?* (A wasp.) *What has colours like a rainbow?* (His sweater.) *What is the third comparison?* (His trousers are compared to a chessboard.) *Why do you think his trousers are compared to a chessboard?* (They have black and white checks.) Move the Screen Shade to reveal the drawing on the left of the page. Highlight the three comparisons in the text. Point out why comparisons improve the text: they bring the writer's descriptions to life, making it easier to form a visual image.

Whole-class shared work
● Use and define the term *simile*: words that create an image in the reader's mind by comparing a subject to something else.
● Explain that the comparisons in the Starter activity are similes.
● Display page 7 of the Notebook file. Point out that similes could add further atmosphere and mood by creating stronger visual images.
● Read the first sentence. Ask the children to think of something that disappears from view very quickly. Agree on something. Ask: *What word should introduce the comparison?* (*Like* or *as*.) Add the simile to the text.
● Continue with a couple more sentences. Ask the children to write ideas on individual whiteboards before you all compare suggestions.
● Encourage imaginative ideas. Stress that there is no 'correct' simile: an unusual comparison will make the visual image stronger in a reader's mind.
● Add the similes to the text and discuss what difference they make.
● Read the sentences to the children and ask them what they 'see'. Share visual images.

Independent work
● Ask the children to re-write the last three sentences of the passage on page 7, extending the passage with a new sentence or two of their own.
● They should use at least three similes. Suggest adding similes to compare with:
  ● twisted trees
  ● menacing branches
  ● metal structures.
● Less confident learners could discuss what to write with a partner before they start work.
● As an extra challenge, ask the children to add similes to their own imaginary world descriptions (see independent work, Lesson 12).

Plenary
● Hold a speaking and listening session. Let the children read their sentences aloud.
● As others listen, ask them to describe the pictures put in their minds by the similes.
● Examples of the similes can be added to page 8 of the Notebook file.

Whiteboard tools
Move the Screen Shade to reveal part of the screen.

 Pen tray
 Select tool
 Screen Shade
 Highlighter pen

English Lesson 15

Apostrophes

Learning objective
PNS: Sentence structure and punctuation
- Use the apostrophe for possession.

Resources
'Apostrophes' Notebook file; photocopiable page 48 'Animal possessions' for each child; individual whiteboards and pens.

Links to other subjects
Science
QCA Unit 4C 'Keeping warm'
- Write a pattern possession poem about the materials and products that keep things warm or cold. (For example: *the sun's rays make me hot; the air's wind makes me cold; the sweater's wool warms me up; the T-shirt's cotton keeps me cool; the freezer's ice saves the food, the bear's coat keeps it snug.*)

Starter
Tell the children you are going to say something, and you want them to decide how often you push words together (made contractions). Then say:
That's very strange. It's the computer: it's never left on! Something's wrong. Someone's definitely been messing around in here. We've got to find out more.

Repeat the words if necessary, then ask the children to show their answers on individual whiteboards.

Display the text on page 2 of the Notebook file and highlight the contractions in the first paragraph. Ask: *What letters have been left out? How should we mark those letters?* (With an apostrophe.) Invite volunteers to add the apostrophes and leave the text on the screen.

Whole-class shared work
- Introduce the term *omission*: letters left out of a shortened form as words are pushed together. This occurs frequently in speech.
- Explain that all the apostrophes used in the Starter are apostrophes of omission. Write an apostrophe in the key at the bottom of the screen, and highlight it with the same colour that you used before. Beside the apostrophe put *O* for *Omission*.
- Ask the children to read the second paragraph to a partner. Can any of them hear something strange about the words?
- Compare ideas. Agree that *of* phrases are clumsy. Ask the children what the more usual, economical way is of explaining who owns something. (An apostrophe followed by *s*.) Explain that possession is the second use of an apostrophe.
- Invite the children to edit the text to make the changes, highlighting the apostrophes in a second colour:
  - **Jasmine's coat** *was on the floor.* **Jade's bag** *was open. The* **boys' instruction books** *were torn in half. The* **children's diaries** *were open.*
- Add another apostrophe to the key and highlight it in the second colour. Label it *P* for *Possession*.
- Now go to page 3 and read out each phrase. Ask the children to say the economical, contracted form. Type up the phrases and add a couple more examples of your own.
- Explain the rules:
  1. Singular owners, and other owners not ending in *s*, add *'s*.
  2. Plural owner ending in *s*, just add *'*.

Independent work
- Ask the children to complete the poem on photocopiable page 48.
- Divide the task in two to support less confident learners: first, write an apostrophe phrase beside each picture; secondly, use the phrases in a poem.
- As an extra challenge, ask more confident learners to write a pattern possession poem about their family.

Plenary
- Use the scanner to view a selection of the children's poems on page 4.
- Invite poets to read their poems aloud to the rest of the class. If a microphone is available, use Windows® Sound Recorder to record the poetry readings.

Whiteboard tools
Add scanned images by selecting Insert, then Picture File, and browsing to where you have saved the image. If a microphone is available, use Windows® Sound Recorder (accessed through Start, then Programs, then Accessories, then Entertainment) to record children reading their poems.

 Pen tray

 Select tool

 On-screen Keyboard

 Highlighter pen

English — Lesson 16

Word order

Learning objectives
PNS: Sentence structure and punctuation
- Clarify meaning and point of view by using varied sentence structure (phrases, clauses and adverbials).
- Use commas to mark clauses.

Resources
'Word order' Notebook file; photocopiable page 49 'Changing order – changing meaning' for each child.

Links to other subjects
History
QCA Unit 7 'Why did Henry VIII marry six times?'
- Link the independent work to the Tudors.

Starter
Go to page 2 of the Notebook file. Ask the children to investigate the sentence pairs. Encourage reading aloud to a partner. What do they notice? Conclude that the pairs of sentences use the same words but change the word order. Do the children think this affects meaning? Ask them to try to make up a similar pair of sentences. Invite volunteers to write their sentences on the board.

Whole-class shared work
- Investigate the sentences from the Starter more closely. Discuss sentence types. Explain that:
  - Sentence 1 is a simple sentence (one clause) with an adverb.
  - Sentence 2 is a simple sentence with a prepositional phrase.
  - Sentence 3 is a compound sentence (two equal clauses).
  - Sentence 4 is a complex sentence (one main clause and a subordinate clause).
- Highlight the words that move in each pair. Identify them:
  - In sentence 1 an adverb is moved.
  - In sentence 2 a prepositional phrase is moved.
  - In sentence 3 the clauses are reversed.
  - In sentence 4 the clauses are reversed.
- Explain that the type of phrases in these sentences means that the word order can be changed without changing the meaning of the sentence. Point out the punctuation changes that occur: when adverbs and prepositional phrases lead the sentence, a comma follows them in sentences 1 and 2, and a comma separates the main and subordinate clauses in sentence 4.
- Display page 3 of the Notebook file. Point out that these sentences also use identical words, but change their order. Ask: *What else has changed?* (The meaning.) Explain that a phrase such as *biggest man* must stay together. If separated, the adjective may describe the wrong noun.
- Go to page 4 of the Notebook file. Experiment with ordering the words in different ways, typing up different sentences. For example:
  - *The dog bit the man nastily.*
  - *Nastily, the dog bit the man.*
- Point out punctuation changes for each version.

Independent work
- Ask the children to complete photocopiable page 49. Remind them to think about punctuation.
- Ask less confident learners to write one sentence from each line of words.
- As an extra challenge, ask the children to create new pairs of sentences about Tudor times.

Plenary
- Invite the children to write their sentences on page 5 of the Notebook file.
- Look at the sentences, discussing meaning and punctuation.
- Use the children's pictures from the photocopiable sheet to show how the meaning of a sentence can change if the word order is changed.
- Press the red box at the foot of page 5 of the Notebook file to see the sentences written out in the correct order.

Whiteboard tools
Convert handwritten words to text by selecting them and choosing the Recognise option from the dropdown menu.

 Pen tray
 Highlighter pen
 Select tool

English Lesson 17

Explanations

Learning objectives
PNS: Text structure and organisation
● Organise texts into paragraphs to distinguish between different information, events or processes.
PNS: Creating and shaping texts

Resources
'Explanations' Notebook file; exercise books and pens.

Links to other subjects
Science
QCA Unit 4D 'Solids, liquids and how they can be separated'
● The Notebook file explanatory text links with this unit.

Starter
Open page 2 of the Notebook file. Write a *How?* or *Why?* question about a process, linking the question to current work in another curriculum area, such as science or geography. For example: *How are map scales used to calculate distances?* Discuss information to answer the question and make notes. Use pictures from the Gallery where appropriate.

Whole-class shared work
● Display page 3. Do the children recognise the text type? (An explanation.) Point out the title. Explain that a *How?* or *Why?* question is often the title for an explanatory text.
● Draw attention to the verbs. Ask the children what tense is used. (The present tense.) Point out the use of the passive voice. (*is placed; is changed.*) Explain that in the passive voice the subject of the verb has something done to it. Highlight examples in the text. Check them using the pull-out screen.
● Ask: *What purpose does the first sentence have?* (It forms an introduction.) Look at the order of the remaining text. The process is explained in sequential steps. Number these steps to highlight the order of the process.
● Highlight the opening words of each step: *The first thing; This means that; After that; As a result.* Establish that the function of these words is to link the paragraphs or steps together. Identify them as connectives.
● Discuss the purpose of organisational devices, such as subheadings, and presentation features, such as diagrams. Agree that they make information more accessible to the reader. Drag the ice cube diagrams into suitable places in the text to illustrate this point.
● Go to page 4 to read and discuss the key features of an explanation text.

Independent work
● Go to page 5 of the Notebook file. Write a question in the space provided at the top of the screen and ask the children to write an explanation that answers it.
● Display page 2 of the Notebook file showing the information the children generated in the Starter.
● Ask the children to write the explanation in their exercise books, following the layout of the writing frame and remembering to include key features of explanation texts.
● Less confident learners may need help with sequential order.
● As an extra challenge, encourage the children to set partners a new question to be answered in a written explanation.

Whiteboard tools
Save the notes made in this Notebook file for a subsequent lesson. Upload scanned images by Selecting Insert, then Picture File, and browsing to where you have saved the image.

 Pen tray
 Gallery
 Highlighter pen
 Select tool

Plenary
● Listen to the children's explanations and use the scanner to view any diagrams the children may have created.
● Use page 6 to make notes on the effective use of diagrams and the types of diagrams that the children chose to use.
● Do the children agree that the presentation and diagrams make the written explanations easier to understand? Record their opinions on page 6.

English — Lesson 18

Common endings

Learning objective
PNS: Word structure and spelling
- Know and apply common spelling rules.

Resources
'Common endings' Notebook file; photocopiable page 50 'Common endings'; individual whiteboards and pens.

Links to other subjects
Citizenship
QCA Unit 9 'Respect for property'
- Ask the children to use some of the following words in a piece of writing suggesting ways to improve a local public space: *through, though, right, obvious, previous, although, ambition, bright, tough, artificial, social, reaction, light, special, partial, serious.*

Starter
Say *tough, fiction* and *trivial* out loud and ask the children to spell the words on their individual whiteboards. Open the Notebook file and go to page 2. Compare the children's spellings. Explain that these are words that are difficult to spell. Can any of the children suggest ways to remember the spellings? Share ideas. These may include: pronunciation and letter sounds; common letter strings; the number of syllables in a word; typical patterns of letter strings; a mnemonic. As children suggest a way of remembering, encourage them to explain it.

Whole-class shared work
- Display page 3 of the Notebook file. Explain that the bag contains words that are commonly misspelled. Drag the words out of the bag and read them together.
- Ask the children to sort the words into groups on their individual whiteboards. Allow brief thinking time before comparing ideas of how the words could be sorted.
- Delete the white box to reveal a table. Place *devious* in one column. Encourage the children to suggest other words that could go in the same group, and why. Guide them towards recognition that *devious, serious* and *obvious* are linked because of their endings (*-ious*). Invite children to move the words together in one column, and write in the heading *-ious*.
- In the same way, work with the children to create groups for these word endings: *-ial, -tion, -ight, -ough*.
- Read aloud the *-ough* words. Ask the children if they notice anything strange about this group of words. Repeat the words if necessary, until the children focus on pronunciation (*-ough* makes a different sound in each word). Explain that *-ough* is the most unpredictable of these five words endings: it can have a number of different pronunciations.
- Focus on the *-ial* group. In these three words, highlight the letter preceding *-ial*. Point out that these words are typical: the letter preceding *-ial* is usually *c* or *t*.
- Talk about word class. In what class are the *-tion* words? (Noun.) Which other group is made up of nouns? (*-ight*.) Which endings usually belong to adjectives? (*-ial* and *-ious*.) Which group is most likely to vary? (*-ough*.)

Independent work
- Ask the children to complete the crossword on photocopiable page 50.
- Emphasise the need to think about spelling.
- Write the common endings of the words used on the whiteboard, if you think the children need this support (*-ial, -ight, -ough, -ious, -tion*).
- Supply less confident learners with the opening letters of answers.
- As an extra challenge, ask more confident learners to list their answers, finding ways to group them according to pronunciation, word class and spelling patterns.

Plenary
- Display the crossword on page 4 of the Notebook file.
- Invite children to come up and fill in the crossword. Press the Clues button to read the clues (if required) and the Answers button to see a completed version of the crossword.
- Identify common spelling patterns and write them on page 5.

Whiteboard tools
 Pen tray
 Select tool
 Delete button

English Lesson 19

Collecting and presenting information

Learning objectives
PNS: Understanding and interpreting texts
- Identify and summarise evidence from a text.
- Use knowledge of different organisational features of texts to find information effectively.

Resources
'Explanations' Notebook file; printed copy of page 3 of the Notebook file for each child; paper and pens.

Links to other subjects
Science
QCA Unit 4D 'Solids, liquids and how they can be separated'
- The children's information charts should link well with this unit.

Starter
Look at any charts of information displayed around the classroom. Ask: *Do you think these charts present information effectively? Which do you find easiest to understand? Why? How would you improve these charts?* Share and list ideas on page 7 of the Notebook file. Ideas could include:
- less text
- more diagrams
- division of chart into sections
- headings
- numbers.

Whole-class shared work
- Read the text on page 8, which explains how plants make their food.
- Focus on the three main paragraphs describing the process. Highlight the words that begin these paragraphs:
  - *The first thing...*
  - *This means that...*
  - *After that...*
- Explain that you want to make a chart about the process. Start by identifying the main information in each paragraph.
- Model how to summarise each paragraph. Highlight key words and phrases.
- On page 9, type a sentence for each paragraph, each in its own separate text box. Agree on a title and type this in a separate text box. For example:
  > **How plants make their food**
  > The plant absorbs water and air.
  > The plant gets energy from the sun.
  > The plant makes its food through photosynthesis.
- Would the children find this a helpful chart? Agree on the need for a better format. Suggest a flow chart format.
- Delete the box on the left-hand side of the screen. The numbered parts of the flow chart represent the three steps in the process.
- Move the phrases next to the correct part of the flow chart.
- Discuss what else to add (for example, diagrams). Let the children comment critically on the proposed chart.

Independent work
- Give each child a printout of page 3 of the Notebook file. Ask them to plan a diagram or chart using the printout. They should focus on the three main paragraphs highlighted earlier.
- Remind the children to highlight key words before summarising each of the three paragraphs in a short sentence or phrase. Their planning should include headings and diagrams.
- The charts can be completed in another session.
- Support less confident learners by helping them to identify key words.
- As an extra challenge, ask the children to think of how they could make a circular chart, by showing how water can be turned back into ice.

Plenary
- Scan and display the children's flow diagrams on page 10.
- Ask the children who produced circular diagrams to explain them to the rest of the class.

Whiteboard tools
Upload scanned images by selecting Insert, then Picture File, and browsing to where you have saved the image.

 Pen tray
 Highlighter pen
Select tool
 On-screen Keyboard
 Delete button

English — Lesson 20

Prefixes

Learning objective
PNS: Word structure and spelling
- Know and apply common spelling rules.

Resources
'Suffixes and prefixes' Notebook file; exercise books and pens.

Links to other subjects
History
QCA Unit 7 'Why did Henry VIII marry six times?'; Unit 8 'What were the differences between the lives of rich and poor people in Tudor times?'
- Link the independent work to information about life at sea in Tudor times, and the importance of the Tudor navy.

Starter
Display page 7 of the Notebook file. Ask the children how the words on the whiteboard could be grouped. Share sorting ideas before recognising the relevance of the prefix in each word. Move the words into the three boxes: *always, almost; affect, afflict; adjective, adverb, advent*. Highlight the prefixes.

Whole-class shared work
- Remind the children of what a prefix is: a sound unit added to the beginning of a word.
- List the three prefixes used in the Starter: *ad-, af-, al-*. Do the children know their meanings? Define them:
  - *ad-* means 'forwards'
  - *af-* means 'tending towards'
  - *al-* is a shortened form of 'all'.
- Using these definitions, investigate the meanings of the groups of words in the Starter. Ask: *How does the prefix's meaning contribute to the meaning of the word? How would you define the word?*
- Let the children check in dictionaries to see if a prefix's meaning is ever contained in the definition of the words.
- Ask the children to work in pairs. Give them time to skim through dictionaries to find words to add to these groups.
- Share the results of this exercise, allowing the children to add words to the whiteboard. Encourage them to look carefully at the additions. Do they think the new words keep to the meaning of the prefix? Delete words that do not relate to the prefix's meaning.
- Use the term *root words*. Explain that the root is a word before the prefix is added. Point out that the addition of the prefix sometimes involves spelling changes in the root word. Investigate these changes:
  - *af-* (the *f* is doubled)
  - *ad-* (no change)
  - *al-* (the prefix loses its second *l*).
- Display page 8 of the Notebook file. Gradually move the filled shapes to reveal the words beginning with the prefix *a-*.
- Highlight the prefix *a-*. Explain that it means *in a state of*.

Independent work
- Ask the children to use the list of *a-* words to write a story, of about 120 words, entitled *Sea Battle*.
- Reduce the number of *a-* words and the length of the story for less confident learners.
- As an extra challenge, ask the children to include words from another prefix group.

Plenary
- Scan and view some of the children's stories, inviting the authors to read them to the class.
- Use page 9 to compare the way in which *a-* words have been used. Investigate the meanings of the *a-* words, asking the children to involve *in a state of* in their definitions.

Whiteboard tools

 Pen tray

 Highlighter pen

 Select tool

English — Lesson 21

Writing poetry

Learning objective
PNS: Creating and shaping texts
- Choose and combine words, images and other features for particular effects.

Resources
'Another world' Notebook file; copy of photocopiable page 51 'A seaside trip'; individual whiteboards and pens.

Links to other subjects
Speaking and listening
Objective 44: Identifying the ways presentational features contribute to message and impact.
- This lesson links well to this objective.

Starter
Read the poem on photocopiable page 51 to the children. (Do *not* display the words.) Discuss what the poem is about and what made it enjoyable to listen to. (Length of lines, rhythm, vocabulary.) Read the poem again. Ask the children to write on individual whiteboards the words or phrases that stick in their mind. Compare results, writing popular words and phrases on page 9 of the Notebook file. Suggest that for a poem to be successful when read aloud, it needs to contain evocative and memorable words and phrases.

Whole-class shared work
- Open page 10 of the Notebook file. Discuss what is meant by *themes*.
- Investigate the text. Identify and circle evocative words that convey the first theme. For example: *speeding, fleeting glimpses, plunged*.
- Separate these words from the rest of the text and drag them into the appropriate box.
- Repeat the process for the second theme (for example, *the twisting line; unfamiliar countryside*) and the third theme (for example, *sinister dream; threatening landscape; twisted trees; menacing branches*).
- Now copy the individual words onto page 11. Explain that you want the children to write a performance poem (a poem that is written to be read aloud). Press the box at the bottom of the page to read the important features of a performance poem. Add more features if the children have any further ideas of performance poems.
- Discuss how to achieve these aims in a performance poem about the strange train journey. Ideas could include: a quick rhythm (to match the train); short, jerky lines; evocative words.
- Suggest that the words and phrases taken from the passage could form the basis of a performance poem. Move these words to the edges of the screen, leaving the central area free.
- With the children's input, use the central area to write sample lines. Introduce new vocabulary, as well as dragging words from the edges of the screen into your lines of poetry.
- Start to build up a poem with the class. Demonstrate making revisions: delete and substitute words, re-organise words and lines, and experiment with figurative language.

Independent work
- Ask the children to write a performance poem about the train journey, using some of the words chosen from the narrative.
- Encourage revision of rough drafts, before producing a polished poem.
- Less confident learners could work with a partner. You could also provide them with the opening lines.
- As an extra challenge, ask more confident learners to write another performance poem on a different subject.

Plenary
- Invite the children to perform their poems. Which words and phrases do listeners remember? Write good examples on page 12.
- If a microphone is available, use Windows® Sound Recorder to record and add the performances to page 12. Select Insert, then Sound, and browse to where you have saved the sound files.

Whiteboard tools
To copy words from the text, double-press on the text, highlight the relevant word and drag it out of the text box. Drag objects to a different page in the Page Sorter to copy or move them to that particular page. Add text to the page using a Pen from the Pen tray or the On-screen Keyboard.

 Pen tray
 Select tool
 On-screen Keyboard
 Page Sorter

English — Lesson 22

Learning objective
PNS: Understanding and interpreting texts
- Use knowledge of word structures and origins to develop their understanding of word meanings.

Resources
'Common roots' Notebook file; photocopiable page 52 'Word webs' for each child; etymological dictionaries.

Links to other subjects
History
QCA Unit 6A 'Why have people invaded and settled in Britain in the past?'
- Investigate words with Latin origins.

Whiteboard tools
Use the Screen Shade to display one sentence at a time in the whole-class shared work. Use the Lines tool to add extra lines to the word webs if necessary.

 Pen tray
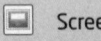 Screen Shade
 Select tool
 Lines tool

Word roots

Starter
Look at page 2 of the Notebook file. Allow thinking time as the children identify what the words have in common. Explain that they have a common root. Use a Highlighter pen to identify the root (*mono*). Explain that it is from the Greek word for *alone*.

Use dictionaries to define the words, using *alone* in the definitions. Ask the children if they can add a word to your collection. Make sure that the meaning of a new word relates to the meaning of the root.

Whole-class shared work
- Display page 3 of the Notebook file. Explain that you are going to show the children some sentences containing words with a common root. Move the Screen Shade to reveal the sentences one at a time. Allow time for the children to think about each sentence, and to write the words on their individual whiteboards. Compare answers before highlighting the two words.
- Investigate the identified words. Ask: *What is the root?* Underline the roots.
- Investigate further, by asking children to use etymological dictionaries to find the meaning and origin of each root. Make sure that they recognise how the meaning of the root affects the meaning of the word.
- Go to page 4 of the Notebook file, and press on the image to open the common roots activity. Explain the page: each definition must be matched to a root word.
- Allow thinking and partner discussion time before agreeing on an answer. Invite children to the whiteboard to match the roots and labels. Check answers by pressing *Am I correct?* The answers are given on page 5.
- On page 6, make a word web together for one of the roots from the Notebook file. (Use the Lines tool to add extra lines if necessary.)

Independent work
- Ask the children to complete the word webs on photocopiable page 52.
- Encourage the use of a dictionary, but remind the children to check the meanings of the words they use.
- Reduce the number of spaces to fill in for each web to support less confident learners.
- As an extra challenge, ask the children to add another word or two to each web.

Plenary
- Use pages 7 to 14 of the Notebook file to go through the independent work.
- Invite the children to fill in the webs with the words they have found.
- Use page 15 to check the children's answers and to see some examples of words that contain the relevant roots.

English — Lesson 23

Punctuation

Learning objective
PNS: Sentence structure and punctuation
● Clarify meaning and point of view by using varied sentence structure.

Resources
'The dilemma' Notebook file; printouts of pages 6 and 7 for each child; individual whiteboards and pens.

Links to other subjects
History
QCA Unit 6A 'Why have people invaded and settled in Britain in the past?'
● Link the text to information about Roman Britain.

Whiteboard tools
Move the Screen Shade to the left of the screen to reveal the text during the whole-class shared work.

 Pen tray
 Screen Shade
 Highlighter pen
    Select tool

Starter
Read the following text aloud. Make sure that punctuation is clear in the way that you read, but do not supply it. Ask the children to record on individual whiteboards the number of sentences they hear:
Titus was a Roman, but he was living in Britain. As a centurion, he had charge of 100 men. Although he tried to treat his men well, he knew they missed home. The north of England was unwelcoming. The landscape was bleak; the terrain was hard-going. The thing his men hated most was the weather. It was cold and rainy.
Compare answers. Read the text out loud again, this time asking the children to record if, what and where punctuation marks are needed. Record their answers on page 2 of the Notebook file.

Whole-class shared work
● Display the paragraph on page 3. Ask the children to punctuate it by pressing the punctuation marks and capital letters at the bottom of the page and dragging and dropping them in the appropriate position in the text. Then move the Screen Shade to reveal the correct punctuation.
● Discuss the use of commas. Point out that writers' use of commas is very variable; some writers would leave out some of these commas.
● Revise the function of capital letters, full stops and commas.
● Go to page 4. Explain that it is possible to link two sentences with colons and semi-colons.
● Explain the use of a colon: to introduce further information. Ask the children to show you a place where a colon could be used in the first sentence. (*The thing his men hated most was the weather: it was cold and rainy.*) Invite a volunteer to drag the colon into position, and move the Screen Shade to see whether they are correct.
● Explain the colon's value: it emphasises the link between two statements, the second one now beginning with a small letter.
● Point out the semi-colon. Explain its use: it can replace a full stop to link two sentences that are related in meaning and are equally balanced. Ask the children where they could use a semi-colon in this paragraph. (*The landscape was bleak; the terrain was hard-going.*) Again demonstrate, moving the Screen Shade to check.
● Tell the children that semi-colons can also be used to separate items in a list, if they have been introduced with a colon.
● Use the text on page 5 to revise the rules for speech marks: where they are placed, how spoken and unspoken words are separated and how new paragraphs are used for each speaker.
● Invite volunteers to add the punctuation. Move the Screen Shade to show the correct punctuation.

Independent work
● Give each child a copy of pages 6 and 7 of the Notebook file. Ask them to add the missing punctuation marks to their sheets. Encourage them to read the sentences aloud to themselves.
● Ask less confident learners to work with partners, with a reduced text.
● As an extra challenge, encourage more confident learners to write more text using semi-colons, colons and speech marks.

Plenary
● Invite volunteers to edit the text on screen to add the punctuation on pages 6 and 7. After they have done this, delete the box at the foot of each page to check that they are correct.

English — Lesson 24

Learning objective
PNS: Creating and shaping texts
- Choose and combine words, images and other features for particular effects.

Resources
'The dilemma' Notebook file; access to computers or a copy of page 12 of the Notebook file, one per child. (Microsoft Word is required to view the embedded text documents in the Notebook file.)

Links to other subjects
History
QCA Unit 6A 'Why have people invaded and settled in Britain in the past?'
- Link the text to information about Roman Britain.

Whiteboard tools
Add text to the page with the On-screen Keyboard, accessed through the Pen tray or the SMART Board tools menu.

 Pen tray
 Select tool
 Highlighter pen
 On-screen Keyboard

Summaries

Starter
Open 'The dilemma' Notebook file and display page 8. Give the children some oral instructions, making them deliberately long-winded. For example:
Look very closely and carefully at the whiteboard. Check absolutely before you go further that you can see properly. Take out just about all the equipment you could possibly need for this lesson.
Ask the children to comment on your language. (Using unnecessary words.) Encourage suggestions as to how these instructions could be given more briefly. Continue this game, one child giving a wordy instruction, somebody else shortening it. Stress the need to retain important meanings.

Whole-class shared work
- Go to page 9 of the Notebook file. Ask the children to help you identify and highlight words that are key to meaning. Identify words that can be deleted, using a different highlighter colour, until you have simpler sentences.
- Erase the blue marks to reveal the sample answers beneath each sentence.
- Read the sentence on page 10. Identify and highlight the key words: *whiteboard; seen*. Discuss the message: whiteboards need to be in the right place to be viewed.
- Type suggestions to summarise the sentence in 12 words or less. For example:
  - *Whiteboards, put in a good spot, can be seen by all.*
  - *Whiteboards in a good spot can be seen by all.*
- Investigate the shortened sentences. Identify the words that were left out. Point out where sentence construction has changed.
- Suggest that new vocabulary can help with summaries. Reveal the final sentence: *Well-positioned whiteboards give good visibility.*
- Point out that *good visibility* (two words) expresses the same meaning as *can be seen by all* (five words).
- Go to page 11. Explain to the children that you want to reduce the paragraph from 41 words to 20 or less.
- Work together to edit the text in the white box using the On-screen Keyboard. Focus on one sentence at a time, reminding the children to think about key words and main messages. For example:
  Titus agreed and disagreed. The camp would run out of special supplies if everyone ate them. What should he do?

Independent work
- Go to page 12. Print out a copy of this text for every child or open the editable documents and make the text accessible on the children's computers.
- The paragraph has 61 words. Ask the children to reduce it to a summary of about 40 words.
- Give less confident learners a target number of words for each sentence.
- As an extra challenge, ask the children to summarise the text from page 7. They can press on the right-hand box on page 12 to view the passage in editable form.

Plenary
- Invite the children to read their summaries out loud.
- The text may be summarised in a variety of ways. Display the children's edited documents or ask them type their versions on page 13. Stress the need to retain important elements.

34

100 SMART Board™ LESSONS • YEAR 4

English — Lesson 25

Its and it's

Learning objective
PNS: Sentence structure and punctuation
● Use the apostrophe for possession.

Resources
'Its and it's' Notebook file; copy of page 7 of the Notebook file for each child.

Links to other subjects
Science
QCA Unit 4B 'Habitats'
● Link the independent work to this unit by asking the children to list common observable features in birds, reptiles and mammals (for example: *Birds have feathers and beaks*).

Starter
Play an oral game, asking the children simple questions. Encourage informal answers, but in sentences. Use questions containing *is it* or *is* + a singular noun, for example: *What day is it? What time is it? What on earth is wrong with this picture? Whose pen is this?*

Extend the game to the children asking you questions. Make a point (without mentioning it) of using *it's* instead of *it is* in the answers. Invite the children to write a sentence to answer the questions on page 2 of the Notebook file.

Whole-class shared work
● Display page 3 of the Notebook file. Can the children spot a difference between the language of each question and its answer? Listen to the children's ideas. Guide them towards noticing that every question word is written in full. Ask: *Is this true of the answer?* (No.)
● Point out the highlighted *it's* in the two answers. Ask the children to name the punctuation mark that has been used here. (An apostrophe.) Establish the reason for its use. (To show that a letter has been omitted.)
● Revise this use of apostrophes. Explain that we often run words together in speech; in informal writing we can do the same. An apostrophe marks the letter(s) left out.
● Look at the page again and ask: *Which letter is missing in it's?* (i) *What would be the full form?* (it is.)
● Point out the highlighted *its* in the two sentences on page 4. Enquire as to whether an apostrophe is needed here. Guide the children towards recognition that no letter is missing. Discuss the meaning of *its* here. Agree on the answer *belonging to it*.
● Go to page 5. The sentences from pages 3 and 4 have been repeated for comparison. Ensure that the children understand why *its* or *it's* has been used in each case.
● Display page 6. Ask the children to decide and then drag the correct word (*its* or *it's*) to complete the sentences.
● Challenge the children to provide sentences using *its* and *it's* and write them on the board. Highlight the *its* and *it's*.

Independent work
● Display page 7 and give a printout of the page to each child.
● Ask the children to fill the spaces on their sheets with either *it's* or *its*.
● Emphasise thinking about what the word means in each sentence.
● Encourage less confident learners to focus on part of the text at a time, advising them of how many of each form to look for.
● As an extra challenge, ask more confident learners to add more text with *it's* or *its* sentences.

Plenary
● Review the independent work using page 7 of the Notebook file.
● Use the Eraser from the Pen tray to rub over the spaces on the screen to reveal the correct answers.
● Ask the children to compare the answers on their worksheets with the version on screen. Discuss any misconceptions they may have had.

Whiteboard tools
Write sentences with a Pen from the Pen tray or use the On-screen Keyboard, accessed through the Pen tray or SMART Board tools menu.

 Pen tray

 Highlighter pen

 Select tool

English Lesson 26

Word endings and classes

Learning objective
PNS: Word structure and spelling
- Know and apply common spelling rules.

Resources
'Word classes' Notebook file; photocopiable page 53 'Same word – different endings' for each child.

Links to other subjects
Speaking and listening
Objective 44: To tell stories using voice effectively.
- Use the children's poems for performance practice.

Starter
Open page 2 of the Notebook file. Discuss the word classes with the children: *noun, verb, adjective* and *adverb*. Then use the Eraser from the Pen tray to erase the red marks to reveal the definitions.

Give oral practice, asking the children to identify classes of words you use in sentences. Say: *The teachers talked to their classes.* Ask: *Which words are the nouns?* (teachers; classes.) *Which word is the verb?* (talked.) Invite them to add an adjective, such as *patient* or *quiet*, and an adverb, such as *loudly*. Move the Screen Shade to reveal the last sentence on the page. Ask volunteers to add their suggested adjective and adverb. They should then highlight the different word types, using the same colours that are used in the definitions.

Whole-class shared work
- Go to page 3 of the Notebook file. Point out the words *dined* and *served* and ask: *What do they have in common?* (Both are verbs and end in *-ed*.)
- Extract *dined* and *served* from the text by double-pressing on the text, highlighting the word and dragging it out from the text. Invite a child to drag the words into the correct column of the word classes table.
- Explain that endings can give clues about word class. Elicit the typical ending of a verb. (-ed.) Put *-ed* under the heading *Verb*.
- Identify endings typical of the other word classes. Label the headings:
  - Noun (plurals end in): *-s, -es*
  - Verb: *-s, -es, -ed, -ing*
  - Adjective: *-er, -est*
  - Adverb: *-ly*
- Point out where endings are typical of more than one word class.
- Investigate further by finding words to agree with the headings, extracting them from the text and moving them into the correct columns.
- Point out that links between word endings and word classes are only generalisations and there are many exceptions. For example, waiter ends in *-er* but it is not an adjective. Ask: *What word class is it?* (A noun.)
- Display page 4 of the Notebook file. Draw attention to the fact that the two sentences use the same root word repeatedly but in different forms, with different endings and in different word classes.
- Drag the highlighted words into the correct column on the table. Point out that *actor* and *buzzer* are nouns.
- Make up more sentences like these. Say the sentences out loud and invite the children to write the words in the chart.

Independent work
- Give out copies of photocopiable page 53 and ask the children to complete the poem. Emphasise that it does not have to make much sense!
- Less confident learners could work with a partner.
- Extend more confident learners by asking them to write a second poem of the same type.

Plenary
- Talk about the varied forms of some words used in the children's poems, making notes on page 5 of the Notebook file.
- Invite some of the children to read their poems aloud.

Whiteboard tools
Extract words from the text by double-pressing on the text, highlighting the word and dragging it out of the text box.

 Pen tray

 Screen Shade

 Highlighter pen

 Select tool

English — Lesson 27

Spelling compound words

Learning objective
PNS: Word structure and spelling
• Use knowledge of phonics, morphology and etymology to spell new and unfamiliar words.

Resources
Photocopiable page 54 'Compound words'; two Notebook pages showing words that can be moved separately – page 1: *pot, life, class, guard, tea, room*; page 2: *dust, bin, grand, parent, bath, room, sand, bag, wind, mill, ship, yard, cart, wheel, rattle, snake, frost, bite, band, stand, rasp, berry, pine, apple, foot, ball, card, board.*

Links to other subjects
History
QCA Unit 6A 'Why have people invaded and settled in Britain in the past?'
• Demonstrate Roman influence on the English language with compound words that reveal Latin influence (for example, *porcupine, porcelain, portfolio, portmanteau*).

Whiteboard tools
- Pen tray
- On-screen Keyboard
- Highlighter pen
- Select tool

Starter
Display the first page of your prepared Notebook file (see Resources). Ask the children to find pairs of words that make a new word. Allow one or two minutes before letting them make suggestions. Encourage them to explain their pairings. Move words on the whiteboard into these pairs:
- tea   pot
- class   room
- life   guard

Join each pair to create three single words: *teapot; classroom; lifeguard*. Explain that these are compound words. Compound words occur when words join to form a new word.

Whole-class shared work
- Explain that the separate parts forming a compound word can help you to spell the word correctly.
- Type *cupboard* on the whiteboard. Say it aloud and ask the children what they notice about your pronunciation. Repeat the word a few times until the children notice that *p* is not heard. Thinking of the word in two parts, *cup + board*, makes it easier to remember to include this letter.
- Consider other examples of compound words where a letter's sound may be difficult to hear because of the way the word is pronounced. Each time:
  - Write the compound word on the whiteboard.
  - Ask the children to look at it as you pronounce it.
  - Encourage them to note on their individual whiteboards a letter they found hard to hear.
  - Compare the children's answers.
- Suitable words might include: *postman, scrapbook, earring, goldfish, football*.
- Type *grand* and *mother*. Elicit that the compound word is *grandmother*.
- Add these sentences to the whiteboard:
  - She is a *grand mother* to her daughter.
  - She is a *grandmother* to her daughter's children.
- Discuss with the children how the meaning of the compound word is not always the same as the meanings of the separate words.
- Point out that some compound words show historical changes. For example, *cloakroom* dates from a time when people usually wore cloaks instead of coats.

Independent work
- Tell the children that they are going to create compound words using photocopiable page 54. Ask them to underline three examples of letters not always heard.
- To support less confident learners, divide the words into first-half and second-half lists.
- As an extra challenge, ask the children to add examples of their own.

Plenary
- Display page 2 of your prepared Notebook file (see Resources). Invite children to move the words to make compound words: *dustbin, grandparent, bathroom, sandbag, windmill, shipyard, cartwheel, rattlesnake, frostbite, bandstand, raspberry, pineapple, football, cardboard*.
- Encourage children to read the words aloud as others look and listen. Are letters hidden in the pronunciation? Highlight these. Emphasise that remembering the original separate parts helps with spelling.

37

100 SMART Board™ LESSONS • YEAR 4

English ▸ Lesson 28

Sentence types

Learning objective
PNS: Sentence structure and punctuation
● Clarify meaning and point of view by using varied sentence structure.

Resources [P]
Photocopiable page 55 'Questions and answers' for each child; individual whiteboards and pens.

Links to other subjects
History
QCA Unit 18 'What was it like to live here in the past?'
● Encourage the children to think of questions about their own area, that they could put to an older person.

Starter
Type the following words and punctuation marks on a blank Notebook page in separate text boxes.
  The   area   been   has   changing   .   ?
Make two sets. Use one set to demonstrate making a statement:
  The area has been changing.
Use the other set to demonstrate making a question:
  Has the area been changing?
Ask the children what they notice about the sentences. Establish that the words used are the same, but that word order and punctuation have changed.

Whole-class shared work
● Use the Screen Shade to hide the question and focus on the statement.
● Ask what the verb is here. Identify and highlight *has been changing*. Explain that this is a *verb string*.
● Explain that a verb string has a main verb and other helping verb(s). Ask: *Which is the main verb?* (changing.) *Which are the helping verbs?* (*has* and *been*.) Label these types of verb.
● Introduce and define the term *auxiliary verbs*: verbs that are used together with other verbs. In the statement, *has* and *been* are auxiliary verbs.
● Now display the second sentence: *Has the area been changing?*
● Ask: *Which is the main verb?* (changing.) *Which are the auxiliary verbs?* (*has* and *been*.) Label these types of verb.
● Discuss what has happened to the verb string. (It has been split up.)
● Now type a new sentence on the whiteboard: *The area changed.* Do the children know what type of sentence this is? (A statement.) What is the verb? (*changed*.)
● Let the children try to make a question from the statement. (It is impossible.) Explain that a statement that contains a verb string can be changed into a question by re-ordering the words. When a statement uses only a main verb, auxiliary verbs are needed to make the question.
● Now try the task again, asking the children to think of auxiliary verbs to help form the question. For example: *Has the area changed? Did the area change?* (Notice in the second example that *changed* has become *change*.)

Independent work
● Ask the children to complete photocopiable page 55. Remind them that they may need to add auxiliary verbs.
● Highlight the starting words for each question to support less confident learners.
● As an extra challenge, ask more confident learners to add five new statements and their questions.

Plenary
● Type some of the statements on the board. Ask the children to identify verb strings.
● Invite volunteers to demonstrate on the whiteboard how words can be re-ordered to become a question.

Whiteboard tools
Use the Screen Shade to reveal sentences one at a time.

- Pen tray
- Select tool
- On-screen Keyboard
- Highlighter pen
- Screen Shade

English — Lesson 29

Learning objective
PNS: Creating and shaping texts
- Choose and combine words, images and other features for particular effects.

Resources
'Advertisement' Notebook file; individual whiteboards and pens.

Links to other subjects
Science
QCA Unit 4C 'Keeping warm'
- Link the advertisements to science experiments on insulation.

Advertisements

Starter
Go to page 2 of the Notebook file. Give the children a minute to think of an advertisement for a product. Ask: *Which advertisement comes most quickly into your mind?* Share results, recording some on the whiteboard.

Focus on one advertisement, particularly if the same one has been thought of by a few children. Ask the children to think of a reason why this advertisement should have been thought of by more than one of them. Allow thinking and partner discussion time before they write a reason on their individual whiteboards.

Whole-class shared work
- Share the reasons children came up with for why this advertisement was remembered. List interesting points on page 3 and add points of your own. The points can be placed in order of importance. Press the blue box to read possible reasons.
- Refer to other advertisements that illustrate some of these points. For example, a memorable slogan: *Have a break. Have a KitKat;* or wordplay: *Beanz meanz Heinz.*
- Talk about what an advertiser is trying to achieve. Agree that they are:
  - making you read about the product
  - making you remember its name
  - making you want to try the product.
- Display page 4 and give the children time to read the advertisement.
- Discuss what the product is. Then ask the children to write on their individual whiteboards the first thing that attracts their attention in the advertisement. Compare their answers.
- Investigate the advertisement further, identifying devices and approaches that it uses to achieve its aims. Point out and label:
  - bold capitals to grab attention
  - appealing layout
  - mixture of text and illustration
  - audience involvement (questions to answer; repeated use of word *you*)
  - clever product name: magimitt is a mixture of *magic* and *mitt* (mitten)
  - varied font
  - product name in large, bold capitals
  - repetition of product name
  - exaggerated claims (permanently hot)
  - dramatic punctuation (exclamation marks).
- Would the children have done this advertisement differently? If so, how?

Independent work
- Ask the children to carry out one of the following tasks:
  - Design a new advertisement for this same product or a different one to keep something warm.
  - Design an advertisement for a product to keep something cold.
- Less confident learners could work with a partner.
- As an extra challenge, ask the children to design two advertisements for the same product but aimed at different audiences.

Plenary
- Go to page 5 of the Notebook file. Use the scanner to view a selection of the children's designs.
- Invite children to present their ideas to the rest of the class.

Whiteboard tools
Upload scanned images by selecting Insert, then Picture File, and browsing to where you have saved the image.

- Pen tray
- Highlighter pen
- Select tool

English ▪ Lesson 30

Connectives

Learning objective
PNS: Sentence structure and punctuation
● Clarify meaning and point of view by using varied sentence structure (phrases, clauses and adverbials).

Resources
'Connectives' Notebook file; printout of page 4 of the Notebook file per child; writing materials; individual whiteboards.

Links to other subjects
Citizenship
QCA Unit 11 'In the media – what's the news?'
● Link the independent writing activity to an argument of local interest.

Starter
Revise and define the term *clause*: a group of words that make sense on their own. Display page 2 of the Notebook file. Discuss ways to link the clauses. Move the Screen Shade to reveal the words at the bottom of the page, and invite the children to use them to join the two sentences. Remind them that they will need to change some letters to capitals, and full stops to commas. For example:
 I was hot **but** the weather was cold.
 Although I was hot, the weather was cold.
 The weather was cold. **On the other hand**, I was hot.
 The weather was cold. **However**, I was hot.
Explain that the words in red are called connectives.

Whole-class shared work
● Investigate the connectives used in the Starter activity. Explain that:
  ● *But* is a **conjunction**, linking clauses within one sentence.
  ● *Although* is a **conjunction** linking clauses within one sentence.
  ● *However* is a **connecting adverb**, connecting ideas, but keeping separate sentences.
  ● *On the other hand* is a **connecting adverbial phrase**, connecting ideas, but keeping separate sentences.
● Write these three terms on the whiteboard beneath the examples.
● Point out the commas in the linked examples.
● Display page 3. Investigate one or two lines at a time, asking the children to identify the connectives. Pull the tab on the left-hand side of the screen to reveal them.
● Explain that connectives help when writing a point of view.
● Display page 4 of the Notebook file. Press the Hints icon in the top-right corner to see what the children have to write in each box:
  ● Paragraph 1: arguments against the supermarket and in favour of village shops.
  ● Paragraph 2: counter-arguments against village shops and in favour of the supermarket.
  ● Paragraph 3: a decision.
● Encourage the children to identify sentences that are relevant to paragraph 1.
● Copy the original sentences and the children's ideas for paragraph 1, placing the copy in the relevant box. Ask for volunteers to experiment with linking the sentences. For example: *The village shops are in the village centre and they are convenient*.
● Look briefly at the sentences that are relevant to the second paragraph.

Independent work
● Hand out printouts of page 4 of the Notebook file and ask the children to write the second paragraph. They will need to add ideas, and then link clauses using connectives.
● Provide less confident learners with a choice of linking words and phrases.
● As an extra challenge, ask children to plan and write the final paragraph.

Plenary
● Invite children to read out the paragraphs they have written on their printouts of page 4. Identify and highlight the connectives used.
● Ask the children to use their individual whiteboards to vote on whether they think the village needs a new supermarket. Take a tally of their votes on page 5, and write notes about their responses.

Whiteboard tools
Use a Pen from the Pen tray or the On-screen Keyboard to add text to the page.

 ▪ Pen tray
 ▪ Select tool
 ▪ Screen Shade
 ▪ On-screen Keyboard

ENGLISH LESSON 2 Name _____

Now and then

Now I eat curry.

Then I ate rusks.

Now I suck my pencil.

Then I _____

Now I sleep in a bed.

Then I _____

Now I wear _____

Then _____

Now I sing _____

Then _____

Now I drink _____

Then _____

Now I have _____

Then _____

Now I am _____

Then _____

PHOTOCOPIABLE 41

ENGLISH LESSON 4   Name _____

The meeting

■ There was a lively meeting of the class council that week. Year 4 children were discussing class rules, and they had a lot to say.

"Play time is too short," Matt called _____.

"_____," Miss Bramble replied _____.

"_____," he continued _____.

"_____," Rafael muttered _____.

Jez spoke _____: "_____"

"_____," Miss Bramble answered _____.

One girl said _____, "_____"

One boy asked _____, "_____?"

"_____," Matt interrupted _____.

"_____," Miss Bramble said _____.

ENGLISH LESSON 5　　　　　　Name _____

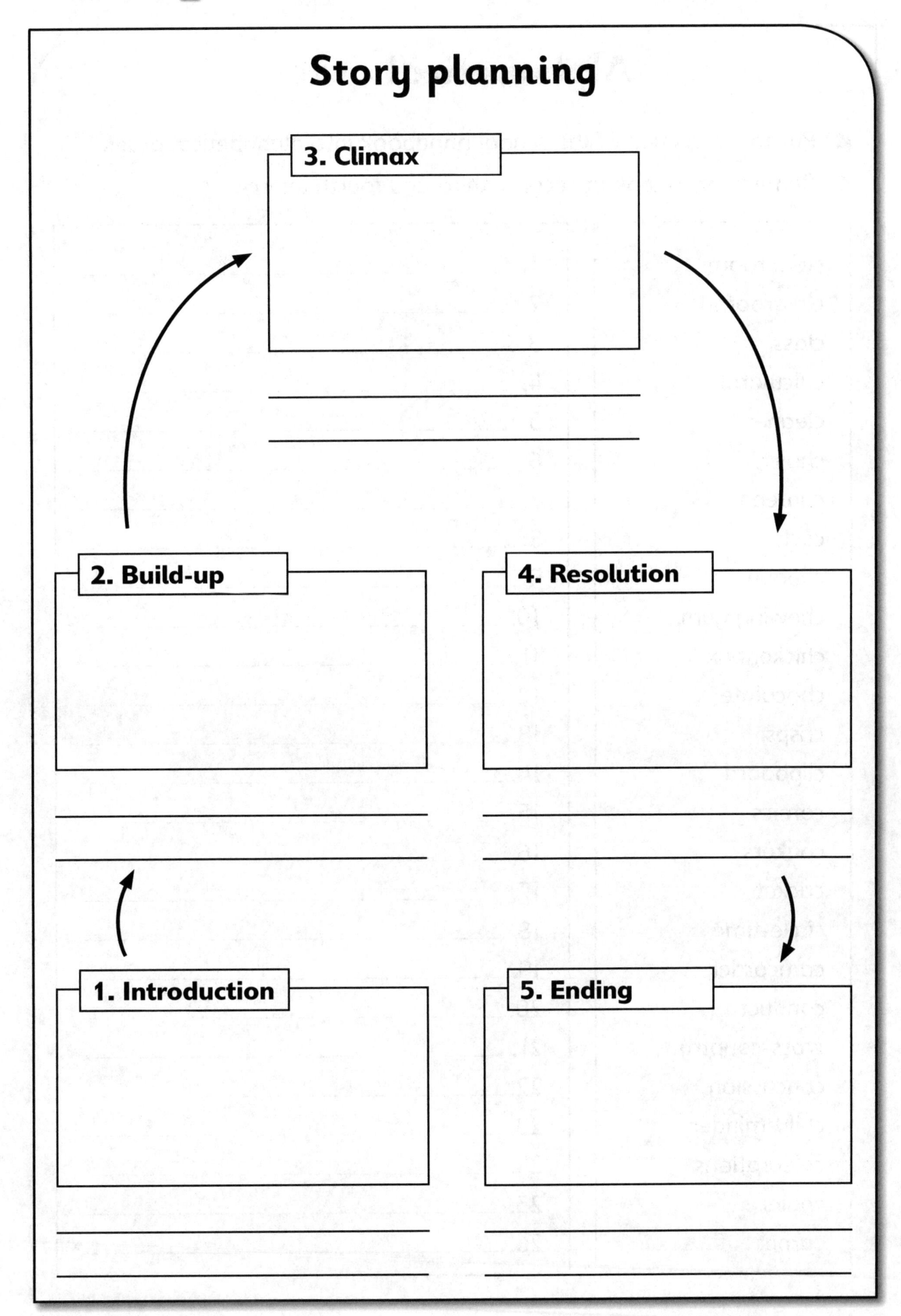

Story planning

3. Climax

2. Build-up

4. Resolution

1. Introduction

5. Ending

ENGLISH LESSON 8

Name _____

Alphabetical order

- Put the 'c' section of the school handbook into alphabetical order.
- Remember to look at second, third and fourth letters.

cloakroom	1. _____
classroom	2. _____
class	3. _____
calculator	4. _____
cleaner	5. _____
choir	6. _____
canteen	7. _____
cash	8. _____
cheque	9. _____
chewing gum	10. _____
chickenpox	11. _____
chocolate	12. _____
crisps	13. _____
clipboard	14. _____
comics	15. _____
conkers	16. _____
cricket	17. _____
circle-time	18. _____
camcorder	19. _____
conduct	20. _____
cross-country	21. _____
concussion	22. _____
child-minder	23. _____
celebrations	24. _____
chairs	25. _____
carpet	26. _____

Story summaries

The Conch Bearer
by Chitra Banerjee Divakaruni (published by The Chicken House)
Anand wants his life to change: he was a happy 12-year-old before ill luck forced him to work on the streets of his home in India. His chance comes the day he meets a strange and ragged old beggar. But who is he? What does he want?

The old man needs Anand's help to protect a treasure of immeasurable value – a tiny, beautiful conch shell. But this is no ordinary conch, it has a potent magical force and must be returned to its rightful home, many hundreds of miles away.

Anand and the old man set out and are soon joined by Nisha, a headstrong but resourceful young sweeper girl. Together they must travel across burning plains and turbulent rivers, facing evil spirits and fantastical creatures, to reach the mountainous Silver Valley. And all the time a dangerous thief, who can sense the force of the conch, is never far behind them.

Buster Bayliss: Night of the Living Veg
by Philip Reeve (published by Scholastic Children's Books)
Buster Bayliss is being forced to stay at his Fake Auntie Pauline's house in the flowery spare bedroom while his mum's away – it's a fate worse than death. Probably. Anyway, Buster is just about to find out for sure, as Smogley is being overrun with giant, man-eating, alien vegetables. Is Buster too weakened by the wallpaper torture to resist the alien advance?

The Stunning Science of Everything
by Nick Arnold (published by Scholastic Children's Books)
Taking a journey from the very small, to the very big, readers will be taken on a glorious tour of everything in science from the smallest thing ever to the horribly huge universe.

Individual chapters cover atoms, molecules, light and sound, microbes, diseases, bugs, humans and the body, animals, the Earth and outer space.

And it's all in glorious full colour!

ENGLISH LESSON 11   Name _____

Letter from Britain

■ Use the words from the Homophones box to complete the letter.

_____ Mother,

_____ can't imagine how cold it is _____! I have _____ warm clothes. Tomorrow we march north to Eburacum. From _____ we go to a _____ near the dreaded Picts. It will _____ even colder there, I am told. We _____ freeze. I am going to help build a wall as high as _____ men. We will guard it day and _____: the Roman _____ will watch everywhere. The enemy will not get _____ our defence. It will be _____ difficult!

   Only _____ years to go before I return across the _____ to Italy. I can't _____ – what a _____ celebration there will be when we get back! _____ to me with the news from home.
Your loving _____,
Titus

Homophones
their/there/they're	plaice/place	deer/dear
to/two/too	mite/might	weight/wait
no/know	for/four	threw/through
eye/I	sun/son	grate/great
bee/be	knight/night	ewe/you/yew
see/sea	right/write	hear/here

46 ■ PHOTOCOPIABLE
100 SMART Board™ LESSONS • YEAR 4

■SCHOLASTIC
www.scholastic.co.uk

ENGLISH LESSON 13 Name _____

A strange shopping list

- Wilf is a sorcerer's apprentice. The sorcerer asks him to write a shopping list for a spell – but Wilf does it all wrong! The sorcerer needs more than one of everything.

- Help Wilf by writing a new shopping list.

One spellbook shelf	Five spellbook shelves
One loaf of magibread	_____
One cat's life	_____
One spare shirt cuff	_____
One starry scarf	_____
One dragon knife	_____
One plum duff	_____
One green elf	_____
One dandelion puff	_____
One Indian chief	_____
One golden calf	_____
One falling leaf	_____

- Write the spell that the sorcerer is going to make.

_____
_____
_____
_____

SCHOLASTIC
www.scholastic.co.uk

PHOTOCOPIABLE 47
100 SMART Board™ LESSONS • YEAR 4

ENGLISH LESSON 15   Name _____

Animal possessions

The giraffe's neck is a useful ladder,

The kangaroo's pouch is the baby's cot,

The _____

The _____

The _____

The _____

The _____

The _____

The _____

The _____

The _____

The _____

48 PHOTOCOPIABLE
100 SMART Board™ LESSONS • YEAR 4

SCHOLASTIC
www.scholastic.co.uk

Illustrations © Jim Peacock / Beehive Illustration

ENGLISH LESSON 16

Name _____

Changing order – changing meaning

■ Use each row of words to make two different sentences.

1. everyone the remembers Henry VIII name of

a _____

b _____

2. six Henry had wives divorces and some

a _____

b _____

3. the king eventually to Pope the spoke selfish

a _____

b _____

4. Pope order asked Henry the for permission in to the law break special

a _____

b _____

5. Pope's unfortunately the to request answer was no Henry's

a _____

b _____

6. Catherine the in Henry end sent away

a _____

b _____

■ Draw two pictures to go with one of your pairs of sentences:

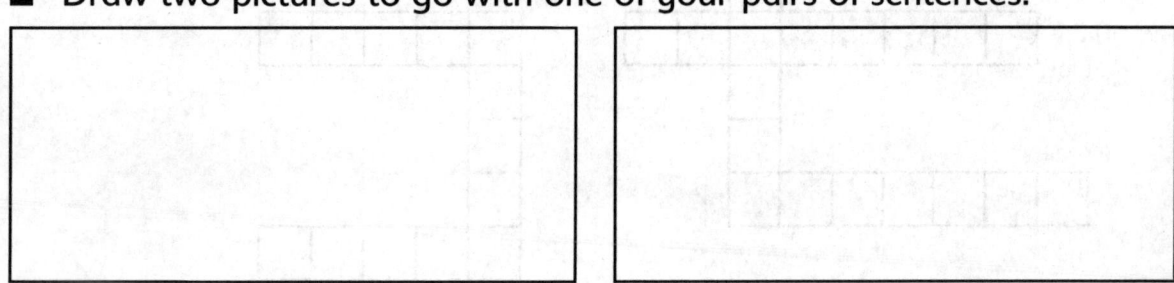

SCHOLASTIC
www.scholastic.co.uk

PHOTOCOPIABLE 49
100 SMART Board™ LESSONS • YEAR 4

ENGLISH LESSON 18   Name _____

Common endings

Across:
4. When a plane is in the sky it is in _____.
5. I don't walk under ladders because I am _____.
8. Another word for branch is _____.
9. The man in the badge and uniform looks _____.
10. 'Two plus two' is an _____ sentence.
11. Harry had a sore throat and a tickly _____.
12. Our cat is very _____ and always wants to know what's going on.
13. After the day comes the _____.

Down:
1. Pigs eat their food from a _____.
2. This is a _____ day for me because it's my birthday.
3. The farmer uses a _____ to turn over the earth in his field.
6. Ella didn't go to school in case her illness was _____.
7. 'Five take away three' is a _____ sentence.

50 PHOTOCOPIABLE
100 SMART Board™ LESSONS • YEAR 4

SCHOLASTIC
www.scholastic.co.uk

ENGLISH — LESSON 21   Name _____

A seaside trip

A seaside trip
is the best of treats because you can
    bake hot
    cool off
    surf waves
    slurp drinks
    lick lollies
    scale rocks
    tunnel under
    slide dunes
    see shells
    sail boats
    enjoy sun
    have fun
at the beach side, seaside.

(by Eileen Jones)

ENGLISH LESSON 22   Name _____

Word webs

■ Complete these word webs.

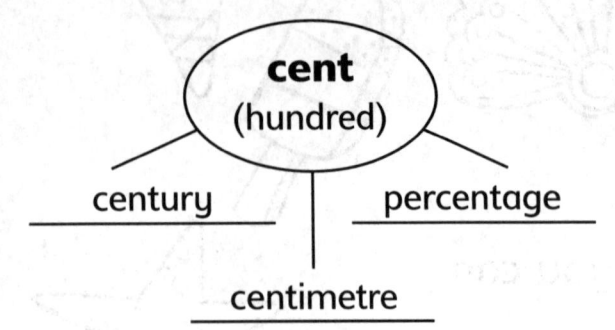

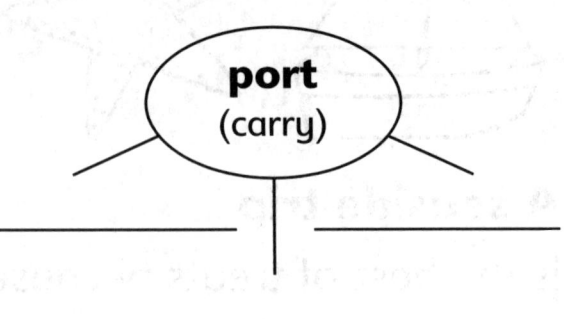

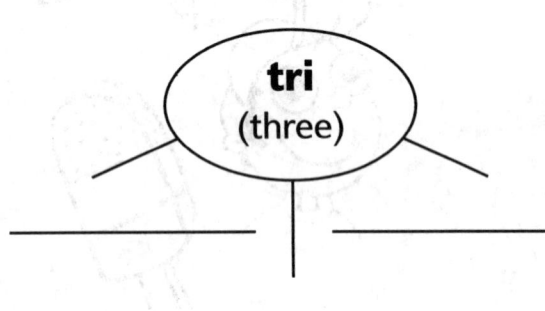

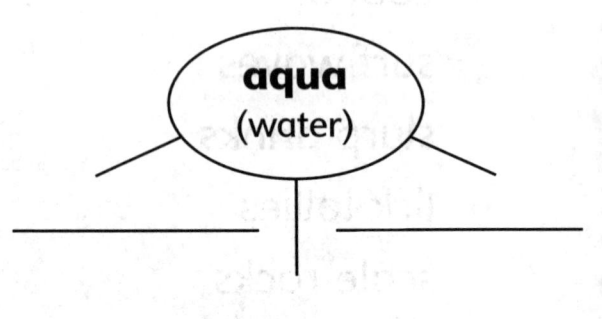

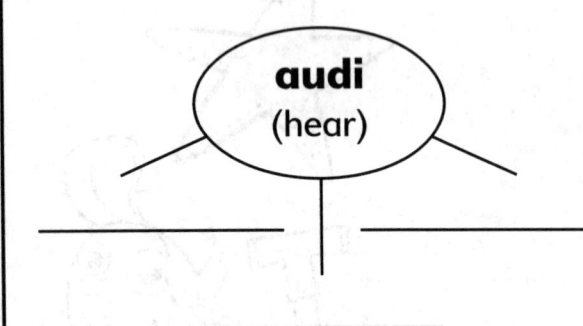

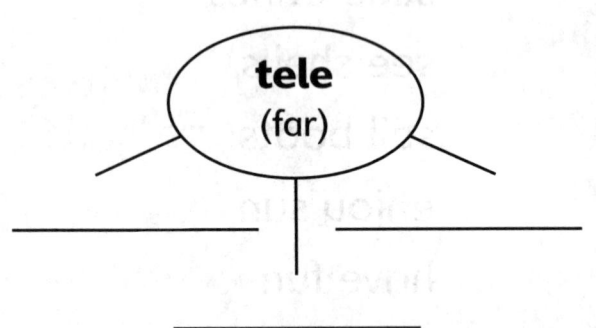

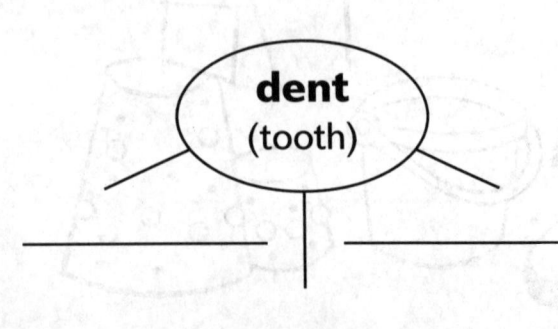

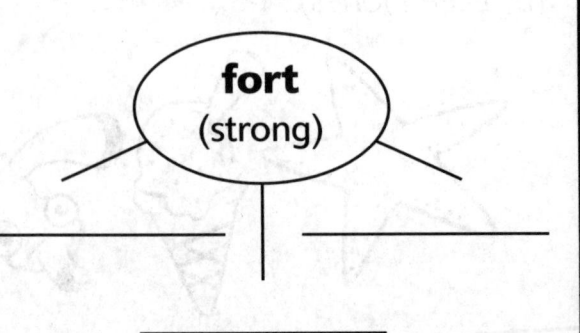

cent
(hundred)

century   percentage

centimetre

port
(carry)

tri
(three)

aqua
(water)

audi
(hear)

tele
(far)

dent
(tooth)

fort
(strong)

ENGLISH — LESSON 26   Name _____

Same word – different endings

■ Finish this poem using the same words but with different endings.

The player, playing, played in plays.

The sailor sailed in a sailing ship with sails.

The worker _____

_____, skipping, _____

_____, _____, _____ in some shops.

_____
_____
_____
_____
_____
_____
_____
_____
_____
_____
_____

Helpful words

play	work	shop	skip	hop	look	teach
farm	sail	look	act	help	fish	write
speak	care					

Helpful word endings

-er   -s   -es   -ing   -ed   -ly   -ful

PHOTOCOPIABLE 53

ENGLISH LESSON 27   Name _____

Compound words

	Separate words	**Compound words**
foot	tea + spoon	teaspoon
grand		
dust		
sand		
wheel		
frost		
wind		
yard		
bite		
bath		
band		
board		
ball		
rattle		
room		
cart		
card		
tea ✓		
apple		
berry		
bag		
bin		
parent		
rasp		
stand		
snake		
ship		
spoon ✓		
pine		
mill		

ENGLISH • LESSON 28   Name _____

Questions and answers

- Kerry has to prepare some questions. She has to ask her gran what the local area was like when she was young.

- Help Kerry by turning these statements into questions. The first one has been done for you.

1. You did live here in the past.

   Did you live here in the past?

2. You did like this area.

   _____

3. The windmill was working.

   _____

4. Prefabs were built in Sheep Street.

   _____

5. Children did walk to school.

   _____

6. You did go to Sunday school.

   _____

7. Children did not wear a uniform.

   _____

8. The town centre looks the same.

   _____

9. You can remember the old cinema.

   _____

10. You did have supermarkets.

   _____

11. Most people walked to the shops.

   _____

Mathematics — Chapter 2

Mathematics

This chapter provides 30 lessons based on the objectives taken from the Primary National Strategy's *Primary Framework for mathematics*, covering all seven strands and a range of objectives. The curriculum grids below are also provided, in editable format, on the accompanying CD-ROM.

The interactive whiteboard can enhance all three parts of the lesson, allowing you to demonstrate concepts and model strategies. Children will become actively involved by highlighting, writing and dragging the particular elements of each lesson. Mathematical resources, such as an interactive 100-square and a random number generator, can appear on screen from a Gallery; a bar chart can take minutes to draw (allowing time to interpret and discuss); picture images allow children to experience mathematics outside the classroom and link it to real-life scenarios or objects.

On the CD-ROM you will also find links to relevant DfES *Interactive Teaching Programs* (ITPs). The whiteboard is an ideal medium for making the most of these exciting and interactive resources.

Lesson title	PNS objectives	NLS objectives	Expected prior knowledge	Cross-curricular links
Lesson 1: Place value	**Counting and understanding number** • Partition and order four-digit whole numbers.	• Partition numbers into thousands, hundreds, tens and ones.	• Reading and writing numbers in figures and words to at least 1000.	**History** QCA Unit 8 'What were the differences between the lives of rich and poor people in Tudor times?'
Lesson 2: Using the symbols < and >	**Counting and understanding number** • State inequalities using the symbols < and > (eg –3 > –5, –1 < +1).	• Read and write the vocabulary of comparing and ordering numbers. • Use symbols correctly, including less than (<), greater than (>), equals (=).	• Comparing two- and three-digit numbers.	**Citizenship** QCA Unit 9 'Respect for property'
Lesson 3: Estimating and approximating	**Knowing and using number facts** • Use knowledge of rounding, number operations and inverses to estimate and check calculations.	• Read and write the vocabulary of estimation and approximation. • Make and justify estimates up to about 250 and estimate a proportion.	• Estimating up to about 100 objects.	**Art and design** QCA Unit 4C 'Journeys'
Lesson 4: Counting patterns	**Counting and understanding number** • Recognise and continue number sequences formed by counting on or back in steps of constant size.	• Recognise odd and even numbers up to 1000, and some of their properties, including the outcome of sums or differences of pairs of odd/even numbers.	• Recognising odd and even numbers to at least 100.	**History** QCA Unit 9 'What was it like for children in the Second World War?'
Lesson 5: Make 100	**Knowing and using number facts** • Use knowledge of addition and subtraction facts and place value to derive sums and differences of pairs of multiples of 10, 100 or 1000.	• Derive quickly: all number pairs that total 100 (for example, 62 + 38, 75 + 25, 40 + 60).	• Being able to use mental calculation strategies for addition of two two-digit integers.	**Geography** QCA Unit 25 'Geography and numbers'
Lesson 6: Pictograms	**Handling data** • Answer a question by identifying what data to collect; organise, present, analyse and interpret the data in tally charts and pictograms, using ICT where appropriate.	• Solve a problem by collecting quickly, organising, representing and interpreting data in tables, charts, graphs and diagrams, including those generated by a computer.	• Making pictograms, using a symbol to represent two units.	**ICT** QCA Unit 4D 'Collecting and presenting information: questionnaires and pie charts'
Lesson 7: Reading scales	**Measuring** • Interpret intervals and divisions on partially numbered scales and record readings accurately, where appropriate to the nearest tenth of a unit.	• Record estimates and readings from scales to a suitable degree of accuracy.	• Reading scales to the nearest half unit.	**Design and technology** QCA Unit 4A 'Money containers'
Lesson 8: Telling the time	**Measuring** • Read time to the nearest minute; choose units of time to measure time intervals; calculate time intervals from clocks.	• Read the time from an analogue clock to the nearest minute, and from a 12-hour digital clock.	• Reading the time to five-minute intervals.	**Geography** PoS (2c) To use maps and plans at a range of scales.

Mathematics Chapter 2

Lesson title	PNS objectives	NLS objectives	Expected prior knowledge	Cross-curricular links
Lesson 9: Polygons	**Understanding shape** • Draw polygons and classify them by identifying their properties, including their line symmetry.	• Classify polygons using criteria such as number of right angles, whether or not they are regular, symmetry properties.	• Describing 2D shapes using appropriate vocabulary.	**Art and design** QCA Unit 3B 'Investigating pattern'
Lesson 10: Identifying angles	**Understanding shape** • Know that angles are measured in degrees and that one whole turn is 360°; draw, compare and order angles less than 180°.	• Begin to know that angles are measured in degrees and that one whole turn is 360° or 4 right angles; a quarter turn is 90° or one right angle; half a right angle is 45°; start to order a set of angles less than 180°.	• Recognising right angles and identifying these in shapes and the environment.	**ICT** QCA Unit 4B 'Developing images using repeating patterns'
Lesson 11: Using *Counter*	**Counting and understanding number** • Recognise and continue number sequences formed by counting on or back in steps of constant size.	• Add/subtract 1, 10, 100 or 1000 to/from any integer, and count on or back in tens, hundreds or thousands from any whole number up to 10,000.	• Adding/subtracting 1, 10 or 100 to any two- or three-digit number.	**Geography** QCA Unit 16 'What's in the news?'
Lesson 12: Multiplying and dividing by 10 and 100	**Calculating** • Multiply and divide numbers to 1000 by 10 and then 100 (whole-number answers), understanding the effect; relate to scaling up or down.	• Multiply or divide any integer up to 1000 by 10 (whole-number answers), and understand the effect; begin to multiply by 100.	• Multiplying single-digit and decade numbers by 10/100.	**Design and technology** QCA Unit 4A 'Money containers'
Lesson 13: Rounding	**Knowing and using number facts** • Use knowledge of rounding, number operations and inverses to estimate and check calculations.	• Round any positive integer less than 1000 to the nearest 10 or 100.	• Rounding two/three-digit numbers to the nearest 10/100.	**Geography** QCA Unit 18 'Connecting ourselves to the world'
Lesson 14: Fractions	**Counting and understanding number** • Use diagrams to identify equivalent fractions (eg ⁶/₈ and ³/₄, or ⁷⁰/₁₀₀ and ⁷/₁₀); interpret mixed numbers and position them on a number line (eg 3½).	• Use fraction notation. • Recognise simple fractions that are several parts of a whole (such as ²/₃ or ⁵/₈), and mixed numbers (such as 5¾). • Recognise the equivalence of simple fractions (such as fractions equivalent to ½, ¼ or ¾).	• Recognising simple fractions that are several parts of a whole, such as ¾.	**ICT** QCA Unit 4B 'Developing images using repeating patterns'
Lesson 15: Difference	**Calculating** • Add or subtract mentally pairs of two-digit whole numbers (eg 47 + 58, 91 − 35).	• Find a difference by counting up.	• Finding differences by counting up, eg where the two integers lie either side of 100.	**English** Sentence structure and punctuation: Use commas to mark clauses.
Lesson 16: Remainders	**Calculating** • Develop and use written methods to record, support and explain multiplication and division of two-digit numbers by a one-digit number, including division with remainders (eg 15 × 9, 98 ÷ 6).	• Find remainders after division.	• Deriving division facts from 2, 3, 4, 5 and 10 multiplication tables.	**Design and technology** QCA Unit 4B 'Storybooks'
Lesson 17: Number puzzle	**Using and applying mathematics** • Identify and use patterns, relationships and properties of numbers; investigate a statement involving numbers and test it with examples.	• Solve mathematical problems or puzzles, recognise and explain patterns and relationships, generalise and predict. Suggest extensions by asking 'What if...?'	• Using hundred squares; recognising and explaining number patterns.	**ICT** QCA Unit 4D 'Collecting and presenting information: questionnaires and pie charts'
Lesson 18: Bar charts	**Using and applying mathematics** • Suggest a line of enquiry and the strategy needed to follow it; collect, organise and interpret selected information to find answers.	• Solve a problem by collecting quickly, organising, representing and interpreting data in tables, charts, graphs and diagrams, including those generated by a computer.	• Making bar charts where intervals are labelled in twos.	**Citizenship** QCA Unit 6 'Developing our school grounds'
Lesson 19: When?	**Measuring** • Read time to the nearest minute; use am, pm and 12-hour clock notation; choose units of time to measure time intervals; calculate time intervals from timetables.	• Read simple timetables and use this year's calendar.	• Reading a simple calendar.	**ICT** QCA Unit 4D 'Collecting and presenting information: questionnaires and pie charts'

Mathematics — Chapter 2

Lesson title	PNS objectives	NLS objectives	Expected prior knowledge	Cross-curricular links
Lesson 20: Reflections	**Understanding shape** • Draw polygons and classify them by identifying their properties, including their line symmetry.	• Sketch the reflection of a simple shape in a mirror line parallel to one side (all sides parallel or perpendicular to the mirror line).	• Recognising lines of symmetry in simple shapes.	**ICT** QCA Unit 4B 'Developing images using repeating patterns'
Lesson 21: Negative numbers	**Counting and understanding number** • Use positive and negative numbers in context and position them on a number line.	• Recognise negative numbers in context (for example, on a number line, on a temperature scale).	• Counting and ordering whole numbers, and using a number line.	**Geography** QCA Unit 24 'A passport to the world' **Science** QCA Unit 4C 'Keeping warm'
Lesson 22: Multiples	**Knowing and using number facts** • Derive and recall multiplication facts up to 10 × 10, the corresponding division facts and multiples of numbers to 10 up to the tenth multiple.	• Recognise multiples of 2, 3, 4, 5 and 10 up to the tenth multiple.	• Knowing 2, 5 and 10 multiplication tables.	**Art and design** QCA Unit 3B 'Investigating pattern' **ICT** QCA Unit 4B 'Developing images using repeating patterns'
Lesson 23: Money	**Counting and understanding number** • Use decimal notation for tenths and hundredths and partition decimals; relate the notation to money.	• Understand decimal notation and place value for tenths and hundredths, and use it in context.	• Recognising all coins and notes.	**History** QCA Unit 9 'What was it like for children in the Second World War?'
Lesson 24: Totalling multiples of 10	**Knowing and using number facts** • Use knowledge of addition and subtraction facts and place value to derive sums and differences of pairs of multiples of 10, 100 or 1000.	• Add three two-digit multiples of 10, such as 40 + 70 + 50.	• Totalling quickly three single-digit numbers.	**English** Sentence structure and punctuation: Use commas to mark clauses.
Lesson 25: Using + and − mental strategies	**Knowing and using number facts** • Use knowledge of addition and subtraction facts and place value to derive sums and differences of pairs of multiples of 10, 100 or 1000.	• Use known number facts and place value to add or subtract mentally, including any pair of two-digit whole numbers.	• Bridging through a multiple of 10 and adjusting.	**Science** QCA Unit 4B 'Habitats'
Lesson 26: Solving word problems	**Using and applying mathematics** • Solve one-step and two-step problems involving numbers; choose and carry out appropriate calculations. **Calculating** • Refine and use efficient written methods to add and subtract two-digit and three-digit whole numbers.	• Choose and use appropriate number operations and appropriate ways of calculating (mental, mental with jottings, pencil and paper) to solve problems. • Develop and refine written methods for column addition and subtraction.	• Using informal methods of recording; beginning to use column addition and subtraction.	**Citizenship** QCA Unit 4 'People who help us – the local police'
Lesson 27: Venn diagrams	**Handling data** • Answer a question by identifying what data to collect; organise, present, analyse and interpret the data in tables, diagrams, tally charts and bar charts, using ICT where appropriate.	• Solve a problem by collecting quickly, organising, representing and interpreting data in tables, charts, graphs and diagrams, including those generated by a computer, for example Venn diagrams.	• Using Venn diagrams to sort data.	**Science** QCA Unit 4B 'Habitats'
Lesson 28: Carroll diagrams	**Handling data** • Answer a question by identifying what data to collect; organise, present, analyse and interpret the data in tables, diagrams, tally charts and bar charts, using ICT where appropriate.	• Solve a problem by collecting quickly, organising, representing and interpreting data in tables, charts, graphs and diagrams, including those generated by a computer, for example Carroll diagrams (two criteria).	• Using Carroll diagrams to sort data.	**Science** QCA Unit 4B 'Habitats'
Lesson 29: Finding positions	**Understanding shape** • Describe and identify the position of a square on a grid of squares.	• Recognise positions and directions: for example, describe and find the position of a point on a grid of squares where the lines are numbered.	• Using coordinates which label spaces, such as a square on a grid.	**Geography** QCA Unit 10 'A village in India'
Lesson 30: Using compass directions	**Understanding shape** • Use the eight compass points to describe direction.	• Use the eight compass directions N, S, E, W, NE, NW, SE, SW.	• Using the four compass points N, S, E and W.	**Geography** QCA Unit 8 'Improving the environment'

58

100 SMART Board™ LESSONS • YEAR 4

Mathematics Lesson 1

Place value

Learning objective
PNS: Counting and understanding number
● Partition and order four-digit whole numbers.

Resources
'Place value' Notebook file; photocopiable page 89 'Partitioning' for each child; individual whiteboards and pens; a set of 0-9 number cards for each pair.

Links to other subjects
History
QCA Unit 8 'What were the differences between the lives of rich and poor people in Tudor times?'
● Ask children to use books and the internet to find population figures for Tudor times and compare these with modern data.

Whiteboard tools
Convert handwritten words to text by selecting them and choosing the Recognise option from the dropdown menu (when writing the whole numbers in words).

- Pen tray
- Select tool

Starter
Explain that you will say a whole number up to 1000. Ask the children to write it, using numerals, on their individual whiteboards and show you. Write the whole number on page 2 of the Notebook file to confirm how it should be written. Invite a volunteer to write the same whole number in words on the Notebook page.
    Repeat this process and include examples where zero is a place holder for tens and/or units, such as *650; 605*. Ask the children questions such as: *What does the zero stand for? What digit is in the hundreds/tens/units place?*

Whole-class shared work
● Extend the number range from the Starter to include thousands. Write an example on page 3 of the Notebook file using figures and words, such as *4256* and *four thousand two hundred and fifty-six*.
● Provide further examples for the children to try for themselves, such as *9043; 7360*. Extend to whole numbers greater than 10,000, writing an example on page 3. For each example, ask: *What does ___ stand for? Which place does the digit ___ hold?*
● Display page 4 of the Notebook file. Ask a child to drag a number from the box at the bottom of the screen into the 'Whole number column' in the table.
● Invite the children to suggest how to fill in each of the columns. Ask a volunteer to drag and drop each digit into place using the numbers at the bottom of the table. Repeat for seven more four-digit numbers dragged from the number box.
● Page 5 can be used to investigate whole numbers greater than 10,000. This can be done as part of this lesson or in a later lesson.

Independent work
● Ask the children to work in pairs. Provide each pair with a set of 0-9 numeral cards, and a copy of photocopiable page 89. The members of each pair take turns to pick four numeral cards. Both children make a four-digit whole number using the cards. They should try to make their integers different. Each child records their whole number on the photocopiable sheet.
● Decide whether to limit the range to three-digit integers for less confident learners by blanking out the thousands column on the sheet.
● Challenge more confient learners to extend the range to five-digit integers. They can draw their own table to complete the work.

Plenary
● Use page 6 of the Notebook file to invite children to take turns to say one of their whole numbers. Write their whole number in the whole number column of the table. Invite other children to drag and drop, or write, the appropriate digits in the partitioning columns.
● Ask questions such as: *Which digit represents thousands/hundreds/tens/units? What would the whole number be if you changed over the tens and hundreds digits?*

Mathematics — Lesson 2

Using the symbols < and >

Learning objective
PNS: Counting and understanding number
- State inequalities using the symbols < and > (eg -3 > -5, -1 < +1).

Resources
Photocopiable page 90 'Using the symbols < and >' for each child; a set of 0-9 number cards for each pair; scrap paper.

Links to other subjects
Citizenship
QCA Unit 9 'Respect for property'
- Follow up this work by asking children to compare crime statistics for two local areas, using newspaper and internet sources. Encourage them to use < and > to compare the statistics.

Whiteboard tools
Use the On-screen Keyboard to type integers in separate text boxes. Use the Random Number Generator from the Gallery to generate random numbers.

- Pen tray
- Highlighter pen
- On-screen Keyboard
- Select tool
- Gallery

Starter
Remind children that < means *is less than* and > means *is greater than*. Use the Random Number Generator from the Gallery to generate pairs of three-digit integers on a blank Notebook page, leaving a gap between the two integers. Invite children to say which is larger and write in < or > correctly. If necessary, highlight digits to help the children to see which integer is smaller or larger. Repeat this for other pairs. Over time, extend to four-digit integers.

Whole-class shared work
- Write the following on a blank Notebook page: 430 < ☐. Ask for suggestions for the missing number.
- Repeat this, using the Random Number Generator to generate four-digit integers. Use both < and >.
- Write 1234 < ☐ < 1563. Invite suggestions for the missing numbers.
- Discuss the range of integers that will fit in the box. Which will not fit?
- Type five four-digit integers on the whiteboard, out of number order. Make sure they are in separate text boxes so that they can be moved independently. Invite the children to re-order these, smallest first. Ask them to insert < between each integer.
- Repeat for another set, this time writing the largest first and inserting > between each integer.

Independent work
- Ask the children to work in pairs. Each pair needs a set of 0-9 number cards. Give each child a copy of photocopiable page 90 and some scrap paper.
- In their pairs, the children take turns to choose four number cards. They each make six different four-digit integers using their chosen cards. They should make a note of these numbers on the scrap paper.
- Next they should record the numbers on the sheet, making sure that they put the numbers in the correct order.
- Decide whether to ask less confident learners to choose three cards to make HTU integers.
- Challenge more confident learners to choose four digits from 1 to 9 (not zero) and to find all possible four-digit integers. (There are 24 possibilities.)
- As the children work, challenge them to tell you which sign would fit between sets of two integers, and why.

Plenary
- Write the following on the interactive whiteboard: 6435 < ☐ > ☐.
- Ask the children to suggest integers that will fit into the boxes. Encourage them to suggest a range of integers that will fit each box. Repeat for another example, such as 2004 > ☐ < ☐.

Mathematics — Lesson 3

Estimating and approximating

Learning objective
PNS: Knowing and using number facts
- Use knowledge of rounding, number operations and inverses to estimate and check calculations.

Resources
'Estimating' Notebook file; transparent containers filled with between 100 and 250 counters; paper plates.

Links to other subjects
Art and design
QCA Unit 4C 'Journeys'
- Children can estimate how much of the surface of a painting or object is covered by a particular design or colour.

Starter
Display page 2 of the Notebook file. Show the image for about five seconds and invite the children to estimate how many counters there are. Hide the screen with the Screen Shade. Ask the children to record their estimates on their individual whiteboards and invite them to share their estimates. Reveal the screen again and ask: *How shall we count these to check?* Invite a child to demonstrate by counting in fives or tens. The counters can be dragged and grouped into sets. Reveal the answer at the top of the page.
   Use the Undo button until the page is reset and delete some of the counters. Repeat the estimating activity.

Whole-class shared work
- Display page 3 of the Notebook file. Ask: *How many stars do you estimate there are? How did you make your estimate?*
- Ask the children to write their prediction of the number of objects on the screen on their individual whiteboards.
- Invite a child to demonstrate how they made their estimate, such as counting a small number of stars and multiplying up.
- Repeat this for pages 4 and 5.
- Now show the children the prepared containers (see Resources). Tell them to work quickly in small groups to make estimates of how many counters there are. Allow about five minutes for this.
- Bring the class back together. Compare and discuss estimates and how these were made. Invite the children to check their estimates by counting the counters in their container.
- Hide the containers, and remove half (or a quarter) of the counters from each. Show each container in turn and ask the children to estimate about how many counters have been removed, and to express this as a fraction.

Independent work
- Ask the children to work in pairs with about 250 counters in a container and a large paper plate. They take turns to spread out some of the counters on the plate. They both estimate how many counters there are, and record their estimate.
- Challenge the children to think of a quick way to count the counters. They then record the actual number.
- Ask the children to repeat the activity ten times.
- Limit the maximum number of counters to 100 for less confident learners.
- Extend more confident learners by increasing the number to 300.

Plenary
- Display page 6 of the Notebook file, and ask the children to estimate how many triangles are on the page. Invite them to explain how they worked this out.
- Repeat this for page 7.
- Invite a child to estimate half of the circles on page 7 by selecting approximately half of the circles and deleting them.
- Then ask another child to estimate half of what is left in the same way. Ask: *What portion is left?* (A quarter.) *Do you agree? Why do you think that?*
- Repeat for other quantities, asking the children to remove estimates of quarters and halves.

Whiteboard tools
Use the Screen Shade to hide the screen in the Starter.

- Pen tray
- Select tool
- Screen Shade
- Undo button

Mathematics Lesson 4

Counting patterns

Learning objective
PNS: Counting and understanding number
- Recognise and continue number sequences formed by counting on or back in steps of constant size.

Resources
Counter software (available on the CD-ROM in the *Using ICT to support mathematics in primary school* training pack, DfES references: DfES0260/2000 for entire training pack; DfES0267/2000 for CD-ROM only - also available through the DfES website www.standards.dfes.gov.uk).
Set Step to +2 for counting up, and then -2 for counting back. Set 361 in the memory.

Links to other subjects
History
QCA Unit 9 'What was it like for children in the Second World War?'
- Ask the children to collect information about rationing. They can use their knowledge of sums of odd and even numbers to determine how many items of food children had in a week, month and year, and whether these are odd or even numbers.

Starter
Set *Counter* to begin to count in twos from 500 to 600. Invite the children to join in the count, keeping a regular counting pace. Repeat, counting back in twos. Ask: *If you count in twos from 500, do you say odd or even numbers? How can you tell whether a number is odd or even?* Repeat for counting in twos starting on an odd number, such as 531.

Whole-class shared work
- Recall the memory in *Counter* (MR button). Ask the children if 361 is an odd or even number. How can they tell?
- Begin the count in twos from 361. Can the children tell you if *Counter* is showing odd or even numbers now? Stop *Counter* and check if they know what would need to be added to the displayed number to make it even.
- Agree the rules for recognising odd numbers (unit digit is 1, 3, 5, 7 or 9), and for even numbers (unit digit is 0, 2, 4, 6 or 8).
- Ask the children questions such as: *Will 4 add 2 give an even or odd sum? What about 6 add 8? And 10 add 14? Do you think that an even plus an even number will always be even? Why do you think that?*

Independent work
- Tell the children that they are going to work in pairs to investigate the sums and differences of odd and even numbers.
- Write the following on a blank Notebook page:
  - odd + odd = ?
  - even + even = ?
  - odd + even = ?
  - even + odd = ?
- Explain to the children that you would like them to decide, in each case, whether the sum is odd or even and to give some examples to demonstrate their findings.
- Work with less confident learners as a group, using small numbers to demonstrate examples for each of the above sums.
- Extend more confident learners by challenging them to explain why, for example, the sum of two odd numbers is always even.

Plenary
- Review each of the above generalised addition sentences, writing appropriate number sentences on the whiteboard, and agree whether the sum is odd or even in each case.
- Ask the more confident learners to explain why the sum of two odd numbers is always even. (An odd number can always be expressed as one more than an even number: for example, 3+3 = 2+1+2+1. So there are always two ones to total to make the sum even.)

Whiteboard tools
- Pen tray
- Select tool

Mathematics — Lesson 5

Make 100

Learning objective
PNS: Knowing and using number facts
- Use knowledge of addition and subtraction facts and place value to derive sums and differences of pairs of multiples of 10, 100 or 1000.

Resources
'Make 100' Notebook file; photocopiable page 91 'Make 100', one copy for each pair; two different-coloured pencils for each pair.

Links to other subjects
Geography
QCA Unit 25 'Geography and numbers'
- Children can use number pairs to 100 to help them compare distances between towns.

Starter
Explain that you will say a small number. Ask the children to call out, together, the number that adds to your number to make a total of 20. So, if you say 13, the children call out 7. Keep a good pace to this to encourage rapid recall.

Alternatively, you can drag random numbers from the Numbers box on page 2 of the Notebook file if the children find it easier to see the number. If children falter for any responses, reveal the hundred square on the Number grid ITP and use this to demonstrate the answer by counting up in appropriate groups.

Whole-class shared work
- Go to page 3 and explain that the children will be finding pairs of numbers that total 100, quickly and easily.
- Begin with the easier pairs, using what is already known: 9 + 1 = 10; 90 + 10 = 100, and so on. Press on the pairs in the hundred grid to highlight them, to mark these numbers so that the children can see which pairs have been found. Use the Pen tool to change the colours of the paired numbers for easy identification.
- Now move to other pairs and ask: *How did you work out the answer?* Praise those children who 'knew' it. Spend about five minutes on finding other pairs.

Independent work
- Ask the children to work in pairs on photocopiable page 91.
- Invite the children to take turns to choose a start number for their partner. The partner finds the other number to total 100. The first child can challenge if they think their partner is wrong, and must find a way to demonstrate that they are correct. Children score a point for a correct answer. Encourage them to colour each pair of numbers, each child using a different colour.
- They should continue until they have found all pairs.
- Work with less confident learners as a group. Invite them to take turns to say a pair that they think totals 100. Discuss strategies for finding answers.
- When the more confident learners have finished playing the game, ask them to write some strategies for finding solutions quickly.

Plenary
- Go to page 4 and put the class into four teams. Appoint a captain for each team and play 'Finding pairs to make 100' as a class game.
- Invite the more confident learners to suggest strategies for finding solutions quickly.
- List these strategies on page 4, and invite all the children to think of which pairs could be made using that strategy. Strategies could include: using decade numbers, using numbers which end in 5 and using number bonds to 10 to find the unit digit of the missing number.

Whiteboard tools
- Pen tray
- Pen tool
- Select tool

Mathematics — Lesson 6

Learning objective
PNS: Handling data
- Answer a question by identifying what data to collect; organise, present, analyse and interpret the data in tally charts and pictograms, using ICT where appropriate.

Resources
'Pictogram' Notebook file.

Links to other subjects
ICT
QCA Unit 4D 'Collecting and presenting information: questionnaires and pie charts'
- This lesson links directly to ICT. Use the other data collected to repeat this lesson so that children become proficient with using and interpreting pictograms where the symbol represents several units.

Whiteboard tools
Use the Lines tool to draw charts, a Pen from the Pen tray to enter the tally and the On-screen Keyboard to add headings to the empty pictogram.

- Pen tray
- Select tool
- Lines tool
- On-screen Keyboard
- Capture tool

Pictograms

Starter
Display page 2 of the Notebook file. Write in a survey question, such as: *What pets do you have?* Agree how to collect the data: for example, by recording the number of children who have dogs, cats or rabbits. Draw a simple data collection chart and enter the information using tallies.

Go to page 3 of the Notebook file and repeat for another question, such as: *What is your favourite type of day out?* Record the number of children who like museums, theme parks, water parks and so on.

Whole-class shared work
- Put the children into mixed-ability groups of about four. Tell them that they are going to gather data from other children. (The quantity of data needs to be large, so agree with other teachers that children can come to their classes in small groups to ask their questions.)
- Display page 4 of the Notebook file. Encourage each group to think of a survey question (for example, month of birth or number of brothers or sisters). Write notes and suggestions on the Notebook file if required.
- Discuss and agree how the children should collect their data. They should make a tally chart and agree the fields (or headings) before they begin.

Independent work
- Children should collect their data and total it for each field.
- Encourage more confident learners to provide support for those who are less confident, if necessary.

Plenary
- Pick one of the groups to share their data.
- Go to page 5 of the Notebook file. Press the button to open the pictogram. Discuss what the headings for each row should be and type these in.
- Discuss how many items one symbol should stand for. Explain that you cannot use a symbol to represent every single item. For example, in many pictograms a symbol represents ten or even twenty items.
- Ask the children to calculate how many symbols are needed for each heading and input these. Discuss how to complete the row where the items do not divide exactly by the number of units chosen for each symbol.
- Fill in the key box.
- Use the Capture tool to insert a screenshot of the finished pictogram on a new Notebook page.
- Ask questions about the data, such as: *How many more ___ are there than ___? Which is the most/least popular? How can you tell that?*
- Encourage children to speculate about their data. Ask: *How accurate do you think this data is? Why do you think that? How could we improve on our data collection?*
- Use the data collected by other groups in subsequent lessons.

Mathematics — Lesson 7

Learning objective
PNS: Measuring
- Interpret intervals and divisions on partially numbered scales and record readings accurately, where appropriate to the nearest tenth of a unit.

Resources
'Reading scales' Notebook file; photocopiable page 92 'Reading scales' for each child.

Links to other subjects
Design and technology
QCA Unit 4A 'Money containers'
- When planning and making items, encourage children to use their measuring skills and to make decisions about estimating and rounding measurements.

Reading scales

Starter
Display page 2 of the Notebook file. Ask the children to look at the first ruler and to say what measurement they see on it. Discuss the scale, and how it is marked. Ask the children to read the scale. Repeat this for the other scales, ensuring that the children understand that for some of the rulers they will need to estimate how many millimetres there are between the markings.

Whole-class shared work
- Display page 3 and discuss the scale, noting that the markings between each centimetre are in millimetres.
- Invite the children to make estimates of the readings and then to look carefully to check the readings. Encourage them to do this accurately. Discuss whether to round up or down to the nearest half centimetre, and why this may be appropriate. Check that the children understand that millimetres can be expressed as a decimal fraction of a centimetre.
- Display page 4 and discuss how the containers are marked, and how to read the scale.
- Ask the children to read the water levels, and to make estimates where necessary. Encourage them to explain their estimates.
- Go to page 5. Again, discuss the scale and invite the children to estimate the readings. Repeat this for page 6.
- Display page 7, which shows three lines. Invite a child to move the ruler until it lines up with the first line. Discuss how to make the measurement to the nearest half centimetre. Repeat for the other two lines.

Independent work
- Give each child a copy of photocopiable sheet 92 to complete.
- As the children work, discuss how they make their estimates, and how accurate they think these are.
- Less confident learners could be asked to read to the nearest cm, nearest 100ml and nearest 10kg.
- Challenge more confident learners to read to the nearest mm, nearest 25ml and nearest 5kg.
- When the children have completed the sheet, ask them to use a ruler to draw some lines on the back of the sheet. They should work with a partner to measure the lines to the nearest half centimetre.

Plenary
- With the children watching, draw some thick lines on page 8 of the Notebook file using the Lines tool. Invite individuals to take turns to move the ruler into place so that it lines up with the drawn line.
- Invite children to read, from the ruler, the length of the line to the nearest half centimetre. They could try using a real ruler as well, to check that the measurements are the same.
- Ask the children: *How do you decide whether to round a measurement up or down?*

Whiteboard tools
Add lines to the page with the Lines tool in the Plenary.

- Pen tray
- Select tool
- Lines tool

Mathematics Lesson 8

Telling the time

Learning objective
PNS: Measuring
● Read time to the nearest minute; use am, pm and 12-hour clock notation; choose units of time to measure time intervals; calculate time intervals from clocks.

Resources
'Telling the time' Notebook file; photocopiable page 93 'How long?', one for each pair.

Links to other subjects
Geography
PoS (2c) To use maps and plans at a range of scales.
● Use string to measure approximate distances on a map. You will also need to talk about the issue of scale when you do this.

Starter
Display page 2 of the Notebook file. Write a time, in words, at the top of the page, and invite a pair of children to place the hands on the analogue clock in the correct place using the Select tool, and write the correct digits into the digital clock. Use times of five-minute intervals, such as twenty past six, quarter to ten. Invite the other children to check that they agree.

Use the Eraser from the Pen tray to delete the writing and invite another pair to try the activity. Repeat for several more pairs.

Whole-class shared work
● Reveal the pair of clocks on page 3 of the Notebook file. Ask: *What time does the first analogue clock show?* Invite a child to write this time on the digital clock. Repeat for the second clock.
● Repeat this for the clocks on page 4. For the second clock ask: *How many minutes past the hour does the clock show?* Invite the children to count the minutes as you point to the minute marks on the clock. Ask: *So what is the time?* Invite a child to write in the time on the digital clock to match.
● Repeat this for the next pairs of clocks on pages 5 to 8.
● Look at the pair of clocks on page 9. Read the problem next to the clocks. Encourage answers and write the answer in the space provided.
● Challenge the children to make up time word problems for the next two pairs of clocks on page 10, and answer them. This page shows a mixture of analogue and digital clocks.

Independent work
● Distribute copies of photocopiable page 93 and ask the children to complete them, working cooperatively.
● Work with the less confident learners in a group. Say the time on each clock together, counting the minutes where necessary. Encourage the children to suggest a word problem for each.
● Provide analogue and digital clock templates for more confident learners. Challenge them to use them to write some times, and to create word problems to go with them. These can be scanned into the computer for the Plenary.

Plenary
● Display the pair of clocks on page 11 of the Notebook file.
● Ask the children to say the difference between the times and suggest a time sentence to go with them. For example, a suitable sentence might be: *The meal started at 12.37 and finished at 1.41 so it lasted for one hour and four minutes.*
● Repeat this for the pair of clocks on page 12.
● Invite the more confident group to reveal one of their scanned-in time word problems for other children to solve. Repeat for the other time word problems.

Whiteboard tools
To upload scanned images, select Insert, then Picture File, and browse to where you have saved the image. Press on the end of the clock hands to rotate them. Use a Pen from the Pen tray to write on the page. Use the Eraser from the Pen tray to erase writing.

- Pen tray
- Select tool

Mathematics · Lesson 9

Polygons

Learning objective
PNS: Understanding shape
• Draw polygons and classify them by identifying their properties, including their line symmetry.

Resources
'Polygons' Notebook file; photocopiable page 94 'Polygons' for each child (you may wish to enlarge the sheet); scissors; shape tiles; paper and glue.

Links to other subjects
Art and design
QCA Unit 3B 'Investigating pattern'
• Provide examples of patterns from other cultures. Invite the children to describe the shapes they see and to explain how each pattern is made. They can search for polygons, explain whether or not these are regular, and why they think that.

Whiteboard tools
Use the Shapes tool for the Starter. Use the Lines tool to create irregular polygons with straight sides.

- Pen tray
- Shapes tool
- Select tool
- Lines tool

Starter
Open the Notebook file and go to page 2. Describe a polygon (for example: *I am thinking of a shape that is regular. It has four right angles*). Ask the children to guess what it is (for example, a square). Use the Shapes tool to place the shape on the page, so that the children can see if they were right. Encourage them to check the shape against your description. Repeat for different polygons.

Whole-class shared work
- Display page 3 of the Notebook file. Discuss the definition of a polygon: *a closed, flat shape with three or more straight sides*.
- Discuss the definition of a regular polygon: *a closed, flat shape with three or more straight sides, and all sides and angles equal*.
- Go to page 4 and tell the children you want them to sort the shapes. Point out the title of the Carroll diagram: *Sorting polygons*.
- Point out the headings: *Triangles; Quadrilaterals; Regular; Not regular*.
- Ask the children to suggest how to sort the shapes and to explain why each shape belongs in its specific place. Invite a volunteer to drag the shapes into the Carroll diagram as they are discussed.
- Point out the shapes that do not fit into the Carroll diagram. Ask the children to explain why they don't belong in the diagram. Emphasise that the remaining shapes are neither triangles nor quadrilaterals because they have more than four sides; however, they are all polygons.
- Use page 5 to discuss the definitions for equilateral (all sides and angles equal), isosceles (two sides and angles equal) and right-angled (one right angle) triangles.
- Complete the polygon sorting activities on pages 6 and 7. Use the ruler if necessary, to measure the sides of the shapes.

Independent work
- Give each child a copy of photocopiable page 94. Ask them to cut out the sets of triangles and to separate them into isosceles, equilateral and right-angled triangles. They should then use the sets to make patterns. The shape tiles in their patterns must touch, leaving no gaps (tessellation).
- When the children have produced patterns they are happy with, these can be stuck onto paper to preserve them.
- Decide whether less confident learners should use plastic shape tiles, and work as a group. Encourage the children to describe the properties of the shapes.
- Provide more confident learners with some assorted shape tiles. Which shapes tessellate and which do not?

Plenary
- Review the patterns that children have made. Discuss the properties of the shapes.
- Ask questions such as: *Are these shapes polygons? Regular polygons? Is a circle a polygon? Why not?*
- Record the children's observations on page 8 of the Notebook file.
- Invite the more confident learners to explain which of the tiles they have been given will tessellate, and to explain why this is so.

Mathematics — Lesson 10

Identifying angles

Learning objective
PNS: Understanding shape
- Know that angles are measured in degrees and that one whole turn is 360°; draw, compare and order angles less than 180°.

Resources
'Angles' Notebook file; photocopiable page 95, 'Identifying angles', one for each pair of children; 45° and 60° set squares, one of each for each pair of children.

Links to other subjects
ICT
QCA Unit 4B 'Developing images using repeating patterns'
- When re-sizing images on screen, ask the children to consider whether the angles of the shape have changed, and in what way.

Starter
Display page 2 of the Notebook file. Ask the children to stand up and face the front of the classroom. Explain that you will say an angle and would like them to turn in the direction that you say. Say, for example: *Turn a right angle to the right. Turn two right angles to the right. Now turn another right angle to the right. How many right angles have you turned? And where have you finished? So how many right angles are there if you turn through a complete circle?*

Repeat with left, and more right, turns, and using 30°, 60°, as well as 90°.

Whole-class shared work
- Display page 3. Ask the children to look carefully at the angles and to say their size. Agree and check with the protractor from the Gallery that these are all 90° angles.
- Go to page 4 and explain that two different types of angles are shown. Ask for volunteers to use the protractor to measure the angles on the page.
- Demonstrate how to record and read the angles in degrees.
- Now display page 5 and ask the children to decide which is the smallest angle, the next smallest, and so on.
- Drag and drop the angles into order from smallest to largest.
- Use the protractor, if necessary, to measure the angles.

Independent work
- Ask the children to work in pairs.
- Provide each pair with a 45° and 60° set square.
- Ask each pair to complete photocopiable page 95.
- Decide whether to work with less confident learners as a group, with an A3 enlargement of the photocopiable sheet and the board set squares.
- If more confident learners complete the work quickly, suggest that they use the set squares to construct some triangles with angles of 45° and 60°.

Plenary
- Use page 6 of the Notebook file to draw an angle, using either a Pen from the Pen tray or the Lines tool.
- Ask the children whether the angle you have drawn is larger or smaller than a right angle.
- Repeat this for other angles, comparing them with 45° and 60° and using the protractor to check.

Whiteboard tools
Use a Pen from the Pen tray or the Lines tool to draw angles. Use the protractor from the Gallery to measure them.

- Pen tray
- Select tool
- Lines tool
- Gallery

Mathematics — Lesson 11

Using *Counter*

Learning objective
PNS: Counting and understanding number
- Recognise and continue number sequences formed by counting on or back in steps of constant size.

Resources
Individual whiteboards and pens; four sets of 0–9 number cards for each pair; *Counter* software (CD-ROM containing the *Counter* software is available from *Using ICT to support mathematics in primary school* training pack, DfES references: DfES0260/2000 for entire training pack; DfES0267/2000 for CD-ROM only). Set the Start number to 54. Set Step to +1 for counting up in ones, and then −1 for counting back in ones.

Links to other subjects
Geography
QCA Unit 16 'What's in the news?'
- Search newspapers for numerical information, such as numbers attending football matches. Discuss what happens if there are 1/10/100 more or fewer.

Starter
Decide upon the number range, such as up to 1000/5000/10,000. Explain that you will say a number and ask the children to write it, using numerals, on their individual whiteboards. Keep the pace sharp. Ask questions such as: *What does the first/second/third/digit stand for? What number would you have if you removed the ___ digit?*

Whole-class shared work
- Explain that you have set *Counter* to count on in ones from 54 (or any number under 100). Begin the count and ask the children to count with *Counter*. Stop the count and ask them what the next number would be.
- Set the Step to −1 and begin the count again. Stop the count. Ask: *What would the next number be? And the next? So how could we describe the count?*
- Repeat this for counting on and back in tens, then in hundreds.
- Write on a blank Notebook page a number such as 546 (or any number under 1000). Ask: *What is one more or less than this? What is ten/hundred more or less than this?*
- Repeat this for other starting numbers, up to 10,000.
- Discuss which digits change when adding/subtracting 1, 10 and 100. Highlight the changed digits on the interactive whiteboard.

Independent work
- Provide each pair of children with number cards. Ask them to generate a starting number, then to write the +1, −1, +10, −10, +100 and −100 number.
- The children can record their work by making a simple table like this:

Start number	+1	−1	+10	−10	+100	−100

- Provide three sets of number cards for less confident learners and ask them to make starting numbers with three digits.
- Provide five sets of cards for more confident learners and challenge them to make integers with five digits, and to add/subtract 1000 to each integer.
- Encourage the children to explain which digit will change as they add and subtract, and why other digits remain unchanged.

Plenary
- Review starting numbers from each group and ask the children to say the numbers which are one, ten and one hundred more or less than this number. Write on the whiteboard the numbers that the children say. Ask: *Which digits could change when we add/subtract 1/10/100? Why is that?*

Whiteboard tools
- Pen tray
- Select tool
- Highlighter pen

Mathematics Lesson 12

Multiplying and dividing by 10 and 100

Learning objective
PNS: Calculating
- Multiply and divide numbers to 1000 by 10 and then 100 (whole number answers), understanding the effect; relate to scaling up or down.

Resources
'Build your own' file; a set of 0-9 number cards for each pair. Open the 'Build your own' file and use it to prepare a Notebook file showing two cakes (from the Mathematics folder under My Content in the Gallery) on the left-hand side and 20 cakes on the right. Cover the 20 cakes with a large rectangle (or use the Screen Shade). Add the Random Number Generator from the same folder under to the second page. Save your prepared Notebook file ready for use.

Links to other subjects
Design and technology
QCA Unit 4A 'Money containers'
- Encourage the children to use the strategies they have learned to change units of measurement (cm to mm, mm to m) as they design a money box.

Whiteboard tools
Use the Screen Shade or Shapes tool to hide the cakes. Use the Random Number Generator in the Gallery to generate numbers.

- Pen tray
- Highlighter pen
- Shapes tool
- Screen Shade
- Gallery
- Blank Page button

Starter
Open your prepared Notebook file (see Resources) and reveal the two cakes. Explain that you have nine people coming to tea and you need to multiply the cakes by 10 to have enough for everyone (including yourself). Write the number sentences on the whiteboard (2 × 10 = 20; 20 ÷ 10 = 2) and ask the children to multiply and divide by 10. Reveal the 20 cakes on the right. Go to a new page and repeat the process of writing a digit on the board and asking the children to multiply and divide by 10. Next, use decade numbers (for example, 20 or 40) and multiply and divide by 100. Keep the pace of this sharp. Discuss the effect of multiplying and dividing by 10 and 100.

Whole-class shared work
- Write the numbers 1 to 9, well spaced, and highlight them.
- Under each number, write the result when it is multiplied by 10 (10 under 1, 20 under 2 and so on).
- Ask: *What has happened to these numbers? What is the pattern? Suppose I multiplied by 1... 2... 100? What would I write then?* On the next line down, write the children's suggestions: 100, 200 and so on.
- Now ask the children what would happen if you multiplied by 1000. Invite them to take turns to complete the next row of this table.
- Challenge the children to say what will happen if you divide by 10. (1000 becomes 100, 100 becomes 10 and 10 becomes 1.)
- Discuss the place value of each zero in the thousands row, and the effect on the digits in each integer of multiplying/dividing by 10 or 100.

Independent work
- Working in pairs, ask the children to generate two-digit numbers using number cards and record the effect of multiplying by 10, then by 100. One group of children could use the Random Number Generator from the Gallery to generate numbers, recording results in a table.
- Challenge the children to write a list of four-digit numbers that can be divided by both 10 and 100.
- Less confident learners should generate unit numbers, and write three-digit numbers that can be divided by both 10 and 100.
- Ask more confident learners to generate three-digit numbers, and write five-digit numbers which can be divided by both 10 and 100.

Plenary
- Ask questions such as: *How many times larger is 350 than 35? How many £1 coins are there in £25... £250... £2500? How many 10p coins in each amount? How did you work that out?* Write the multiplication and division by 10, 100 and 1000 as appropriate for each of these questions.

Mathematics Lesson 13

Learning objective
PNS: Knowing and using number facts
- Use knowledge of rounding, number operations and inverses to estimate and check calculations.

Resources
'City distances' Notebook file; individual whiteboards and pens.

Links to other subjects
Geography
QCA Unit 18 'Connecting ourselves to the world'
- The children can use maps and the internet to find places in the world and compare distances between them.

Rounding

Starter
Display page 2 of the Notebook file. Agree the rules for rounding to the nearest 10: unit digit of 5 to 9 rounds up; unit digit of 1 to 4 rounds down. Write the rules on the Notebook file. Explain that you will say a two-digit number. Ask the children to decide whether to round it up or down to the nearest 10. If it rounds up, ask them to point up; if it rounds down, they point down. Keep the pace of this sharp.

Whole-class shared work
- Go to page 3. Explain that you will write a three-digit number in the table. Challenge the children to round it up or down to the nearest 10, then the nearest 100, recording the answers in the appropriate columns.
- Display page 4 of the Notebook file. Ask: *To round these distances, is it more sensible to round to the nearest 10 or 100 miles? Why do you think that?*
- Delete the box with the heading *Rounded to 10 or 100?* to reveal the heading *Rounded to nearest 10.*
- Invite the children to round some of these distances to the nearest 10. Use the Eraser from the Pen tray to reveal the correct answers in the answer column.
- Repeat for the map and distances on page 5.

Independent work
- This should take no longer than ten minutes. Allow extra time for the Plenary.
- Display page 6 of the Notebook file, showing the larger distances for Europe. Ask: *Is it more sensible to round the distance between ___ and ___ to the nearest 10 or 100? Why do you think that?*
- Explain that you will use this page to look at distances between London and various cities in Europe. Tell the children to write down the cities and the distances on their individual whiteboards.
- Now ask them to round these distances to the nearest 10 miles and 100 miles and to record their results.
- Work with the less confident learners to check that they understand the rounding rules.
- Challenge the more confident learners to undertake a web search to find further distances for the Plenary.

Plenary
- Review the roundings from the independent work. Discuss which would be more sensible: rounding by 10 or by 100 for each distance.
- Use page 7 to round by both 10 and by 100 to observe the effect. Write the rounded distances in the first column under each heading.
- Use the Eraser from the Pen tray to reveal the answers in the yellow boxes. For each example, ask: *Would it be more sensible to round by 10 or by 100? Why do you think that?*

Whiteboard tools
Use the Eraser from the Pen tray to reveal the answers.

- Pen tray
- Select tool

71

100 SMART Board™ LESSONS • YEAR 4

Mathematics Lesson 14

Learning objective
PNS: Counting and understanding number
• Use diagrams to identify equivalent fractions (eg $^6/_8$ and $^3/_4$, or $^{70}/_{100}$ and $^7/_{10}$); interpret mixed numbers and position them on a number line (eg $3^1/_2$).

Resources
'Build your own' file; centimetre-squared paper and pens.

Links to other subjects
ICT
QCA Unit 4B 'Developing images using repeating patterns'
• The children can follow up this work by using the shapes made by their fractions to create repeating patterns.

Fractions

Starter
Open the 'Build your own' file, which consists of a blank Notebook page and a ready-made Gallery collection of resources located in My Content. Use the Fraction Maker, from the Mathematics folder under My Content, to write $^1/_2$ on the blank Notebook page. Ask the children to suggest another fraction that is equivalent to this (for example, $^2/_4$). Now write $^1/_{10}$ and ask them how many tenths make one whole. Repeat this for other fractions, such as $^1/_4$, $^1/_5$ or $^1/_8$. Write $^3/_{10}$ and ask: *How many more tenths do I need to make one whole?* Repeat for other fractions such as $^2/_5$ or $^7/_8$.

Whole-class shared work
• Place an empty number line on a blank Notebook page. Label one end 0 and the other 1. Invite a child to write in where they estimate $^1/_2$ should go. Now ask where $^2/_4$ will go. Agree that $^1/_2$ and $^2/_4$ are equivalent.
• Repeat this for other pairs of fractions, such as $^1/_5$ and $^2/_{10}$; $^1/_4$ and $^2/_8$; $^3/_4$ and $^6/_8$.
• Draw a set of eight triangles using the Shapes tool. Ask: *How many triangles are there? So how many would $^5/_8$ be? What about three-quarters?* Allow the children to drag and drop the shapes to count them if necessary. Repeat for other sets of shapes.
• Extend to mixed numbers, such as $2^3/_4$, by drawing two sets of four shapes, and then three more.

Independent work
• Explain that you will write some fractions on the interactive whiteboard. Challenge the children to draw the fraction, using centimetre-squared paper. For example, if you wrote $^1/_4$, the children would draw a shape with four squares and shade one square. Then ask them to draw a shape for, and write, an equivalent fraction. For example, they could draw a shape with twelve squares and shade three of them, and write the equivalent fraction $^3/_{12}$.
• Write up the following fractions: $^1/_4$, $^1/_3$, $^2/_3$, $^1/_5$, $^3/_5$, $^1/_8$, $^5/_8$, $^1/_{10}$ and $^7/_{10}$, using the Fraction Maker. Ask the children to continue the exercise using these.
• Decide whether less confident learners should work as a group. The children could model each fraction using counters.
• Challenge more confident learners by extending the range of fractions to include ninths and twelfths.

Plenary
• Review each fraction. Ask the children to suggest equivalents. These can be drawn on the board using shapes made of squares with the fractions shaded.
• Say: *Tell me an equivalent fraction for $^2/_6$ ... $^4/_6$ ... $^4/_8$ and so on.* Insert an empty number line and mark one end 0 and the other 1. Say: *Where does $^1/_2$ ... $^1/_4$ ... $^3/_8$ ... $^5/_{10}$ ... fit?* Invite a child to mark up the fractions.
• Encourage the children to suggest some fractions that are greater than $^1/_2$ and to write these on the number line.

Whiteboard tools
Use the Fraction Maker (from the Mathematics folder under My Content in the Gallery) and the Shapes tool to demonstrate fractions. Use a Pen from the Pen tray to write on the Fraction Maker and then press on the arrow using the Pen.

- Pen tray
- Shapes tool
- Gallery
- Select tool

Mathematics — Lesson 15

Difference

Learning objective
PNS: Calculating
• Add or subtract mentally pairs of two-digit whole numbers (eg 47 + 58, 91 − 35).

Resources
'Build your own' file; individual whiteboards and pens. Open the 'Build your own' file and use it to prepare a Notebook file showing 22 parrots on the page. Insert text: *22 parrots are in a pet shop. 18 are bought in a week, so how many are left?* Prepare two more problems with text only. Use differences of 9 or less.

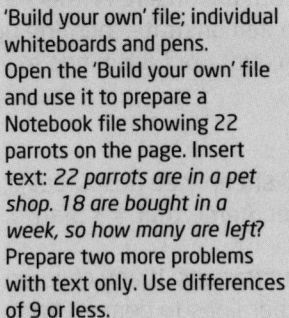

Links to other subjects
English
Sentence structure and punctuation: Use commas to mark clauses.
• Ask the children to incorporate difference problems within sentences, using commas appropriately.

Whiteboard tools
Select parrots from the Mathematics folder under My Content in the Gallery (in the 'Build your own' file). Use the Timer's count-down function to keep the pace brisk in the Starter.

- Pen tray
- Gallery
- Select tool

Starter
Display the first page of your prepared Notebook file (see Resources). Talk the children through the problem. Ask them to write the difference on their individual whiteboards and, when you say *Show me*, they should hold up their boards for you to see. Limit their response time by setting the Timer. Repeat using the following pages of your prepared file, showing problems without illustrations. Ask how the children worked out each answer and discuss the strategies used.

Whole-class shared work
- Explain that you will be using the interactive whiteboard to model finding small differences between pairs of numbers. Insert an empty number line on the board and write 95 − 88 = ?
- Ask: *How can we use the empty number line to help us to work this out?* Agree this:

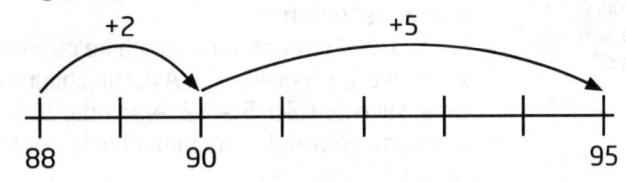

```
        +2              +5
   ┌────────┐    ┌──────────────┐
   │        ↓    │              ↓
───┼────┼───┼────┼────┼────┼────┼───
  88        90                  95
```

- Repeat for other pairs of two-digit and three-digit integers, such as 97 and 106, 388 and 407, or 9000 and 8994.
- Now ask the children to work out mentally the differences between pairs of numbers that you say. Encourage them to count up in the same way that they have done with the empty number line. They can write their answer on their whiteboards and hold these up for you to see.

Independent work
- Write the following integers on a blank Notebook page: 106; 507; 631; 5000; 6994. Ask the children to find the integers that have a difference of 8, 12 and 15 with these numbers. So, for 106 they would write: 98 and 114; 94 and 118; 91 and 121.
- Ask the children to choose a pair of numbers with a small difference and write a word problem using these numbers.
- For less confident learners, provide a separate list of two-digit integers.
- Challenge more confident learners to choose their own pairs of four-digit integers with a difference of 14.
- Encourage the children to use a mental, rather than written, number line where possible.

Plenary
- Review the children's answers. Discuss how they calculated, and whether they used a mental or written number line.
- Invite a child from each ability group to read out their word problem for the others to solve. Establish how they solved the problem. Discuss how, by counting up, it is possible to find small differences quickly and easily.

Mathematics Lesson 16

Remainders

Learning objective
PNS: Calculating
- Develop and use written methods to record, support and explain division of two-digit numbers by a one-digit number, including division with remainders (eg 15 × 9, 98 ÷ 6).

Resources
'Build your own' file; two sets of 0-9 number cards for each pair; exercise books and pens. Open the 'Build your own' file and use it to prepare a Notebook file showing 23 pictures of sheep and 4 pens. Write: *A farmer sorts 23 sheep into 4 pens. He wants the same number of sheep in each pen. How many sheep will be left over?*

Links to other subjects
Design and technology
QCA Unit 4B 'Storybooks'
- Ask the children to work out how many book pages they can cut from a piece of card. Encourage them to use division to find the answer.

Starter
Explain that you will ask some division questions. Ask the children to use their multiplication table facts to help them to find the answers. Ask, for example: *What is 40 divided by 5? 30 divided by 3? 45 divided by 9?* Ask questions where there is no remainder. If any children are unsure of the answer to a question, use an empty number line to demonstrate counting up in equal groups. (For example, for 56 divided by 8, count up 7 × 8 times to reach 56.)

Whole-class shared work
- Display your prepared Notebook file with the 23 sheep (see Resources). Write on the board 23 ÷ 4 and ask for the answer. Agree that 4 × 5 = 20, so the answer is 5 remainder 3.
- Repeat for other examples but without using illustrations. If any children are unsure, use near table facts and empty number lines to demonstrate the nearest multiple.
- Extend this to questions which lie outside the normal range of table facts, such as 63 ÷ 5 or 46 ÷ 3. Ask the children to give the multiplication each time, such as 63 ÷ 5 = 12 remainder 3; 63 = (12 × 5) + 3.
- Over time, extend to include division of three-digit integers.

Independent work
- Ask the children to work in pairs. Explain that you would like them to generate two-digit integers using the number cards. Each integer should be divided by 2, then 3, 4, 5, 6, 7 and 10. Ask the children to record each division on paper, and show any remainders. Encourage them to generate at least five numbers and write the divisions.
- Decide whether to limit the range of divisions to those by 2, 3, 4, 5 and 10 for less confident learners.
- Challenge more confident learners to include divisions by 8 and 9.

Plenary
- Ask the class to work in pairs. Explain that you will say a remainder. Challenge each pair to write five different division sentences that contain this remainder.
- Give the children a couple of minutes and then ask each pair, in turn, to come to the whiteboard and write up one of their divisions.
- Explain that each division must be different from any that have gone before. When the children have run out of ideas, repeat the activity for a different remainder.

Whiteboard tools
Select sheep and a sheep pen from the Mathematics folder under My Content in the Gallery (in the 'Build your own' file).

- Pen tray
- Gallery
- Select tool

Mathematics Lesson 17

Number puzzle

Learning objective
PNS: Using and applying mathematics
- Identify and use patterns, relationships and properties of numbers; investigate a statement involving numbers and test it with examples.

Resources
Paper and pencils; *Monty* (available from the DfES website **www.standards.dfes.gov.uk**).
For the Starter: set to grid 1 and a ten seconds delay.
For whole-class shared work: set to grid 3 and a 120 seconds delay.
For independent work: reduce the time to about 20 seconds delay.

Links to other subjects
ICT
QCA Unit 4D 'Collecting and presenting information: questionnaires and pie charts'
- When children collect numerical data, ask them to search for any number patterns in the data.

Whiteboard tools
Use the Floating tools, including the On-screen Keyboard, for this lesson.

- Pen tray
- Floating tools
- Select tool

Starter
Explain that the children should look at the *Monty* grid (see Resources) and identify the way the numbers are ordered. They will have ten seconds to do this. Press on the box next to the word *Monty* to start, and after a few seconds press anywhere on the screen. Invite the children to suggest which numbers *Monty* is concealing and use your computer keyboard to type these into the box at the top of the screen. Encourage the children to explain their thinking. Repeat, pressing on Start to use another grid 1.

Whole-class shared work
- Display grid 3. Explain that the children will have 120 seconds to look at the grid and understand how the numbers work.
- Start *Monty* and when he stops, invite the children to say which numbers the snake is covering and to explain their thinking. Type the numbers into the box.
- Reveal the grid again, by pressing on Grid. The children can check if they identified correctly where their chosen numbers are.
- Repeat this for another grid 3.
- Now show a different grid 3 and let *Monty* start. Press on the screen to stop him.
- Encourage the children to explain carefully why they think that particular numbers are under *Monty*. Ask: *Why do you think the number ___ is under Monty? Do you all agree? Why/why not?*
- Repeat this for other grid 3s.

Independent work
- Ask the children to work in pairs. They will need paper and pencils.
- Display another grid 3. Ask them to agree the number range and to try to spot the pattern.
- Stop *Monty* and invite the pairs to discuss and write down all the numbers that they think are under him.
- Take feedback, asking questions such as: *How did you work out that ___ was under Monty? Does this give us a clue about other numbers that are under Monty? Tell me some numbers that you are sure are not under Monty. How do you know that?*
- Reveal the grid again, by pressing on Grid. The children can check if they identified correctly where their chosen numbers are.
- All children can tackle this task. Less confident learners can work as a group with an adult. More confident learners can be challenged to explain in further detail how they made their decisions.

Plenary
- Display a grid 5, counting in ones. This is more difficult, and will give a diagonal pattern of numbers, starting in the top right corner.
- Invite the children to say how the number pattern is displayed.
- Repeat the *Monty* activity, again asking children to suggest what numbers are hidden by *Monty*.
- Ask questions such as: *Tell me some numbers that are not under Monty. Where do you think these numbers will be?*
- Reveal the grid again, by pressing on Grid, to show the answers.

Mathematics — Lesson 18

Bar charts

Learning objective
PNS: Using and applying mathematics
- Suggest a line of enquiry and the strategy needed to follow it; collect, organise and interpret selected information to find answers.

Resources
'Bar charts' Notebook file; small safety mirrors; large sheets of sugar paper.

Links to other subjects
Citizenship
QCA Unit 6 'Developing our school grounds'
- Follow up this work by undertaking a school-wide survey about opinions on changes that could be made to the school grounds. They can record data using tally charts and create bar charts from these.

Whiteboard tools
Use a Highlighter pen to draw attention to data in the bar charts. Use the Select tool to alter the height of the bars in the bar chart. Use the On-screen Keyboard to amend the headings and labels for the bar chart.

- Pen tray
- Highlighter pen
- Select tool
- Undo button
- On-screen Keyboard

Starter
Open page 2 of the Notebook file and prompt the children with questions to analyse the bar chart and the data that it represents:
- What is the title of this bar chart? What do you think it will tell us?
- What is the scale?
- How many children went on holiday to ___?
- Which was the most/least popular destination?
- How many fewer/more children went to ___ than ___?
- If everybody went on holiday, how many children are in the school?

Whole-class shared work
- Discuss the survey question on page 3 of the Notebook file.
- Give each child a small safety mirror. Ask them to count their own teeth and make a note of the result.
- Discuss how to gather the data. Children could put their hands up if they have 20 teeth, 21 teeth, and so on.
- When the data has been gathered, reveal the blank bar chart on page 4. Ask the children to suggest the title and axes headings.
- Discuss what scale should be used, and why. (This is likely to be in twos or fives, but will depend upon the data gathered.)
- Edit the headings and complete the bar chart. Discuss any data that needs a fraction of a bar and how this can be represented.
- Discuss the data and highlight comparisons. Ask questions such as: How many children have ___ teeth? Are there more/fewer children with ___ teeth than ___?

Independent work
- Ask the children to work in mixed-ability groups of four or five. Each group will collect data about the colour of the family car from a different class in the school. (You will need to agree this with the relevant teachers beforehand.)
- The children should agree how to collect the data and what the headings on their tally chart should be.
- Once they have collected the data, they should use it to make a bar chart on large sheets of sugar paper. They should agree the scale, the title and the axes headings.
- Allow one group to use the bar chart file on page 4 of the Notebook file.
- Encourage more confident learners to support those who are less confident.

Plenary
- Invite each group, in turn, to show their data.
- Use the Undo button to reset the bar chart on page 4 to compile a collective bar chart, using all of the data that the children have collected.
- Invite the children to suggest axes headings, scale and title.
- Ask questions about the data, such as:
  - How many more red than blue cars are there?
  - Which is the most popular colour?
  - How would the chart look if we changed the scale to ___? Would this be helpful? Why/Why not?
  - Is the data from each class the same? Why not?
- Make a note of the children's observations on page 5 of the Notebook file.

Mathematics Lesson 19

When?

Learning objective
PNS: Measuring
● Read time to the nearest minute; use am, pm and 12-hour clock notation; choose units of time to measure time intervals; calculate time intervals from timetables.

Resources
'Calendar and timetable' Notebook file; photocopiable page 96 'When?' for each child. (Microsoft Excel is required to view the embedded calendar spreadsheet in the Notebook files.)

Links to other subjects
ICT
QCA Unit 4D 'Collecting and presenting information: questionnaires and pie charts'
● Ask the children to collect dates of birthdays from friends and family. They can then use this year's calendar to find out the day each birthday will fall upon.

Whiteboard tools
Use a Highlighter pen to highlight relevant dates and times. Use the count-down function on the Timer from the Gallery to time the first part of the independent work.

- Pen tray
- Select tool
- Highlighter pen
- Gallery

Starter
Display page 2 of the Notebook file 'Calendar and timetable'. Remind the children of the months of the year and, together, arrange them in the correct order.

Whole-class shared work
● Display the month of January on page 3 and ask: *What day of the month is the seventh of January? How many days has January? How many Sundays are there in this month?* Ask the children to come up and highlight some of the answers. Continue asking questions about January and its dates, to check that the children can read the calendar for a month correctly.
● Go to another month (the months of the year are on pages 3 to 14) and ask children to highlight different dates. Ask questions such as: *What date is the third Tuesday in April? How many Wednesdays are there in September? How many days between ___ and ___? How many weeks between ___ and ___?*
● Some symbols have been supplied at the bottom of the relevant pages. Invite the children to find out what festival or special day they represent, and when these days occur. They can then drag the symbols to the correct day on the calendar (the symbol can be duplicated if the celebration lasts for several days).
● Press on the text on page 15 to open the calendar in a spreadsheet format. Explain that this shows the same year, but in a different format. Ask questions about the composition of the year: number of months, weeks, days. Discuss leap years and how and why these have an extra day.
● Go to page 16 of the Notebook file. Can the children explain how to read the bus timetable?
● Ask questions about the data. For example: *How long does it take to get from ___ to ___? Which bus should I catch if I want to get the train that leaves at 10.48?*

Independent work
● Explain that the individual work is in two parts and that you will give the children ten minutes for each part. Provide each child with a copy of photocopiable page 96.
● Provide the children with printouts of the calendar to help them with answering the calendar questions.
● After ten minutes, change to the bus timetable for the children to answer the rest of the questions.
● Decide whether to work with less confident learners as a group. Check that the children can read and interpret calendars and simple timetables.
● Challenge more confident learners to make up further questions about the calendar.

Plenary
● Review each of the questions from the photocopiable sheet. Display the calendar or timetable as appropriate, and invite children to point to the relevant information.
● Highlight relevant data such as, for question 3, all the Mondays in July.
● Invite more confident learners to read out their further questions for the other children to answer. Again, highlight relevant data on the calendar.
● Go to page 17 to access hyperlinked pages that show the answers to the questions on the photocopiable sheet.

Mathematics — Lesson 20

Learning objective
PNS: Understanding shape
- Draw polygons and classify them by identifying their properties, including their line symmetry.

Resources
'Reflections' Notebook file; photocopiable page 97 'Reflections' for each child; centimetre-squared paper; rulers; safety mirrors.

Links to other subjects
ICT
QCA Unit 4B 'Developing images using repeating patterns'
- Encourage the children to repeat and reflect shapes when they make their patterns and to discuss their reflections using the vocabulary of symmetry.

Reflections

Starter
Explain that you will be asking the children to draw the reflection of an image. Display page 2 of the Notebook file. Discuss what a reflection is and how you would draw one. Ask the children to draw the image on page 2 on squared paper, using the lines to help, and to put in the mirror line. Invite individual children to describe lines of the image using vocabulary such as *horizontal* and *vertical*. Then ask the children to draw the reflection of the image on their squared paper. Ask them to show you this, then invite them to explain how the reflection is the same as, and different from, the original image. Invite individuals to come up and draw the reflective image on the Notebook page.

Drag the arrow to check the answer. This will reveal the reflected image of the shape, which should be dragged to the correct place. Repeat for the next shape on page 3 of the Notebook file, checking the reflected image in the same way.

Whole-class shared work
- Go to page 4 of the Notebook file. Invite the children to draw the image on squared paper and then to sketch its reflection.
- Ask individuals to come up and draw the reflection on the whiteboard. Drag the arrow to reveal the correct reflection.
- Use the squares on the grid or the ruler from the Gallery to compare the distances between the mirror line and points on the image, and the mirror line and the reflected point.
- Encourage the children to do the same with their rulers.
- Discuss how equivalent points on the image and its reflection are the same distance from the mirror, or line of symmetry.
- Repeat for the next images on pages 5, 6 and 7.

Independent work
- Provide each child with a copy of photocopiable page 97, a ruler and a safety mirror.
- Ask them to complete the sheet individually, but tell them that they can compare and discuss what they are doing with a partner.
- Decide whether to bring less confident learners together as a group and to discuss what they see on the sheet. Encourage them to use the vocabulary of symmetry as they describe shapes and lines.
- Challenge more confident learners to work in pairs. Using squared paper they can draw an image of their own, then swap sheets and draw the reflection of their partner's image.

Plenary
- Invite individuals to come up and draw their images on page 8 of the Notebook file. Ask another child to draw the reflected image.
- Clear the page using the Eraser, or press Edit and then Clear Page. Repeat this several times.

Whiteboard tools
Select the Lines tool to draw straight lines. Use the ruler from the Gallery to compare distances.

- Pen tray
- Lines tool
- Gallery

Mathematics Lesson 21

Negative numbers

Learning objective
PNS: Counting and understanding number
● Use positive and negative numbers in context and position them on a number line.

Resources
'Thermometer' Notebook file; today's newspaper; photocopiable page 98 'Negative numbers' for each child.

Links to other subjects
Geography
QCA Unit 24 'A passport to the world'
● Follow up your work on negative temperatures by looking at an area in the world that is cold (below 0°C).
● Encourage the children to compare the temperatures of home and the chosen area.
Science
QCA Unit 4C 'Keeping warm'
● Talk about how weather affects body temperature – what do you need to do to maintain body temperature?

Starter
Ask the children to count in ones from 10 to 100 and back again. Continue the exercise, counting up from 0 to 10, then back beyond 0. If children find counting back beyond zero difficult, use the empty number line on page 2 of the Notebook file, writing the numbers on the line as they say them.
Repeat this for other starting and finishing numbers which use both positive and negative numbers.
Reset the page and invite children to estimate and write on the number line where 10 would go, and then 4, 0, -3 and so on.

Whole-class shared work
● Display the thermometer on page 3 and introduce the concept of temperature.
● Move on to discuss where the children may have seen negative numbers used, such as on thermometers, and the temperatures in colder climates.
● Go to page 4 and ask the children to read the temperature. Agree that the temperature is marked in degrees Celsius and that the end of the alcohol line marks the temperature.
● Move the Screen Shade to reveal the second thermometer at the foot of the page and repeat, drawing attention to the negative numbers.
● Display the thermometers on page 5. Adjust the length of the alcohol line and mark in two readings, such as -4 on one and +6 on the other. Invite the children to find the difference between the two readings. Use the Undo button to reset the page and repeat for other pairs of readings where one is negative and one positive.

Independent work
● Provide each child with a copy of photocopiable page 98. Ask them to use what they know about reading and comparing temperatures to find the answers to the thermometer problems and word problems. Suggest that the children draw their own number line to help, if necessary.
● Work with less confident learners as a group. Use the empty number line on page 2 to act as an aid. Mark in 0 and the negative and positive temperatures.
● Challenge more confident learners to find out about world temperatures from today's newspaper, and to find the difference in temperature between London and the coldest and hottest places.

Plenary
● Review the answers to the questions on the photocopiable sheet. Invite children to explain how they worked out the answers, such as using an empty number line, or mental counting up. The answers can be checked on pages 7, 8 and 9 of the Notebook file.
● Invite the more confident learners to give the maximum and minimum temperatures that they have found in the newspaper for others to find the difference.

Whiteboard tools
Move the Screen Shade to reveal the hidden thermometer on page 4. Use the Undo button to erase any unsaved changes.

🖥 Pen tray
▶ Select tool
▭ Screen Shade
↶ Undo button

Mathematics Lesson 22

Multiples

Learning objective
PNS: Knowing and using number facts
● Derive and recall multiplication facts up to 10 × 10, the corresponding division facts and multiples of numbers to 10 up to the tenth multiple.

Resources
'Build your own' file; photocopiable page 99 'Hundred square', one for each pair; coloured crayons; individual whiteboards and pens. *Counter* software (available on the CD-ROM in the *Using ICT to support mathematics in primary school* training pack, DfES references: DfES0260/2000 for entire training pack; DfES0267/2000 for CD-ROM only). Set to count in twos, threes, fours, fives and tens, starting from zero, with Controls not showing. Then set the count to start from a small number.

Links to other subjects
Art and design
QCA Unit 3B 'Investigating pattern'
● Follow up this work by getting the children to create a patchwork pattern based on the patterns they have created in their hundred squares.
ICT
QCA Unit 4B 'Developing images using repeating patterns'
● Challenge the children to recreate and repeat the patterns they find in hundred squares, for different multiples, using the computer.

Whiteboard tools
Use the Pen tool to select different colours for values on the interactive hundred square. Use the Pen tool to change the colour of the Pen.

- Pen tray
- Gallery
- Pen tool
- Select tool

Starter
Begin with multiples of 2. Explain that *Counter* will make a number pattern. Ask the children to identify what the next number will be, and the next, and so on. Ask them to say which multiplication table the pattern belongs to. Repeat for other tables. Then repeat, but this time starting from a different number.

Whole-class shared work
● Open the 'Build your own' file, which consists of a blank Notebook page and a collection of resources located in My Content in the Gallery. Display the hundred square from the Mathematics folder under My Content, and set it to 1–100.
● Ask the children to identify multiples. Begin with multiples of 2. Set the Pen tool to green and press the multiples as the children say these (or ask individuals to come up and press on them). Go up to 30.
● Repeat for multiples of 3, up to 30, this time changing the Pen tool to pink. Invite the children to suggest which multiples will be common to both the two- and three-times tables.
● Repeat for multiples of 5, highlighted in red, and 10, in yellow.
● Ask: *Which numbers are in both the two- and three-times tables? The two- and five-times tables? The three- and five-times tables? Which number is in all of these tables?* (30.)
● Ask the children to write on their individual whiteboards all the table facts with a product of 30. Discuss how one integer can be formed from different multiples.

Independent work
● Ask the children to work in pairs. Give each pair a copy of photocopiable page 99.
● Tell them they are going to continue the multiplication patterns from 30 to 100. Explain that they should use the same colours for the multiples as used on the hundred square on the whiteboard.
● Before they start, ask the pairs to make a list of the numbers that they think will be products in all of the two-, three-, five- and ten-times tables. (60 and 90.)
● Work with the less confident learners as a group, using the hundred square on the whiteboard. Discuss how to count on to find the next multiple using the hundred square.
● Challenge the more confident learners to continue the patterns beyond 100.

Plenary
● Ask the children questions about the number patterns that they have found. For example:
  ● *Which numbers are multiples of 2 and 3? 2 and 5? 2, 3 and 5?*
  ● *Which numbers did you predict would be products in all of the two-, three-, five- and ten-times tables? Did you make a good prediction?*
  ● *Which number do you think will be the next product that is in the two-, three-, five- and ten-times tables?* (120.) *How did you work that out?*

80
100 SMART Board™ LESSONS • YEAR 4

Mathematics Lesson 23

Money

Learning objective
PNS: Counting and understanding number
• Use decimal notation for tenths and hundredths and partition decimals; relate the notation to money.

Resources
Individual whiteboards and pens; *Toy Shop* software (available on the CD-ROM in the *Using ICT to support mathematics in primary school* training pack, DfES references: DfES0260/2000 for entire training pack; DfES0267/2000 for CD-ROM only. Also available through **www.standards.dfes.gov.uk**). Set to the third level (up to £2.49); name the players Team 1 and Team 2.

Links to other subjects
History
QCA Unit 9 'What was it like for children in the Second World War?'
• The children can use what they have learned in this lesson to find out about the cost of different types of food in the Second World War, and compare to today's prices.

Starter
Write: £12, £15, £8, 40p, 70p, 90p, 3p, 8p, 1p on a blank Notebook page. Point to one amount for pounds, then one for tens of pence, then one unit pence and ask the children to write on their whiteboards how much this comes to in total, using the £ and decimal point signs. When you say *Show me*, the children show you their boards. Repeat for other examples, including some where there are no unit pence, and others where there are no tens of pence.

Whole-class shared work
- Play the *Toy Shop* game in two teams. A toy is selected and the price displayed. The teams take it in turns to tender a coin to buy a toy. The team who offers the coin that makes up the correct price wins. You need to press on *New game* to get a new item.
- Discuss how the amounts of money are displayed, using the £ sign and the decimal point.
- Keep a list of toys and amounts of money paid.
- When you have finished playing the game, choose two of these amounts and ask how the children would total these.
- Demonstrate some of the methods, including formal pencil and paper methods.
- Repeat, this time asking for totals and change from £10.

Independent work
- Ask the children to work in pairs and to take turns in the following activity: One child says an amount of money. The other child first counts it out using as few coins as possible. Then he/she finds the change for the amount from £15. The amount of money should be recorded as a decimal fraction of £s. The change from £15, and the method used to work it out, should also be recorded.
- Give more confident learners a maximum of £20 and less confident a maximum of £5 or £10.
- Discuss with different pairs what they are doing. Ask: *How do you know you have found the least number of coins? How did you calculate the change?*

Plenary
- Play the *Toy Shop* game again and keep a points score of which team wins each round. Play six rounds and keep a list of the amounts of money.
- Challenge the children to work in pairs to find a way to total these amounts and to calculate the change from £20. Ask questions such as: *How did you calculate the total? How did you calculate the change?* Ask the children to demonstrate their methods.

Whiteboard tools
- Pen tray
- Select tool

Mathematics Lesson 24

Totalling multiples of 10

Learning objective
PNS: Knowing and using number facts
● Use knowledge of addition and subtraction facts and place value to derive sums and differences of pairs of multiples of 10, 100 or 1000.

Resources
'Build your own' file; a set of 1-9 number cards for each pair; exercise books and pens.

Links to other subjects
English
Sentence structure and punctuation: Use commas to mark clauses.
● When the children write down their word problems, encourage them to use commas correctly, and to revise and edit their work.

Starter
Ask questions about adding tens to make a total of 100. For example: *What is 30 add 70? What is the difference between 100 and 80?* Keep the pace sharp. If children are unsure, open the 'Build your own' file (which consists of a blank Notebook page and a ready-made Gallery collection of resources located in My Content) and model the question using an empty number line or a hundred square, located in the Mathematics folder under My Content.

Whole-class shared work
● Write 5 + 2 + 4 and ask for the total. Now write 50 +20 + 40 and ask: *How can we find the solution to this?* Remove the zeros to demonstrate the link with the first question. Children may suggest totalling 50 and 40, then adding 20. Use the empty number line to demonstrate the addition.
● Compare the two totals of 11 and 110. Remind the children that, when totalling multiples of tens, they can check by totalling just the tens digit and multiplying by 10.
● Repeat for other examples and time the children's responses using the Timer's count-down function. Use the empty number line to model each example.
● Make up a word problem. Ask the children to solve the problem and to explain how they found the answer. Repeat for another word problem.

Independent work
● Ask the children to work in pairs with a set of 1-9 number cards.
● They should choose three cards, multiply each number by 10, write down these decade numbers and find the total. For each addition, they write a word problem. Give them time to write five or six word problems. One group of children can use the Random Number Generator from the 'Build your own' file to generate their numbers on the whiteboard.
● Now ask the children to work in fours, but not with their partner. They must take turns to say one of their word problems for the others to solve.
● Give each group of four a couple of minutes to invent another two-word problem, using addition of multiples of tens.
● Provide less confident learners with empty number lines to model the additions.
● More confident learners can try adding four two-digit multiples of 10.

Plenary
● Invite each group to ask the whole class to solve one of their problems. Encourage them to explain how they found the answer. Model this, as necessary, using an empty number line.
● Repeat, until all the word problems have been tried by the other children.
● Challenge the children to total four decade numbers and to explain how they worked this out. Try, for example, 40 + 70 + 60 + 20. (40 + 60 = 100; 70 + 20 = 90; 100 + 90 = 190.)

Whiteboard tools
Use the Timer's count-down function to put a time limit on children's responses.

- Pen tray
- Select tool
- Gallery

Mathematics — Lesson 25

Using + and – mental strategies

Learning objective
PNS: Knowing and using number facts
- Use knowledge of addition and subtraction facts and place value to derive sums and differences of pairs of multiples of 10, 100 or 1000.

Resources
'Build your own' file; photocopiable page 100 'Add and subtract' for each child.

Links to other subjects
Science
QCA Unit 4B 'Habitats'
- The children can use mental methods to find the overall total of different organisms they find in a given area.

Starter
Open the 'Build your own' file, which consists of a blank Notebook page and a collection of images located in My Content in the Gallery. Invite a child to use the Random Number Generator, from the Mathematics folder under My Content, to generate a teen number. Ask the children to suggest addition and subtraction sentences with this integer as the answer (for example, 17: 19 - 2 = 17 and 9 + 8 = 17) and write them up on the interactive whiteboard. When several number sentences are on the board, ask the children to use these to find others. Ask: *How did you use what you can see to find this?*

Whole-class shared work
- Explain that the children will use mental methods to total pairs of two-digit whole numbers. Begin by totalling decade numbers, such as 50 + 70.
- Ask the children how this might be calculated and record their suggestions. For example: 50 + 50 + 20 = 120.
- Discuss why the methods work. Repeat for other examples. Include subtraction, such as 160 - ☐ = 90.
- Move on to examples where one number is a decade and the other not, such as 43 + 60 and ☐ - 60 = 43. Discuss different methods. If children are unsure, demonstrate with an empty number line.
- If the children are confident with the above, then extend to adding or subtracting any pair of two-digit numbers, such as 56 + 39 and 95 - ☐ = 39. Record methods and, where necessary, use the empty number line to demonstrate a mental method of counting up or back.

Independent work
- Provide each child with a copy of photocopiable page 100. Ask them to think about how they can solve the questions and to be ready in the Plenary to explain their chosen methods.
- Remind the less confident learners that they can draw empty number lines to help them to work mentally.
- More confident learners can write a set of four number sentences for each of the open questions at the end of the photocopiable sheet, using the same numbers for each set. This will produce two add and two subtract sentences.
- Target children to ask for explanations of the mental methods they choose to use for specific questions.

Plenary
- Review the photocopiable sheet together. Invite individual children to write up their addition sentences and to explain their mental methods.
- Repeat this for the subtraction sentences.
- Ask questions such as: *How did you work this out? Who used a different method? Do you think that one of these methods is better? Why do you think that?*

Whiteboard tools
Use the Random Number Generator from the Gallery to generate random numbers.

- Pen tray
- Select tool
- Gallery
- Highlighter pen

Mathematics ◗ Lesson 26

Learning objectives
PNS: Using and applying mathematics
● Solve one-step and two-step problems involving numbers; choose and carry out appropriate calculations.
PNS: Calculating
● Refine and use efficient written methods to add and subtract two-digit and three-digit whole numbers.

Resources
'Word problems' Notebook file; photocopiable page 101 'Word problems', one for each child.

Links to other subjects
Citizenship
QCA Unit 4 'People who help us – the local police'
● Invite a police spokesperson to talk about their role. Set some further word problems which relate to police work in the community.

Solving word problems

Starter
Display page 2 of the Notebook file. Read the question out loud and ask the children for the answer. Invite them to share their answers and count the legs to check. Repeat this for pages 3 and 4.

Explain that you will now ask a series of simple word problems for the children to solve mentally, without pictures. They should state the answer and explain their mental method. Say, for example: *I'm thinking of a number. I add 22 to it, and the answer is 44. What was my number?* or: *Jodie has 42 felt-tipped pens. Dilshad has half as many. How many has Dilshad?* Write the answers as number sentences on page 5.

Whole-class shared work
● Explain that the children will be solving complex word problems involving multi-step operations.
● Reveal the problem on page 6. Ask: *What information does this give us? What do we need to find out? How can we do this?*
● Ask the children how they would complete the first step in the problem. They will need to total the books on the top and bottom shelves. Invite them to suggest which method to use. Use a pencil and paper method, writing this on the Notebook page.
● Discuss what the next step should be. (Subtracting the total for the two shelves from the overall total.) Again, record this on the whiteboard using a pencil and paper method.
● Delete the book to check that you are right.
● Repeat this for the other problems on pages 7 and 8.

Independent work
● Provide each child with a copy of photocopiable page 101. Ask them to work individually to solve the first problem. They should then compare their method with a partner and discuss which method (if there is a difference) is more appropriate, and why.
● They should repeat this for the other three problems on the photocopiable sheet.
● Decide whether to work together as a group with less confident learners. Demonstrate recording methods on paper or on the whiteboard. Ask the children to write down the recording method on their sheets.
● More confident learners could invent their own word problem, which should have multiple steps.

Plenary
● Review each problem from the photocopiable sheet. Invite children from each ability group to explain how they worked out the answer. Ask: *Which method do you think is best? Why do you think that?*
● Invite one child to demonstrate how they recorded by writing on page 9 of the Notebook file.
● Discuss the recording method chosen and its suitability.
● Use pages 10 to 13 to check the answers and methods.
● Invite the more confident learners to take turns to read out their invented word problems for the others to try to solve.

Whiteboard tools
Use a Pen from the Pen tray to record methods of working out the answers.

🖥️ Pen tray
🔖 Select tool

Mathematics — Lesson 27

Venn diagrams

Learning objective
PNS: Handling data
- Answer a question by identifying what data to collect; organise, present, analyse and interpret the data in tables, diagrams, tally charts and bar charts, using ICT where appropriate.

Resources
'Build your own' file; individual whiteboards and pens, or pencils and paper. Open the 'Build your own' file and use it to prepare a Notebook file showing a two-circle Venn diagram on four or five pages. Type the numbers 1 to 50, in separate text boxes, at the top of the first two pages.

Links to other subjects
Science
QCA Unit 4B 'Habitats'
- Encourage the children to use Venn diagrams to record data about observable features of the organisms being grouped.

Starter
Display the first Venn diagram from the Mathematics folder under My Content in the Gallery (see Resources) and write in the headings: *Multiple of 6* and *Multiple of 3*. Ask the children to suggest where each integer from 1 to 40 should fit and invite individuals to drag and drop the integers into the correct position. Discuss where each number fits: for example, 12 is both a multiple of 3 and 6; but 8 is a multiple of neither. If time allows, extend to integers up to 60.

Whole-class shared work
- Display the next Venn diagram in your prepared Notebook file and explain to the children that they are going to do a class task. Tell them that you want them to draw a Venn diagram to sort the numbers 1 to 50 into odd numbers and multiples of 7. Help them to decide on a title and labels for the new diagram.
- Give the children about five minutes to complete the task on their individual whiteboards, or with pencils and paper.
- When they have done this, ask individuals to come up and sort the numbers into the Venn diagram on the Notebook file.
- Discuss the numbers that fit in the intersection. (Numbers that are odd and are multiples of 7. For example: 35 is an odd number and it is a multiple of 7.)
- Repeat on the next diagram for multiples of 4 and multiples of 9.

Independent work
- Set another task to sort the integers 50 to 100 into multiples of 3 and multiples of 4.
- Ask the children to work in pairs to draw their own Venn diagrams, writing their own titles and labels.
- Ask less confident learners to use the integers 1 to 50.
- Challenge more confident learners to also try multiples of 7 and multiples of 8 for the integers 50 to 100.
- As the children work, ask them to explain why particular integers fit where they do.

Plenary
- Review the task together. Go to the next Venn diagram in your prepared Notebook file, and invite the children to write in their headings and labels.
- Discuss any differences in wording and agree on the best form of wording.
- Discuss which numbers fit in the intersection of the Venn diagram.
- Invite the more confident learners to demonstrate their challenge. Ask questions such as: *Which integers are both a multiple of 7 and 8? What do you think will be the next one? Why do you think that?*

Whiteboard tools
Use a Pen from the Pen tray to add extra numbers to the Venn diagrams.

- Pen tray
- Highlighter pen
- Select tool
- Gallery

Mathematics — Lesson 28

Carroll diagrams

Learning objective
PNS: Handling data
- Answer a question by identifying what data to collect; organise, present, analyse and interpret the data in tables, diagrams, tally charts and bar charts, using ICT where appropriate.

Resources
A prepared Notebook file: several copies (about five or six) of an empty Carroll diagram (you could use the Carroll diagrams in the 'Polygons' Notebook file: delete all the shapes and save the file under a new name); photocopiable page 102 'Carroll diagrams' for each child.

Links to other subjects
Science
QCA Unit 4B 'Habitats'
- Encourage the children to use Carroll diagrams when they study habitats, to record data about where animals live.

Starter
Reveal the first empty Carroll diagram in your prepared Notebook file and write in the headings: *Even* and *Not even* (across the top); *Numbers greater than 20* and *Numbers not greater than 20* (down the side). Invite the children to suggest some numbers to fit into each box and to write these in. Continue until there are at least four or five numbers in each box. Ask: *Which number does not fit?* (20.) *Why is that?*

Repeat, if there is time, using different criteria, such as *Is/is not a multiple of 5* and *Is/is not a multiple of 4*.

Whole-class shared work
- Display the next Carroll diagram and group the children in pairs.
- Provide each pair with a copy of photocopiable page 102. Give them the following task: sort the numbers 20 to 60 into *Is/is not even*; *Has/has not three tens*. Remind them that they need to complete the title and region headings boxes.
- Give the children about five minutes to do this. Use the count-down option on the Timer from the Gallery to time them.
- Invite the children to take turns to suggest what the title should be and what should go in the region headings boxes.
- Now encourage them to suggest which numbers go into which boxes and ask volunteers to come up and write them in.
- Repeat this for another sorting activity, such as *Is/is not a multiple of 6* and *Is less than/is not less than 20*. Set the number range as 0 to 60.

Independent work
- Ask the children to continue to work in their pairs. Hand out fresh copies of photocopiable page 102.
- Provide the criteria for sorting a range of numbers from 0 to 80. For example: *Is/is not odd* and *Numbers that are/are not multiples of 8*, or *Is/is not a multiple of 2 and 3* and *Is/is not a multiple of 4*.
- Allow less confident learners to work as a group and record on the whiteboard.
- Challenge more confident learners to try *Is/is not a multiple of 12* and *Is/is not a multiple of 9* for the number range 0 to 150.

Plenary
- Review each of the sortings and allow the children to write the numbers on a fresh copy of a Carroll diagram on the Notebook file.
- Ask questions such as: *What do you think will be the next number that could go into the box that 'Is...' and 'Is...'? What properties must this number have?*
- Invite the more confident learners to show their results for the challenge. They can sort their numbers on a Carroll diagram on the whiteboard. Challenge them to say what the next number would be that *Is a multiple of 12 and 9* after 108.

Whiteboard tools
Use the Shapes tool and the Lines tool to create Carroll diagrams. Add numbers to the page with the On-screen Keyboard.

- Pen tray
- On-screen Keyboard
- Shapes tool
- Lines tool
- Gallery

Mathematics Lesson 29

Finding positions

Learning objective
PNS: Understanding shape
- Describe and identify the position of a square on a grid of squares.

Resources
'Position and direction' Notebook file; photocopiable page 103 'Finding positions' for each child; squared paper.

Links to other subjects
Geography
QCA Unit 10 'A village in India'
- Encourage the children to use maps with simple coordinate markings when they study other countries. Invite them to give the position of key towns and cities using the coordinates and to find places from coordinates given to them.

Starter
Display page 2 of the Notebook file. Discuss how positions where lines cross can be written as a coordinate, and the convention for doing this: (row, column). Use a phrase, such as: *Walk along the corridor and then go up or down the stairs*, to help children remember the order. Discuss and show the children how to write the coordinate of the star.

Mark a chosen coordinate, such as (3, 2), with a cross and ask: *What is the coordinate of this point?* Agree how this should be written. Invite a child to write the coordinate in the form (3, 2). Repeat for other coordinates.

Clear the page using the Eraser from the Pen tray (or press Edit and then Clear Page) and name a coordinate. Invite a child to mark with a cross where it should be. Repeat for other coordinates.

Whole-class shared work
- Display page 3 of the Notebook file, showing the map of an island.
- Discuss with the children what they can see on the map.
- Ask for the coordinate of the treasure chest. Invite a child to write this next to the treasure chest icon beside the map.
- Repeat for the other items on the map.
- Now ask the children to identify points where there is nothing on the map.
- The icons on the map can be moved if you wish to check the children's understanding of coordinates. For example, move the parrot to (5,1).
- Return to page 2 of the Notebook file and delete the star.
- Mark a cross at (5, 1) and explain that you want to draw a square, four squares high.
- Ask: *What will the coordinate of the top of the line above (5, 1) be?* Mark the cross and draw the line.
- Repeat for the other two crosses and draw the lines.
- Reset the page as before and repeat for drawing another shape.

Independent work
- Provide each child with a copy of photocopiable page 103. Ask them to work individually to note the positions on the map.
- Less confident learners could use an A3 enlargement of the photocopiable sheet and work together as a group. Encourage them to say the coordinates out loud, pointing to the row and column position each time.
- Ask more confident learners to draw their own map, marking in special places and the coordinates for these.

Plenary
- Display page 4 of the Notebook file.
- Explain that you would like to draw a rectangle on the grid with sides that are three units in height and six units in length.
- Give a starting point of (1, 1) and ask the children to suggest where the other crosses should go.
- Go to page 5, give a starting point of (1, 1) and this time draw a right-angled triangle. The two sides containing the right angle should both be four units in length. Discuss how one side of the triangle is a diagonal line.

Whiteboard tools
Use the Eraser from the Pen tray to re-use the grid.

- Pen tray
- Lines tool
- Select tool

Mathematics — Lesson 30

Using compass directions

Learning objective
PNS: Understanding shape
- Use the eight compass points to describe direction.

Resources
'Position and direction' Notebook file; photocopiable page 104 'Using compass directions' for each pair.

Links to other subjects
Geography
QCA Unit 8 'Improving the environment'
- Ask the children to make maps of the school on squared paper and to give coordinates and compass points. The children can use the maps to describe routes around the school and its grounds.

Starter
Ask if the children can remember the names of the directions of a compass. Display the NSWE compass on page 6 of the Notebook file and label it. Explain that you will draw lines to show the different angles between the directions. Ask the children to say how many right angles there are between, for example, north and west, north and south, and so on. Let them use the protractor from the Gallery if necessary. Delete the lines and repeat for different movements. Include clockwise and anticlockwise turns and ask the children to say in which direction the turn is.

Whole-class shared work
- Reveal the eight-point compass on page 7. Label the points for north, south, east and west.
- Explain that between, for example, north and east there is another direction. This direction is 45° from north and east and is called north-east. Label it on the compass.
- Repeat for the other directions.
- Use lines to mark an angle between north-east and south-east and ask: *How many degrees of turn is this?* Let the children use the protractor if necessary.
- Repeat for other 90° turns.
- Now extend this to include turns of 135°. Include turns that are anticlockwise as well as clockwise.
- Now reveal the 0–10 grid on page 8. Draw attention to the eight-point compass. Ask the children to suggest how to move south-west from coordinate (8, 6) for four units. List all the coordinates and mark the points visited with crosses.
- Repeat for other directions and starting points.

Independent work
- Ask the children to work in pairs on photocopiable page 104, taking turns to mark in the directions. If they wish, let them use counters to mark their routes.
- Less confident learners may need to practise using just a four-point compass.
- Suggest to more confident learners that they describe movements that combine two directions, such as south-east for three units, then north-west for four.

Plenary
- Go to page 9 of the Notebook file, which shows a forest. The forest is on a grid and some of the squares contain obstacles.
- Point to a coordinate on the map and say: *Give me a route from (9, 1) in a north-westerly direction.* Explain that the children will need to think about how to move around the squares that cannot be used. List the coordinates that they suggest at the side of the whiteboard and put crosses on the coordinates to mark the route.
- When the route is finished, draw it on the page.
- Ask: *Was all of the route in a north-westerly direction? Tell me what was not. What direction was the rest in?*
- Use the Eraser from the Pen tray (or press Edit and then Clear Page) to clear the page and repeat for other starting coordinates and compass directions.

Whiteboard tools
Use the Lines tool to mark direction arrows on the compass. Use the protractor from the Gallery to measure the angles between compass directions.

- Pen tray
- Lines tool
- Select tool
- Gallery

MATHEMATICS LESSON 1   Name _____

Partitioning

- Work with a partner.
- You will need a set of 0 to 9 number cards.
  - Take turns to choose four cards.
  - Both of you make a four-digit integer with the cards. Try to make your integers different!
  - Record your integer and its partition in the grid below.
  - Do this nine more times.

Integer	Thousands	Hundreds	Tens	Units

- Now write your integers again, this time using words.

1. _____
2. _____
3. _____
4. _____
5. _____
6. _____
7. _____
8. _____
9. _____
10. _____

MATHEMATICS LESSON 2   Name _____

Using the symbols < and >

- Work with a partner.
- You will need a set of 0 to 9 number cards.
  - Take turns to choose four cards.
  - Make six four-digit integers with your cards. Make a note of each number on some scrap paper.
  - Record your numbers below in the first line. Make sure you put each number in the right place!
  - Do this nine more times.

☐ < ☐ < ☐ < ☐ < ☐ < ☐

☐ < ☐ < ☐ < ☐ < ☐ < ☐

☐ < ☐ < ☐ < ☐ < ☐ < ☐

☐ < ☐ < ☐ < ☐ < ☐ < ☐

☐ > ☐ > ☐ > ☐ > ☐ > ☐

☐ > ☐ > ☐ > ☐ > ☐ > ☐

☐ > ☐ > ☐ > ☐ > ☐ > ☐

☐ > ☐ > ☐ > ☐ > ☐ > ☐

☐ > ☐ < ☐ < ☐ < ☐ > ☐

☐ > ☐ < ☐ < ☐ < ☐ > ☐

MATHEMATICS LESSON 5

Make 100

- Work with a partner to find pairs of numbers to total 100.
- Colour each pair of numbers. Choose a different colour from your partner.

1	2	3	4	5	6	7	8	9	10
11	12	13	14	15	16	17	18	19	20
21	22	23	24	25	26	27	28	29	30
31	32	33	34	35	36	37	38	39	40
41	42	43	44	45	46	47	48	49	50
51	52	53	54	55	56	57	58	59	60
61	62	63	64	65	66	67	68	69	70
71	72	73	74	75	76	77	78	79	80
81	82	83	84	85	86	87	88	89	90
91	92	93	94	95	96	97	98	99	100

MATHEMATICS ▪ LESSON 7   Name _____

Reading scales

▪ Read the measurement on each ruler. Write the measurement to the nearest 0.5cm.

measurement _____ cm

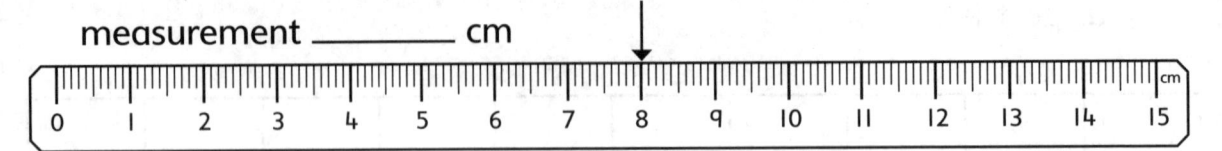

measurement _____ cm

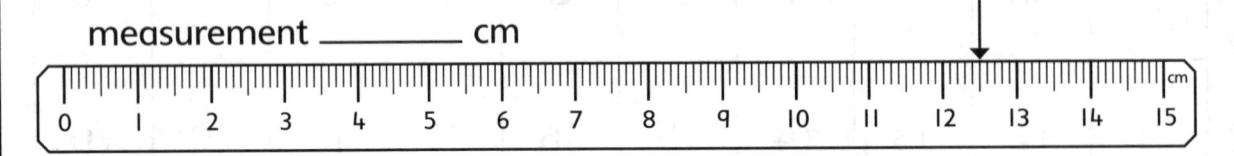

measurement _____ cm

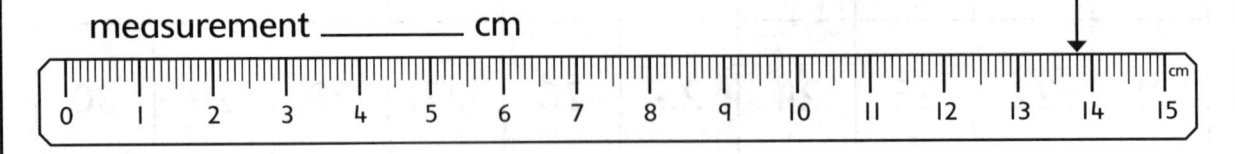

measurement _____ cm

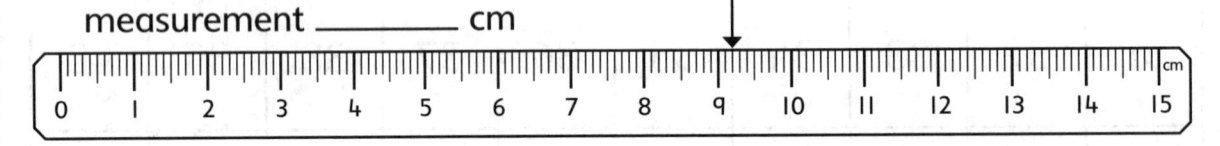

▪ Read the scale on each beaker. Record the water level to the nearest 50ml.

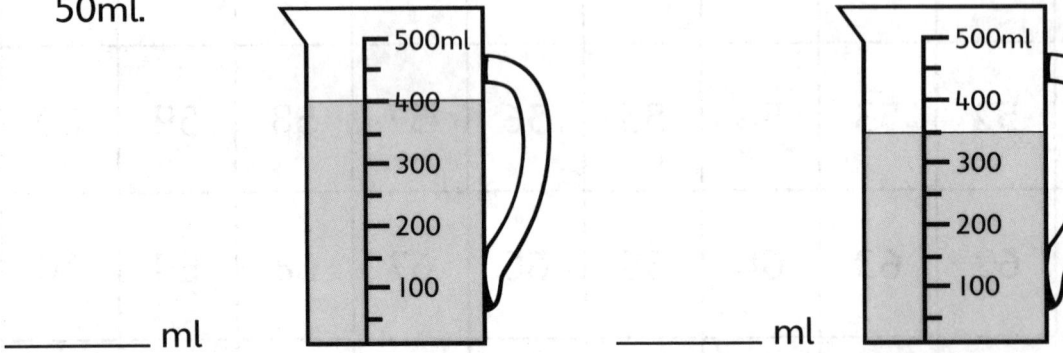

_____ ml   _____ ml

▪ Read the bathroom scales. Write the weight to the nearest 10kg.

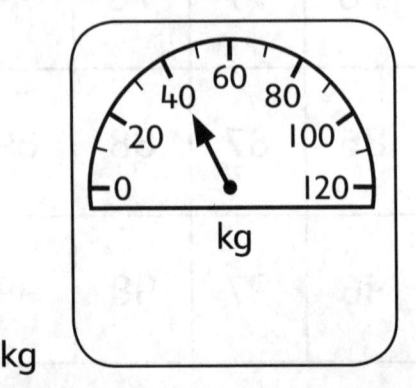

_____ kg 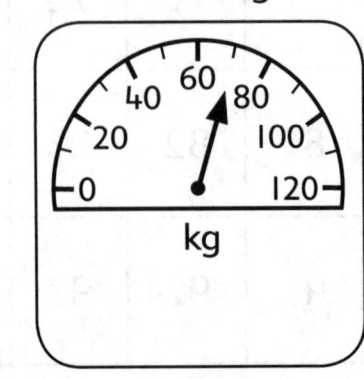   _____ kg

92 ▪ PHOTOCOPIABLE

100 SMART Board™ LESSONS • YEAR 4

▪ SCHOLASTIC
www.scholastic.co.uk

Jug illustrations © Jim Peacock / Beehive Illustration

MATHEMATICS LESSON 8   Name _____

How long?

■ Work with a partner.

  □ Look at each set of clocks in turn.

  □ Work out how long between the times on the first and second clocks.

  □ Write this in the box at the end of the set.

  □ Write a sentence using all three clock times.

1. _____

   [clock]   8.42   The difference is _____

2. _____

   [clock]   6.48   The difference is _____

3. _____

   [clock]   12.07   The difference is _____

4. _____

   [clock]   3.19   The difference is _____

5. _____

   [clock]   11.24   The difference is _____

MATHEMATICS LESSON 9   Name _____

Polygons

- Cut out the shape tiles.
- Sort them into three sets.
- Use each set to make a pattern. Try to leave no gaps in your pattern.

MATHEMATICS LESSON 10   Name _____

Identifying angles

- Work with a partner.
- You will need a 45° set square and a 60° set square.
- Measure these angles and write their measurements.

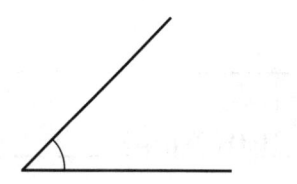

Measurement 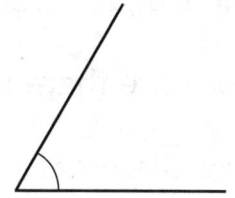 _____   Measurement _____

- Order these angles from smallest to largest and write their letters in order.

1. a. 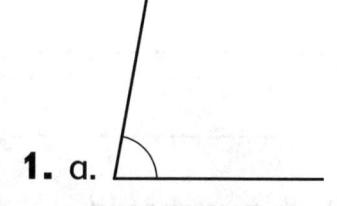   b. 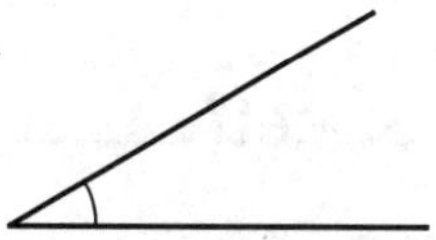   c.    d.

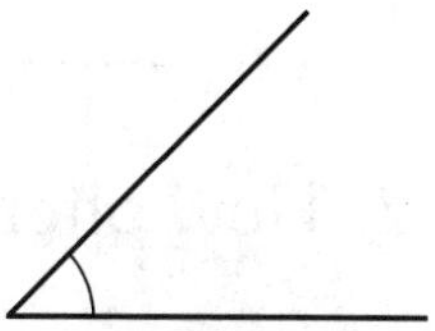

smallest _____ largest

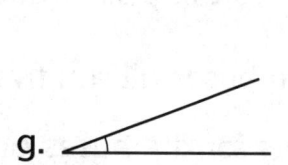

2. e. 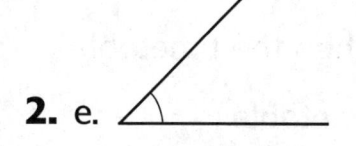   f. 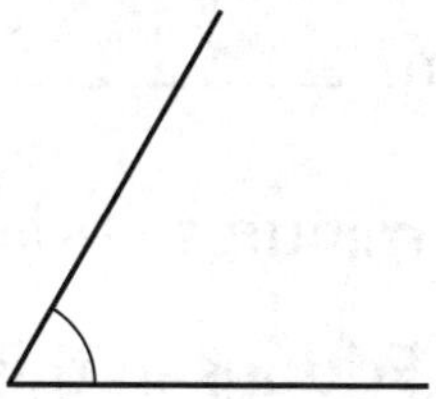   g.   h.

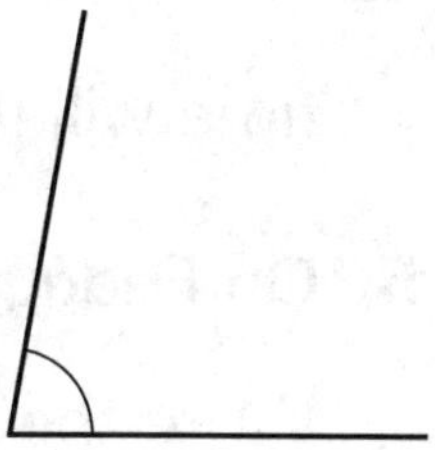

smallest _____ largest

- Challenge!
  ☐ On the back of this sheet, use the set squares to draw angles of 45°, 60° and 90°.

SCHOLASTIC
www.scholastic.co.uk

PHOTOCOPIABLE 95
100 SMART Board™ LESSONS • YEAR 4

MATHEMATICS — LESSON 19   Name _____

When?

- Use the calendar to help you to answer these questions.

1. Which months have 30 days? _____

2. On what day is 2nd August? _____

3. How many Mondays are there in July? _____

4. How many days are there between 3rd June and 24th June? ____

5. Which day of the week is New Year's Day? _____

- Use the timetable to help you to answer these questions.

1. How long does it take to get from Esplanade to the train station?

_____

2. How often does a bus leave Low Street? _____

3. I need to be at the bus station by half past ten. Which bus should I catch from High Street? _____

4. The 10 o'clock bus from Esplanade is running ten minutes late. What time will it get to the train station? _____

5. On Fridays the buses all run five minutes earlier than the timetable. Write the times for the buses on Fridays in this timetable.

Esplanade				
High Street				
Low Street				
Bus station				
Train station				

96 PHOTOCOPIABLE
100 SMART Board™ LESSONS • YEAR 4

SCHOLASTIC
www.scholastic.co.uk

MATHEMATICS LESSON 20   Name _____

Reflections

■ Draw the reflections of these shapes. You can use your ruler to check that the reflection is drawn correctly.

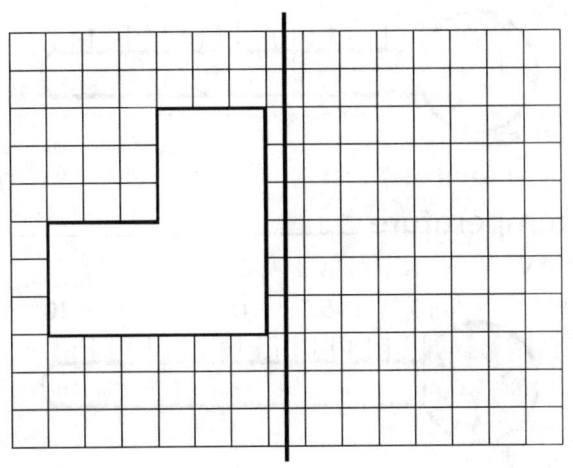

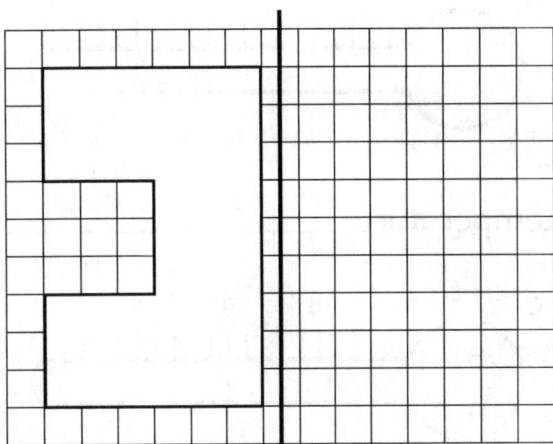

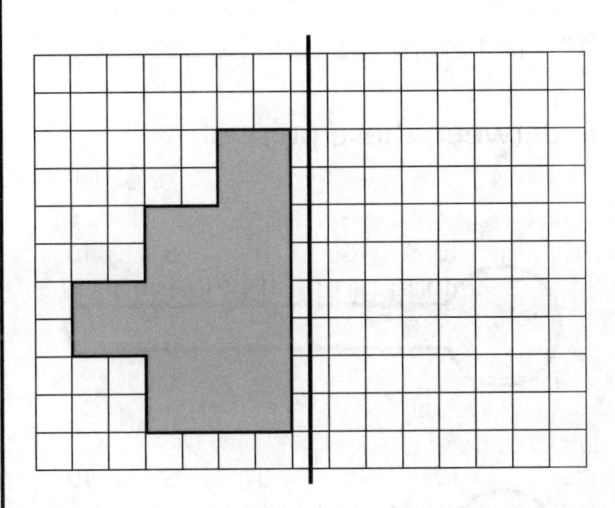

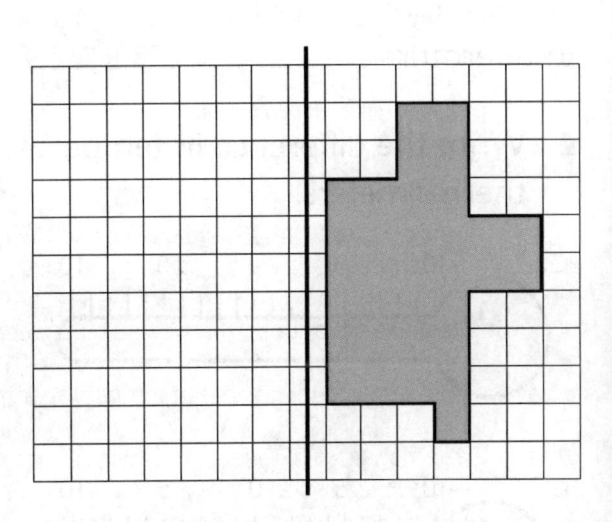

■ Now draw two images of your own. Make sure the lines are vertical or horizontal. Draw the reflection of each of your images.

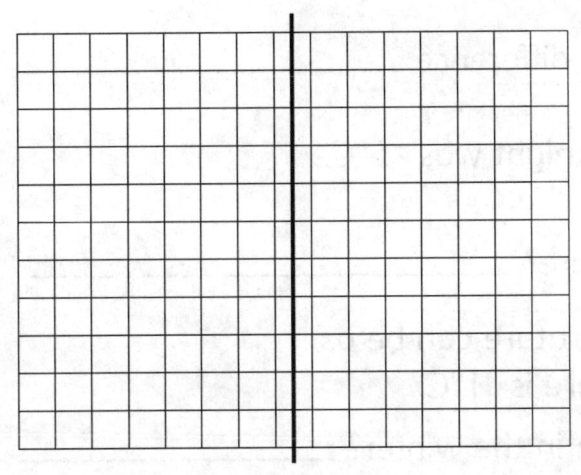

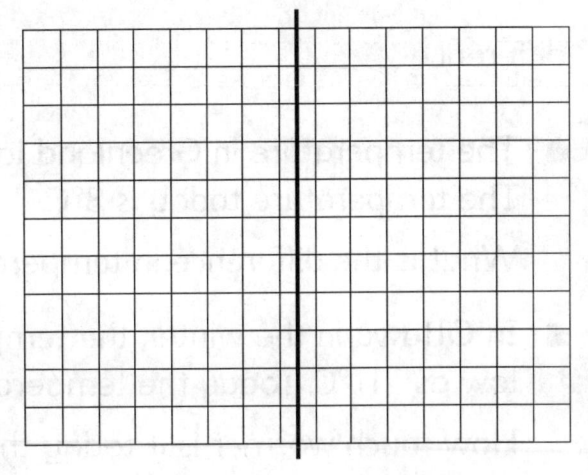

SCHOLASTIC
www.scholastic.co.uk

PHOTOCOPIABLE 97
100 SMART Board™ LESSONS • YEAR 4

MATHEMATICS LESSON 21   Name _____

Negative numbers

■ Write the temperature readings for each of these thermometers.

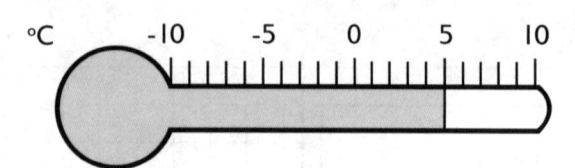

temperature 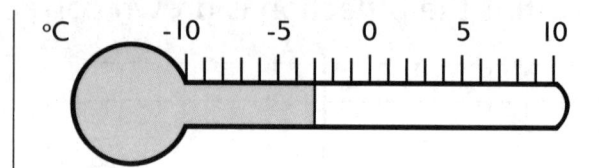 _____   temperature _____

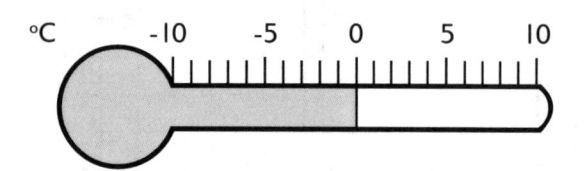

temperature 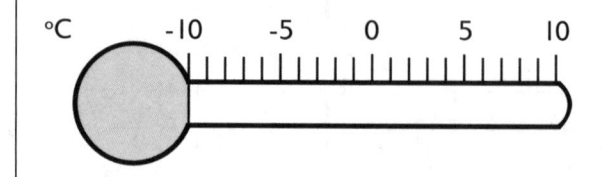 _____   temperature _____

■ Write the difference in temperatures between these pairs of thermometers.

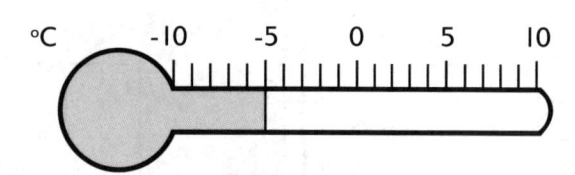

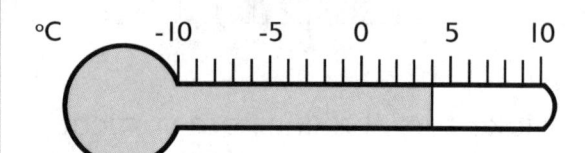

difference 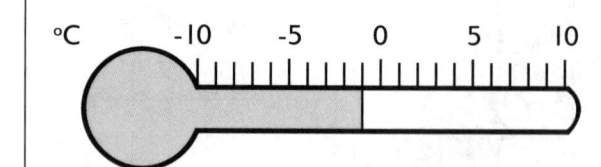 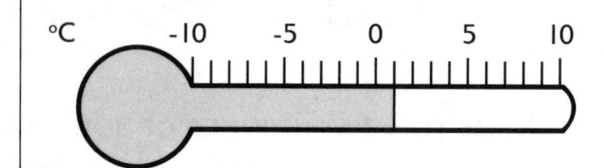 _____   difference _____

■ The temperature in Greenland last night was −5°C. The temperature today is 8°C.

What is the difference in temperature? _____

■ In Ottawa in the winter, the temperature can be as low as −11°C. Today the temperature is 11°C.

How much warmer is it today than in the winter? _____

MATHEMATICS LESSON 22   Name _____

Hundred square

- Circle the multiples of 2, 3, 4, 5 and 10 in different colours.
- Complete the key to record what each colour represents.

Key			multiple of 4
	multiple of 2		multiple of 5
	multiple of 3		multiple of 10

1	2	3	4	5	6	7	8	9	10
11	12	13	14	15	16	17	18	19	20
21	22	23	24	25	26	27	28	29	30
31	32	33	34	35	36	37	38	39	40
41	42	43	44	45	46	47	48	49	50
51	52	53	54	55	56	57	58	59	60
61	62	63	64	65	66	67	68	69	70
71	72	73	74	75	76	77	78	79	80
81	82	83	84	85	86	87	88	89	90
91	92	93	94	95	96	97	98	99	100

SCHOLASTIC
www.scholastic.co.uk

MATHEMATICS LESSON 25   Name _____

Add and subtract

- Choose a pair of numbers from the grid.
- Find their total.
- Write the addition sentence.
- Cross out your chosen numbers in the grid.
- Do this nine more times.

45	36	70	90	80	72	15	63	40	52
21	37	69	43	60	20	28	63	44	30

_____   _____   _____
_____   _____   _____
_____   _____   _____
_____

- Now write the answers to these subtraction sentences.

1. 90 – 30 = ☐
2. 45 – ☐ = 20
3. ☐ – 30 = 42
4. 60 – ☐ = 19
5. 80 – 36 = ☐
6. ☐ – 37 = 56

- Decide how to complete these number sentences. Make each one different.

1. ☐ + ☐ = ☐
2. ☐ + ☐ = ☐
3. ☐ + ☐ = ☐
4. ☐ – ☐ = ☐
5. ☐ – ☐ = ☐
6. ☐ – ☐ = ☐

MATHEMATICS LESSON 26   Name _____

Word problems

- Read each problem and decide how to answer it.
- Write your working out on the back of this sheet.

1. I think of a number and subtract 4. Then I multiply by 3. The answer is 15. What was my number? _____

Now compare with your partner.

Did you both use the same method? _____

Did you both get the same answer? _____

2. There are 234 red cars in the car park. The rest of the cars are silver. 48 cars leave. Now there are 295 cars left in the car park. How many silver cars were there altogether? _____

Now compare with your partner.

Did you both use the same method? _____

Did you both get the same answer? _____

3. There are four stacks of jotters. In the first stack there are 12 jotters. The second stack has twice as many as the first stack. The third stack has half as many as the first stack. Altogether, there are 58 jotters. How many jotters are there in the fourth stack? _____

Now compare with your partner.

Did you both use the same method? _____

Did you both get the same answer? _____

4. Sam has half as many CDs as Jon. Jon has half as many CDs as Peter. Peter has 48 CDs. How many CDs does Jon have? _____
How many does Sam have? _____

Now compare with your partner.

Did you both use the same method? _____

Did you both get the same answer? _____

SCHOLASTIC
www.scholastic.co.uk

PHOTOCOPIABLE 101
100 SMART Board™ LESSONS • YEAR 4

MATHEMATICS LESSON 28   Name _____

Carroll diagrams

MATHEMATICS LESSON 29   Name _____

Finding positions

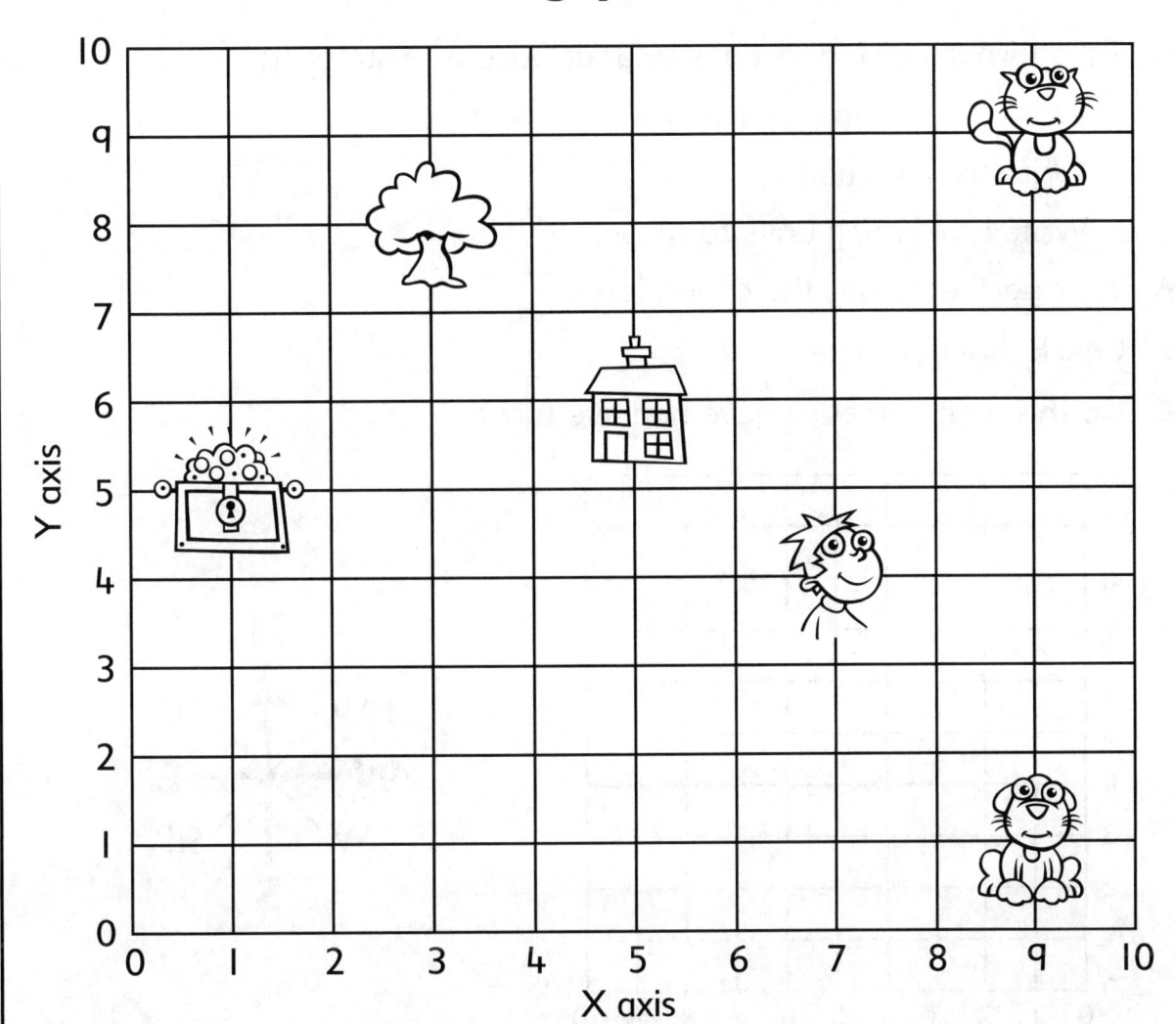

Write the coordinates of the items on the map.

Treasure chest _____   Tree _____
Cat _____   Dog _____
House _____   Boy _____

Now put a cross on the map at these coordinates:
(4, 1)   (4, 4)   (1, 4)   (1, 1)

Join the crosses with straight lines.
What shape have you made? _____

Draw a small rectangle on the map.
Write its coordinates here. _____

Draw your own shape on the map.
Write its coordinates here. _____

PHOTOCOPIABLE 103
100 SMART Board™ LESSONS • YEAR 4

MATHEMATICS LESSON 30   Name _____

Using compass directions

- Take turns to give directions to your partner. You must:
  - Write the starting coordinate.
  - Write the direction.
  - Write how many units to move.
- Your partner writes the coordinates.
- Check that you agree.
- Do this until you each have had five turns.

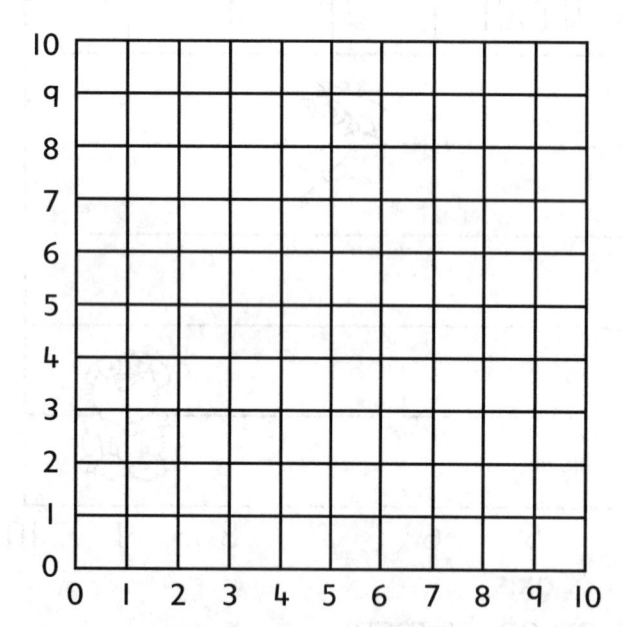

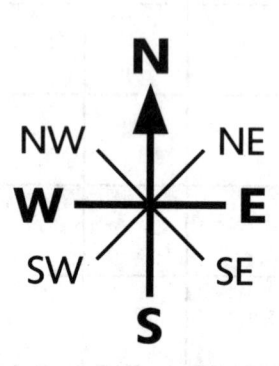

Starting coordinate	Direction	Number of units	Finishing coordinate

Science ▭ Chapter 3

Science

The following lessons offer ways to use an interactive whiteboard to teach science, using different whiteboard tools to target different learning styles. Using an interactive whiteboard gives teachers and children a unique opportunity to project, annotate and save large-scale images.

In science lessons, the whiteboard can be used to aid practical activities such as investigations. It can also display experiments and tests that would normally not be considered safe to perform in a classroom. The use of peripherals, such as the digital microscope or the digital camera, adds an extra dimension to lessons: organisms can be observed at close proximity and habitats can be photographed for children to explore.

Using a combination of tools, the whiteboard can assist the children's structured written work: word banks, photographs and video clips can be projected onto the whiteboard as an aide-mémoire; children's results can be shared using data-handling programs and resultant bar charts or line graphs can be projected to encourage class discussions and analysis.

Lesson title	Objectives	Expected prior knowledge	Cross-curricular links
Lesson 1: Similar skeletons	QCA Unit 4A 'Moving and growing' • To know that humans (and some other animals) have bony skeletons inside their bodies and to raise questions about different bony skeletons • To make and record relevant observations of bones and skeletons.	• Know that our skeletons help us to move and that they support our bodies.	ICT QCA Unit 4C 'Branching databases'
Lesson 2: Skeleton investigation	QCA Unit 4A 'Moving and growing' • To learn that human skeletons are internal and grow as humans grow. • To identify a question, make a prediction and test it. • To decide and make a body measurement. • To use bar charts to present measurements. • To say what the evidence shows and whether it supports the prediction.	• Know that our skeletons help us to move. • Know how to take accurate measurements.	Mathematics Measuring: Choose and use standard metric units and their abbreviations when estimating, measuring and recording length, weight and capacity. Handling data: Answer a question by identifying what data to collect; organise, present, analyse and interpret the data in tables, diagrams, tally charts and bar charts.
Lesson 3: Supporting skeletons	QCA Unit 4A 'Moving and growing' • To learn that the skeleton supports the body.	• Know that a skeleton protects the soft, delicate parts of an organism.	English Sentence structure and punctuation
Lesson 4: Muscles and bones	QCA Unit 4A 'Moving and growing' • To learn that animals with skeletons have muscles attached to the bones. • To learn that a muscle has to contract (shorten) to make a bone move. • To learn that muscles work hard when you exercise. • To make observations and comparisons relating to exercise and rest.	• Know that bones do not move freely on their own.	PE PoS (4a) How exercise affects the body in the short term; (4b) To warm up for different activities.
Lesson 5: Different organisms	QCA Unit 4B 'Habitats' • To group organisms according to observable features. • To use keys to identify plants or animals.	• Know that groups of organisms share similarities.	ICT QCA Unit 4C 'Branching databases'

Science — Chapter 3

Lesson title	Objectives	Expected prior knowledge	Cross-curricular links
Lesson 6: Food chains	**QCA Unit 4B** 'Habitats' • To identify the structure of a food chain in a specific habitat. • To be aware that animals are suited to the habitat in which they are found. • To know that most food chains start with a green plant.	• Know that different animals are found in different habitats.	**Geography** QCA Unit 10 'A village in India'
Lesson 7: Different habitats	**QCA Unit 4B** 'Habitats' • That different animals are found in different habitats. • To make predictions of organisms that will be found in a habitat. • To learn that animals are suited to the environment in which they are found.	• Be aware that all organisms need a habitat, and that all habitats are different.	**Geography** QCA Unit 8 'Improving the environment' **History** PoS (2a) To learn about characteristic features of periods and societies studied.
Lesson 8: Changing habitats	**QCA Unit 4B** 'Habitats' • To recognise ways in which living things and the environment need protection.	• Be aware that all organisms need a habitat, and that all habitats are different.	**Geography** QCA Unit 21 'How can we improve the area we see from our window?' **English** Creating and shaping texts
Lesson 9: Temperature and thermometers	**QCA Unit 4C** 'Keeping warm' • To be aware that the sense of touch is not an accurate way of judging temperature. • To use a thermometer to make careful measurements of temperature. • To know that something hot will cool down and something cold will warm up until it is the same temperature as its surroundings. • To explain temperature and temperature changes using scientific knowledge and understanding.	• Know that temperature is a measure of how hot or cold things are. • Be aware of the importance of accurate measurements.	**Mathematics** Measuring: Interpret intervals and divisions on partially numbered scales and record readings accurately.
Lesson 10: Keeping things cold	**QCA Unit 4C** 'Keeping warm ' • To turn an idea about how to keep things cold into a form that can be investigated. • To decide what evidence to collect. • To make a table and record results in it. • To draw conclusions from their results.	• Know what happens to food when it is taken out of the freezer.	**Geography** QCA Unit 24 'Passport to the world' **English** Understanding and interpreting texts: Use knowledge of word structures and origins to develop their understanding of word meanings.
Lesson 11: Keeping warm	**QCA Unit 4C** 'Keeping warm ' • To make careful measurements of temperature at regular time intervals. • To record results in a table and to use these to draw conclusions. • To know that some materials are good thermal insulators.	• Know how to keep themselves warm during the cold winter months.	**Geography** QCA Unit 24 'Passport to the world'
Lesson 12: Flowing materials	**QCA Unit 4D** 'Solids, liquids and how they can be separated' • To make careful observations and measurements of volume, recording them in tables and using them to draw conclusions. • To understand that liquids do not change in volume when they are poured into a different container. • To understand that solids consisting of very small pieces behave like liquids in some ways.	• Know that liquids will run freely into a space when poured or pushed.	**Mathematics** Measuring: Choose and use standard metric units and their abbreviations when estimating, measuring and recording length, weight and capacity.

Science ▸ Chapter 3

Lesson title	Objectives	Expected prior knowledge	Cross-curricular links
Lesson 13: Mixing solids and liquids	QCA Unit 4D 'Solids, liquids and how they can be separated' • To understand that changes occur when some solids are added to water. • To make careful observations, recording results in tables, and make comparisons.	• To know what happens when they mix a drink such as coffee, hot chocolate, or milkshake.	Art and design PoS (2b) Pupils should be taught to apply their experience of materials and processes.
Lesson 14: Sieving and filtering solids	QCA Unit 4D 'Solids, liquids and how they can be separated' • To understand that when solids do not dissolve or react with the water they can be separated by filtering. • To choose apparatus to separate an undissolved solid from a liquid.	• Know that when materials are mixed, a change occurs.	ICT QCA Unit 4D 'Collecting and presenting information'
Lesson 15: Dissolving solids	QCA Unit 4D 'Solids, liquids and how they can be separated' • To understand that some solids dissolve in water to form solutions and that although the solid cannot be seen it is still present. • To predict whether sugar can be separated from a solution by filtering and to test the prediction. • To decide what apparatus to use. • To know when it is safe to taste things to test them.	• Be aware of the properties of solids and of liquids.	PSHE PoS (3a) To consider what makes a healthy lifestyle.
Lesson 16: In a spin	QCA Unit 4E 'Friction' • To know that air resistance is a force that slows objects moving through air. • To plan a fair test saying what to change, what to keep the same and what to measure. • To make measurements of time. • To identify a pattern in the results and to explain it in terms of air resistance.	• Be aware that all objects when dropped from a height will fall, but that all objects do not necessarily fall in the same way.	ICT QCA Unit 4D 'Collecting and presenting information'
Lesson 17: Complete circuits	QCA Unit 4F 'Circuits and conductors' • To learn that a circuit needs a power source. • To learn that a complete circuit is needed for a device to work.	• Know how to construct a simple circuit.	PE PoS (4b) To warm up and prepare appropriately.
Lesson 18: Circuits and switches	QCA Unit 4F 'Circuits and conductors' • To understand that a circuit needs a power source. • To know that a complete circuit is needed for a device to work. • That a switch can be used to make or break a circuit to turn things on or off (using batteries or mains).	• Know how to construct a simple circuit.	Design and technology QCA Unit 4E 'Lighting it up'
Lesson 19: Using switches	QCA Unit 4F 'Circuits and conductors' • To know that a circuit needs a power source and needs to be complete for a device to work. • To understand that a switch can be used to make or break a circuit to turn things on or off. • To construct a circuit with a switch.	• Know how to construct a simple circuit. • Know how switches are used in everyday life.	English Creating and shaping texts Word structure and spelling Design and technology PoS (5c) Design and make assignments using a range of materials.
Lesson 20: How bright?	QCA Unit 4F 'Circuits and conductors' • To make predictions about the effect of including additional batteries in a circuit, and check whether results support the prediction made. • That bulbs can burn out if components in a circuit are changed. • To know how to change the brightness of bulbs in a circuit. • To plan to change one factor and keep others constant.	• Know that components need power in order to work.	Design and technology QCA Unit 4E 'Lighting it up'

Science Lesson 1

Similar skeletons

Learning objectives
QCA Unit 4A 'Moving and growing'
- To know that humans (and some other animals) have bony skeletons inside their bodies and to raise questions about different bony skeletons.
- To make and record relevant observations of bones and skeletons.

Resources
'Bones' Notebook file; examples of animal bones, thoroughly cleaned and sterilised (if available); photocopiable page 128 'Similar skeletons?' for each child; pictures of different skeletons, enough for two per group; large pieces of sugar paper; white paper; pencils; glue.

Links to other subjects
ICT
QCA Unit 4C 'Branching databases'
- Challenge the children to create a branching database to identify the two skeletons they investigated during the independent work.

Whiteboard tools
Use the Lines tool to link written ideas on the concept map. Delete objects by selecting them and then pressing the Delete button.

- Pen tray
- Lines tool
- Select tool
- Delete button
- Gallery

Starter
Display page 2 of the Notebook file and build a concept map with the children to find out what they know about bones. Ask: *Why do we have bones? Are bones all the same size? Where do you have/can you feel bones in your body? Can you name any of the bones?* Label any bones that the children know. Images from 'The Human Body' in the Gallery can be used as an extra support for this activity.

Whole-class shared work
- Together with the children, read pages 3, 4 and 5 and answer the questions. Select the panels and press the Delete button to reveal the answers. Discuss any new and interesting facts.
- If possible, show examples of animal bones to the children. Explain which part of the (animal) body they are from.
- Go to page 6. Look carefully at the picture of the skeleton and ask the children what they notice. What type of skeleton do they think is shown here? How does it compare to a human skeleton? What type of animal does it belong to? Press the *What is it?* button to find the answer. Are the children surprised by the answer?
- Repeat this process for the skeleton on page 7.
- Remind the children of the bone words collected during the Starter. Can they identify different bones in the skeletons on pages 6 and 7? Add their suggestions to the Notebook file.

Independent work
- Give each child a copy of photocopiable page 128 to complete as they carry out the following activity.
- Put the children into small mixed-ability groups. Give each group two pictures of different skeletons or examples of bones, a large piece of sugar paper, white paper, scissors, pencils and glue.
- Ask the groups to make two sets of labels using the words in the word bank. They should then put the skeleton pictures in the middle of the sugar paper and arrange the labels around the outside to identify the different parts of the skeletons. When they are satisfied with the result they can stick down the pictures and labels.
- As the children work, encourage them to notice similar parts of each skeleton (for example, the skull) and to discuss how they are the same or different.
- Ask the children to write down the similarities and differences between the two skeletons. For example: one had longer arm bones than the other; both skeletons had the same number of ribs.
- If there is enough time, ask the children to draw pictures of the skeleton or bones on the back of the photocopiable sheet or on separate sheets of paper.
- Mixed-ability groups should support less confident learners. Monitor the groups to ensure that everyone contributes to the task.

Plenary
- Show the children pictures of bones and ask them to think of adjectives to describe them, such as *long, thin, smooth, fragile, tough, hard*. Make a note of the words that they suggest on page 8.
- Show the children the x-ray photographs of a human ankle and knee on page 9 and ask them to describe what they see. Ask: *Has anyone had an x-ray? Why did you have one? What was used to take the x-ray? How do you think the machine works?*

Science Lesson 2

Skeleton investigation

Learning objectives
QCA Unit 4A 'Moving and growing'
- To learn that human skeletons are internal and grow as humans grow.
- To identify a question, make a prediction and test it.
- To decide and make a body measurement.
- To use bar charts to present measurements.
- To say what the evidence shows and whether it supports the prediction.

Resources
'Skeleton investigation' Notebook file; photocopiable pages 129 and 130 'Investigation report 1' and '2', one of each for each child; tape measures and rulers. (Microsoft Excel is required to view the embedded spreadsheet in the Notebook file.)

Links to other subjects
Mathematics
Measuring: Choose and use standard metric units and their abbreviations when estimating, measuring and recording length, weight and capacity.
Handling data: Answer a question by identifying what data to collect; organise, present, analyse and interpret the data in tables, diagrams, tally charts and bar charts.
- The children should record the body measurements accurately and use bar charts to present their results.

Whiteboard tools
Use the Lines tool to draw a simple table.

- Pen tray
- Highlighter pen
- Lines tool

Starter
Display page 2 of the Notebook file and ask the children to compare the size of their forearm with their neighbour's. Ask: *What do you notice about the size of your neighbour's forearm? Whose arm is bigger? Why do you think this is?* Make notes of the children's ideas.

Whole-class shared work
- Go to page 3. Ask: *Who has the biggest head size in the class? Do you think my head will be the same size, bigger or smaller than yours? Why? How could we find out?*
- Demonstrate how to measure your head size using a tape measure. Ask for a suitable unit of measurement. (Centimetres.) Encourage the children to predict what the measure will be.
- Compare the measurement of your head size with a child's head size and discuss whether the children's predictions were correct.
- Explain that our bones grow as we grow, so adults have longer or bigger bones than children. Ask: *Does this mean that all the children in this class are the same size?*
- Go to page 4 of the Notebook file. Ask the children whether the boys and girls in their class are the same size. Explain that, as a class, they will design an investigation to find this out. Invite them to suggest what they could measure (for example, head size, hand span, or forearm length). Make notes on the board.
- Give the children copies of photocopiable pages 129 and 130 to help them write up their investigation.
- Work through pages 5 to 8 of the Notebook file with the children, adding their suggestions to the board.

Independent work
- Organise the children into groups of four or five.
- Display page 9 of the Notebook file. Discuss how they will record results. Draw a table, using the Lines tool for them to copy onto their photocopiable sheet.
- Allow the children enough time to take measurements of their chosen bone, filling in their sheets as they do so.
- Provide less confident learners with adult support in measuring bones.

Plenary
- Go to page 10 of the Notebook file. Press the icon to open the Measurement investigation spreadsheet. An example table and example chart have been provided to illustrate how the children can record data and use it to create a suitable bar chart.
- Fill in the data fields on the Table worksheet.
- Ask the children to predict what the bar chart will look like.
- Bring up the Chart worksheet and ask the children questions about the bar chart. For example: *Which group of people had the smallest head? How do you know?*
- Use the other headings on page 11 to discuss how to write the conclusion to, and evaluation of, the investigation. The children can finish their reports as follow-up work.

Science | Lesson 3

Learning objective
QCA Unit 4A 'Moving and growing'
● To learn that the skeleton supports the body.

Resources
'Supporting skeletons' Notebook file; a range of reference books containing information about different invertebrates.

Links to other subjects
English
Sentence structure and punctuation
● Encourage the children to think about how invertebrates move and to use powerful verbs, such as *slithered*. More confident learners will also be able to add adverbs to describe the movement.

Whiteboard tools
Add text to the page with the On-screen Keyboard, accessed through the Pen tray or the SMART Board tools menu.

- Pen tray
- Select tool
- On-screen Keyboard

Supporting skeletons

Starter
Play the video clip on page 2 of the Notebook file. Ask: *What do you notice about how this animal moves? How quickly does it move? Does it move in a certain way? Do you think this animal has a backbone or not?*

Whole-class shared work
● Show the children page 3 and ask them what the animal is. (A jellyfish.) Reveal the correct answer using the Eraser from the Pen tray. What do the children notice about the jellyfish? Encourage them to point out the structural differences between this animal and a mammal.
● Ask the children to think about how their own skeletons support their bodies: they would not be able to stand if they had no leg bones! Go to page 4 to show how the skeleton acts as a framework for the human body.
● Go to page 5, and ask the children to work in pairs to discuss where they think each animal should go. Invite pairs to the board to drag pictures into the correct space, giving reasons for their choices.
● Explain that animals with a skeleton are called *vertebrates* because they have a backbone, which is the supporting column of the body. Ask the children: *What does having a backbone enable you to do? What does it not allow you to do?*
● Explain that the animals without an internal skeleton are called *invertebrates*.

Independent work
● Display page 6. Ask the children to work in pairs to create a fact file about an animal without an internal skeleton. They should choose one invertebrate and find out information about it, using the questions on the board as a guide: *How does it move without a skeleton? What shape is it? How does it protect itself?* Encourage the children to think of further questions.
● Provide them with a selection of reference books that give information about different invertebrates.
● Mixed-ability pairs should provide support for less confident learners. Monitor pairs to ensure that they both contribute to the task.
● Challenge more confident learners to think about how they want to present their information in a fact file.

Plenary
● Ask the children to share what they have discovered about their chosen invertebrates. Display page 6 and add interesting facts that the children have gathered about how these animals support or protect themselves.
● The children should understand that all bodies need some sort of support, but not all animals have an internal structure to do this. Point out that animals without an internal skeleton often have strong muscles to help them to move, whereas other animals, like spiders, have an *exoskeleton* (a skeleton on the outside of the body).
● Go to page 7 and summarise what the children have learned.

Science Lesson 4

Muscles and bones

Learning objectives
QCA Unit 4A 'Moving and growing'
● To learn that animals with skeletons have muscles attached to the bones.
● To learn that a muscle has to contract (shorten) to make a bone move.
● To learn that muscles work hard when you exercise.
● To make observations and comparisons relating to exercise and rest.

Resources
'Build your own' file; a room with space for children to move around; paper and pencils.

Links to other subjects
PE
PoS (4a) How exercise affects the body in the short term; (4b) To warm up for different activities.
● During PE lessons, remind the children that every movement requires muscles. Use a digital camera to film certain movements and display these on the whiteboard. Discuss which muscles are being used.

Whiteboard tools
Display an image of a person from the Gallery for the Starter. Use the Timer from the Science folder under My Content in the Gallery to time the children's activities.

- Pen tray
- Select tool
- Gallery

Starter
Ask the children to find a space in the room. Tell them to pick up a book and lift it up and down. What helps them to do this? Is it their bones alone? Explain that muscles are attached to their bones, and that these help to support their movements. Ask the children to point out any muscles that they know.

Open the 'Build your own' file, which consists of a blank Notebook page and a collection of images located in My Content in the Gallery. Display a Gallery image of a person on a blank Notebook page and annotate it with the children's suggestions about muscles.

Whole-class shared work
● Ask the children to discuss in pairs what they think muscles do. Allow three to five minutes' thinking time.
● Invite the children to share their ideas and note them down on a new Notebook page.
● Explain that muscles help us to move parts of our bodies. Every movement we make involves muscles, such as smiling, writing and clapping. Ask the children to try a few of these movements and to identify where muscles are being used.
● Ask the children to roll up their sleeves, then stretch one arm right above their head. Tell them to bend their arm slowly and to look at it while they perform this action. Ask: *What do you notice when you bend your arm? What do you think is happening inside your arm?*
● Tell the children that muscle contraction is an active process and that muscles work in pairs. Ask them to feel their upper arm as they flex their arm. The biceps contracts (it gets rounder and harder) and the triceps relaxes as the arm is flexed.
● Tell the children that they will be doing some short exercises and, as they do so, you'd like them to think about the muscles they are using.

Independent work
● Move to a room where there is space for the children to move around.
● Ask the children to organise themselves into pairs and find a space.
● Give each pair a sheet of paper and a pencil. Ask them to list the following five activities in a column on the left-hand side of the page:
  ● sit-ups
  ● marching
  ● stretching out arms and touching shoulders
  ● running on the spot
  ● star jumps.
● Use the Timer's count-down function to time the children as they carry out each of the five activities for 60 seconds.
● After each activity, ask the children to write which muscles they think they used. They do not need to know the specific names, but should be able to identify whether they are using their leg/arm/shoulder muscles and so on.

Plenary
● Go back to the classroom and go through the exercises and muscles used on the board. Ask the children how they feel after the exercises.
● Explain that their muscles are working a lot harder when they move around than when they are sitting still. That is the reason why it is important to warm up before they take part in longer exercises, so that their muscles are ready for the movement.

Science ▪ Lesson 5

Different organisms

Learning objectives
QCA Unit 4B 'Habitats'
● To group organisms according to observable features.
● To use keys to identify plants or animals.

Resources
'Grouping and identifying organisms' Notebook file; photocopiable page 131 'Organisms cards' cut up and made into cards – each group of children will need one set of cards.

Links to other subjects
ICT
QCA Unit 4C 'Branching databases'
● Ask the children to create their own branching databases for sorting organisms, using a suitable software package and a bank of clip art.

Starter
Display the pictures on page 2 of the Notebook file and ask the children to discuss in pairs how they would sort them. There is no single correct way but it is important to think about the similarities and differences. The children should look at the features of each organism, such as the legs, wings, eyes and colours. Invite pairs to sort the animals on the board and ask them to explain their reasons for sorting them in a particular way.

Whole-class shared work
● Go to page 3. Give the children five to ten minutes to group similar organisms together. Use the Timer's count-down function to time them.
● Invite groups to explain how they sorted the organisms and what criteria they used. Write their ideas on page 3.
● Explain that they have sorted these organisms based on similarities, or features that the organisms shared.
● Ask the children to sort one of the groups into two smaller groups. What would happen if they took one of the groups and sorted it, and then did it again and again? (They should eventually end up with a single organism.)
● Go to page 4 and explain that this page shows a key to identify some of the animals that the children looked at during the Starter. They will be asked questions to sort the animals into two groups, and then into two groups again, and so on, until they are left with one animal in each group.
● Slowly pull the Screen Shade down from the top of the screen. Read and discuss the questions one at a time.
● When the full screen is revealed, demonstrate how each question sorts the animals.
● Tell the children that a key provides an easy way to identify an organism. It is like a signposted diagram; at each post you can either go one way or the other.

Independent work
● Provide groups of three to four children with a set of 'Organisms' cards, made from photocopiable page 131.
● In pairs, ask the children to shuffle their sets of Organisms cards and place them upside down. They should then choose six cards and create their own key (following the same procedure as on page 4 of the Notebook file) for this group of organisms.
● Let the less confident learners choose four cards only.
● Challenge more confident learners to create a key for eight organisms.

Plenary
● Display page 5. Tell the children that there is an animal hidden behind the box on the right. Can they guess what it is?
● Pull the first question from the red box and place it on the white area to read it. Then drag it onto the orange box below to reveal the yes or no answer. When all the questions have been revealed, encourage the children to guess the animal. Select the box on the right-hand side of the page and press the Delete button to reveal the answer.
● Finish the lesson by asking the children what kind of yes or no questions they could ask to identify a human being. For example: *Can it talk? Can it fly? Can it crawl? Can it walk? Does it stand on two legs?*

Whiteboard tools
Move the Screen Shade on page 4 to reveal the questions one at a time.

- Pen tray
- Select tool
- Delete button
- Screen Shade

Science ◼ Lesson 6

Food chains

Learning objectives
QCA Unit 4B 'Habitats'
● To identify the structure of a food chain in a specific habitat.
● To be aware that animals are suited to the habitat in which they are found.
● To know that most food chains start with a green plant.

Resources 💿 📘
'Food chains' Notebook file; photocopiable page 132 'Food chains' for each child; scissors; glue.

Links to other subjects
Geography
QCA Unit 10 'A village in India'
● Find out about animals that are native to India and construct a variety of food chains. Are some animals and plants only found in India?

Starter
Remind the children of the word *habitat*. Ask: *What does the word 'habitat' mean? How many types of habitat can you name? Which habitat do we live in?* Write their suggestions on page 2 of the Notebook file.

Whole-class shared work
● Go to page 3. Ask the children to match the organisms to their correct habitat. Choose a few animals and ask the children what those animals eat. Are some of the foods in the picture?
● Enable the Spotlight tool 🔦 and go to page 4 of the Notebook file. Focus on one of the words at the top of the page using the spotlight. Ask the children to think about what it means. Allow them some quiet thinking time. Do the same for the other word. Encourage the children to share their ideas.
● Reveal the whole screen and point out the producers and consumers on the page. Tell the children that the word *producer* means *maker*. The producers are usually plants, and they make their own food. The word *consumer* means *eater* or *drinker*. The consumers are usually animals. They either eat plants, or other animals.
● Use the Select tool to match the producers on the page with the correct consumers.
● Repeat this process for the words *predator* and *prey* on page 5. Ask the children to share ideas first, and then explain what the words mean. The word *predator* means *an animal that hunts other animals for food* and the word *prey* means *an animal that is hunted for food*. Point out to the children that more than one predator can hunt for the same prey.
● Go to page 6. Ask the children to group pictures together that illustrate a producer and consumer (a plant and one animal), or a producer, prey and predator (a plant and two animals). Invite children to the board to demonstrate their choices and their reasons.
● Emphasise the arrows and the direction in which they are pointing. What does it mean if you rotated the arrow to face the other direction?

Independent work
● Provide each child with a copy of photocopiable page 132. Ask the children to cut out the pictures, labels and arrows and use them to create food chains.
● Invite less confident learners to pair together a producer and a consumer.
● Challenge more confident learners to create a complete food chain and identify, using the labels, the predator, prey, consumer and producer.

Plenary
● Ask the children to talk about the examples of food chains that they have created.
● Go to page 7 and, as a class, create a fact file for a human being and an owl. Use images from the Gallery 🖼 to choose suitable foods to place in the food chain.

Whiteboard tools
Use the Spotlight tool in the SMART Board tools menu to focus on words on the screen. Use the Gallery to find images of suitable animals and plants for a food chain.

🖥 Pen tray
▶ Select tool
🔦 Spotlight tool
🖼 Gallery

◼ 113
100 SMART Board™ LESSONS • YEAR 4

Science ▫ Lesson 7

Different habitats

Learning objectives
QCA Unit 4B 'Habitats'
- To know that different animals are found in different habitats.
- To make predictions of organisms that will be found in a habitat.
- To learn that animals are suited to the environment in which they are found.

Resources
Prepared Notebook file showing a habitat and some animals that might live there (the animals should be hidden behind shapes); individual whiteboards and pens; digital camera (if available); video clips or images of different types of habitat (copyright permitting), such as fresh water, seaside, woodland; picture of a local habitat – if possible, organise a visit to this habitat to collect organisms (alternatively focus on the habitat of the school grounds).

Links to other subjects
Geography
QCA Unit 8 'Improving the environment'
- Investigate litter problems around the school and think about how this affects the habitat of creatures that live on the school grounds.

History
PoS (2a) To learn about characteristic features of periods and societies studied.
- Use a similar technique to prompt children to guess the purpose of artefacts placed on an historical background.

Whiteboard tools
Create a habitat using images from the Gallery and digital images (copyright permitting). Use the Shapes tool to create shapes to hide the animals.

- Pen tray
- Gallery
- Shapes tool
- Select tool

Starter
Show the prepared Notebook file (see Resources) to the children and ask them to guess what animals are living in this habitat. They can only ask ten questions for each animal and you can only answer *yes*, *no* or *sometimes*. Reduce the size of the shape to reveal each animal, or drag them out from their hiding places.

Whole-class shared work
- Ask the children to organise themselves into groups of three. Provide each group with an individual whiteboard and pen to record their decisions.
- Tell the children that they are going to play a game called 'Who lives here?' You will show them a habitat. They have to identify the habitat and predict what kind of animals would live there. They also need to think of good reasons for their choices.
- Show your pictures and/or video clips of different habitats. Ask the children to tell you what kind of habitats they saw and what kind of animals would live in them. How would they describe the habitats? Why did they choose these animals? Would those animals be able to live in any of the other habitats? Invite the children to write their suggestions on their individual whiteboards.
- Annotate the children's suggestions around the images.

Independent work
- Put a heading on a new Notebook page, 'Our class field trip', and show a picture of a local habitat.
- Explain that the children will be going on a field trip to this place to collect animals. Emphasise that this must be done with care, to ensure that the animals are not harmed or their habitat damaged.
- Tell the children you want them to make some notes to prepare for their field trip. Ask them to:
  - predict the different types of organisms they might find in the habitat that they are going to visit, and explain their predictions;
  - suggest equipment for collecting the animals, and explain why the equipment is appropriate and necessary;
  - suggest what information they should plan to collect, and how they will collect it.
- Suggest that a digital camera could be used to take pictures of the organisms and the location(s) in which they were found. Another idea is to design a table to collect information about the conditions in which each organism is found. (For example: How much light/shade did the organism have? Was the organism found near water? What type of soil was it found in? How hot or cold was the place where it was found?)

Plenary
- Discuss the children's ideas, making notes on the Notebook page.
- Explain the importance of returning any animal collected to its original habitat.
- Discuss with the children why we should respect an animal's habitat.

Science Lesson 8

Changing habitats

Learning objective
QCA Unit 4B 'Habitats'
- To recognise ways in which living things and the environment need protection.

Resources
'Build your own' file. Use the 'Build your own' file to prepare a Notebook page showing a busy woodland scene – use the 'Outdoor scene' background from the Science folder under My Content in the Gallery, along with trees and animals such as a badger, fox, rabbit, owl, blackbird and hedgehog. Presentation software such as Microsoft PowerPoint (optional).

Links to other subjects
Geography
QCA Unit 21 'How can we improve the area we see from our window?'
- Study the local area and identify good places to site a pond.
English
Creating and shaping texts
- Write a formal letter of complaint about the pond.

Whiteboard tools
Remove objects on the Notebook page by selecting them and pressing the Delete button. Alternatively, choose the Delete option from the dropdown menu.

- Pen tray
- Delete button
- Select tool
- Gallery

Starter
Ask the children if they have ever moved house or stayed in a place away from home. How did it feel to be somewhere different? How long did it take for them to get used to it? Did it feel strange that things they were used to weren't there any more? Write their responses on a blank Notebook page.

Whole-class shared work
- Display the prepared page in the 'Build your own' file (see Resources). Ask the children to describe the habitat they can see on the screen, and the animals living in it.
- Tell the children that the wood has been sold to a construction company to build houses on the land. Delete the trees one at a time until only the animals remain. Ask them what will happen to the habitat and the animals.
- Explain that organisms are affected when changes occur in their habitat.
- Ask the children to imagine that a local pond is going to be drained and covered over, so that a new playground can be built on it.
- Ask: *Is it so bad to fill in the pond if it means that children will have somewhere to play?*
- Tell the children to discuss with a partner what the effects would be, and why the habitat is important to the organisms and to the local area. Ask: *What do plants give back to people that we need? What will happen to the plant life and animals if the pond is drained?* Write down their suggestions on a blank Notebook page.

Independent work
- Split the class in two. In pairs, one half of the class will prepare notes on why the change you have been discussing is bad. (For example, the pond provides a valuable habitat for plants and animals, and a valuable resource for humans.) The other half will argue why this change is good. (For example, it will improve the habitat of humans by giving children somewhere safe to play.)
- At the end of the lesson, the two groups will take turns to debate why this is a good or bad change, giving reasons for their argument.
- Mixed-ability pairs should provide support for less confident learners.
- Challenge more confident learners to prepare a presentation using appropriate software, such as Microsoft PowerPoint, if resources are available.

Plenary
- Seat the two groups on opposite sides of the room. Invite pairs from each group to speak in turn, stating their argument.
- Encourage the opposing group to respond to the statements. Tell them they must abide by the rules: no interruptions!
- Make a note of the children's arguments on a new Notebook page.
- Conclude the lesson by asking all the children to vote on whether they believe the change is good or bad. They do not have to vote for the side for which they debated, but they should instead look at all the arguments presented and make their own balanced judgement.

Science — Lesson 9

Temperature and thermometers

Learning objectives
QCA Unit 4C 'Keeping warm'
- To be aware that the sense of touch is not an accurate way of judging temperature.
- To use a thermometer to make careful measurements of temperature.
- To know that something hot will cool down and something cold will warm up until it is the same temperature as its surroundings.
- To explain temperature and temperature changes using scientific knowledge and understanding.

Resources
'Temperature' Notebook file; non-mercury thermometers; three bowls containing the following: ice cubes, water at room temperature, warm water - one bowl for each group and one set of all three for the Starter. (Microsoft Excel is required to view the embedded spreadsheet in the Notebook file.)

Links to other subjects
Mathematics
Measuring: Interpret intervals and divisions on partially numbered scales and record readings accurately.
- Use the ITP to work out different temperature word problems. For example: *In the morning, it is 18°C in the classroom. By the afternoon, the temperature drops by 5°C. What is the temperature in the afternoon?*

Whiteboard tools
Use the On-screen Keyboard to enter data into the spreadsheet.

- Pen tray
- Select tool
- Capture tool
- On-screen Keyboard

Starter
Place three bowls containing ice cubes, water at room temperature and warm water on a table. Invite a few children to judge how hot the contents in the bowls are using their fingers. Write their answers on page 2 of the Notebook file.

Whole-class shared work
- Go to page 3. Ask: *What is a more accurate way of measuring temperature?* (A thermometer.) *What is a thermometer? How is it used?* Write the children's ideas on the board.
- Press the thumbnail image on page 4, which opens the Interactive Teaching Program (ITP) *Thermometer*.
- Demonstrate how to read a thermometer. Point out where the pointer is placed. (It is at 0 when the ITP is initially opened.) What do the children think the negative numbers mean?
- Practise changing the temperature on the thermometer and working out the differences between readings.
- Encourage the children to place the pointer where they think the current temperature is.
- Show the children a real thermometer. Check the temperature of the room and set the actual temperature on the ITP. Take a snapshot of the thermometer using the Capture tool and add it to the Notebook page. Write the room temperature next to the snapshot.

Independent work
- Provide each group of four with a thermometer and a container of water (each group should have water of a different temperature).
- Ask each group to write the time and record the temperature of their water. Tell them they will be repeating this every ten minutes.
- Use the Timer on page 4 of the Notebook file to count down ten-minute intervals.
- Each child should draw up a table to record their results.
- While the children are waiting they could work out the difference between the last two readings.

Plenary
- Press the link on page 5 to open the spreadsheet. Collect the results from all the groups in the table on the first worksheet. Each group's chart will be automatically completed on the relevant worksheet.
- Discuss the results as a class. Ask: *Which bowls of water got warmer? Which bowls of water got colder? What is the difference between the coldest and warmest temperature at the beginning of the experiment? At the end of the experiment?* Write the children's responses on page 5.
- Lead the children to realise that all the bowls of water gradually returned to the temperature of the room. Remind them of this temperature by looking again at page 4 of the Notebook file.

Science — Lesson 10

Keeping things cold

Learning objectives
QCA Unit 4C 'Keeping warm'
- To turn an idea about how to keep things cold into a form that can be investigated.
- To decide what evidence to collect.
- To make a table and record results in it.
- To draw conclusions from their results.

Resources
'Ice cube insulators' Notebook file; photocopiable pages 129 and 130 'Investigation report 1' and '2', one of each per child; one very cold ice cream; a selection of materials of differing textures (such as polythene, aluminium foil and bubble wrap), four pieces per group; four ice cubes and four jars for each group; backpack. (Microsoft Excel is required to view the embedded spreadsheet on page 7.)

Links to other subjects
Geography
QCA Unit 24 'Passport to the world'
- Investigate houses around the world, looking at how the construction materials insulate against heat or cold.

English
Understanding and interpreting texts: Use knowledge of word structures and origins to develop their understanding of word meanings.
- Investigate the common root for *thermal* and *thermometer* (from the Greek for *heat*).

Whiteboard tools
Use the Timer's count-down function as a reminder to the children to take their readings. Use the On-screen Keyboard to enter data into the spreadsheet.

- Pen tray
- Select tool
- On-screen Keyboard

Starter
Show the children an ice cream and a backpack. Ask them to imagine that you want to carry the ice cream in the backpack on a very hot day. What do they think will happen to the ice cream? Write their predictions on page 2 of the Notebook file.

Whole-class shared work
- Discuss why the bag would not keep the ice cream cold, focusing on the properties of the material. Ask: *What would cause the ice cream to melt?* (The heat.) Add these ideas to the children's predictions on page 2.
- Go to page 3. Ask the children how you could stop the ice cream from melting. Add their ideas to the board.
- Show the children the materials you have brought (see Resources) and list them on page 4. Demonstrate wrapping the ice cream in one of the materials. Ask: *Which material do you think would keep the ice cream cold?* Use voting methods to collect the children's predictions and make a note of the results.
- Ask them to investigate this, using the ice cubes instead of ice cream. What will they keep the same and what will they change to ensure this investigation is a fair test? Make notes on page 5.

Independent work
- Give each group of four children four ice cubes, four pieces of different material and four jars. Ask them to wrap each ice cube in a different material and place it in a jar.
- To find out how quickly the ice cubes melt, the children should measure the amount of water in the jar after the following intervals: 5 minutes, 15 minutes, 30 minutes, 45 minutes and 60 minutes.
- Go to page 6. Set the Timers on the page to count down the appropriate intervals to remind the children to measure the water and write down the measurement and time.
- Ask the children to use photocopiable pages 129 and 130 to write a report.
- Support less confident learners by reviewing the annotated Notebook pages to remind them of what was discussed during the lesson.

Plenary
- Open the spreadsheet on page 7 and collect the results from all the groups on the first page of the spreadsheet. Ask: *Which materials kept our ice cubes the coolest for the longest amount of time? Which materials let the most water out? Which let out the least?*
- Each group's results will be automatically transferred to the line graphs on the relevant pages of the spreadsheet. These can be printed out and kept as records.
- Explain to the children that a material that keeps warmth or cold in is called a *thermal insulator*. (The word *thermal* refers to heat.) Challenge them to suggest a material which is an excellent thermal insulator and another which is a really poor insulator.

Science · Lesson 11

Keeping warm

Learning objectives
QCA Unit 4C 'Keeping warm'
● To make careful measurements of temperature at regular time intervals.
● To record results in a table and to use these to draw conclusions.
● To know that some materials are good thermal insulators.

Resources
'Keeping warm' Notebook file; materials to test thermal insulation (bubble wrap, aluminium foil, thick and thin fabrics, paper); selection of summer and winter clothes; plastic containers (eg beakers); hot water (not so hot that it will soften plastic containers); box or tray for each group; thermometers; photocopiable pages 129 and 130 'Investigation report 1' and '2', one of each per child; graph paper. (Microsoft Excel is required to view the embedded spreadsheet in the Notebook file.)

Links to other subjects
Geography
QCA Unit 24 'Passport to the world'
● Investigate what people wear in different parts of the world. What kinds of fabric are worn in places near the north pole and the equator?

Whiteboard tools
Use the Timer's count-down function as a reminder to record the thermometer readings. Use the On-screen Keyboard to enter data into the spreadsheet.

- Pen tray
- Select tool
- Fill Colour tool
- On-screen Keyboard

Starter
Display page 2 of the Notebook file. Ask the children to sort the clothes you have brought in into two piles: summer and winter clothes. What would they wear to keep warm? To stay cool? Why? Identify that different materials have been used to make the clothes and discuss the properties of these materials. Annotate the Notebook page with their suggestions.

Whole-class shared work
● Ask: *What else do you do to stay warm?* Make notes on page 3.
● Go to page 4. Read the problem together and encourage the children to suggest possible solutions. Discuss their ideas.
● Look at the materials named on page 5. Ask: *Would these materials help? Why? Why not?* Change the colour of the bad choices to red, using the Fill Colour tool, and drag them out of the circle. Fill the good choices in blue and leave them in the circle.
● Tell the children that they will be conducting an investigation to see which materials keep a hot liquid the warmest for the longest amount of time.
● List the materials you have brought for the investigation on page 6. Can the children predict which material will keep the hot chocolate hotter for longer, and give their reasons why? They could using voting methods to vote on their prediction.
● On page 7, discuss how to make this a fair test. What will the children keep the same and what will they change? (They should use one control container with no insulation, and two with different materials.)

Independent work
● Give each group of four children three containers, two pieces of material and a tray or box. Also provide each group with a sheet of graph paper and a thermometer.
● The children should wrap each container in a different material, ensuring that the containers can stand upright in the box or tray.
● Fill the containers with hot water and tell the children to measure the temperature of the water every ten minutes. They should record the material, temperature and the time in a suitable table on their graph paper.
● Go to page 8. Set the Timers on the page to count down the appropriate intervals to remind the children to record the thermometer readings.
● Hand out photocopiable pages 129 and 130 to help the children write their reports.
● Provide extra support to less confident learners by looking at the pages annotated during this lesson to remind them of what was discussed.

Plenary
● Open the spreadsheet on page 9 and collect the children's results. Ask: *Which materials kept the water the hottest for the longest amount of time? Which materials kept the water warm? Which did not?*
● Each group's results will be transferred automatically to the relevant pages in the spreadsheet to create line graphs. These can be printed out and kept as records.
● Explain that the materials that kept the water hot for the longest time are good thermal insulators because they stop the heat from getting through. Remind them that the word *thermal* relates to heat.

Science Lesson 12

Flowing materials

Learning objectives
QCA Unit 4D 'Solids, liquids and how they can be separated'
- To make careful observations and measurements of volume, recording them in tables and using them to draw conclusions.
- To understand that liquids do not change in volume when they are poured into a different container.
- To understand that solids consisting of very small pieces behave like liquids in some ways.

Resources
'Flowing materials' Notebook file; photocopiable page 133 'Flowing materials' for each child; writing materials; different-shaped measuring containers (six per group); a range of different materials for the children to pour, such as water, undiluted squash, sand, rice, salt, small plastic blocks.

Links to other subjects
Mathematics
Measuring: Choose and use standard metric units and their abbreviations when estimating, measuring and recording length, weight and capacity.
- Support the children in making accurate measurements. Use measuring containers with different scales to show that 500ml is the same as 0.5l.

Whiteboard tools
Convert handwritten words to text by selecting them and choosing the Recognise option from the dropdown menu.

- Pen tray
- Select tool

Starter
Display page 2 of the Notebook file, which shows pictures of different kinds of materials. In pairs, ask the children to discuss how to sort the materials. Invite them to sort the pictures on the whiteboard by dragging and dropping them into different groups. Ask them to explain their reasons. Encourage them to describe the properties of the materials.

Whole-class shared work
- Go to page 3 and watch the video clips. Ask: *What type of material is this? Does it move or stand still? What sound does it make? What do you think it feels like?* Make a note of the children's responses. Repeat for the video clips on page 4.
- Go to page 5 and invite the children to sort these pictures into two groups. Ask them to explain their reasons.
- Introduce and discuss the terms *solids* and *liquids*, exploring similarities and differences, and thinking about the properties that solids and liquids possess.
- Ask the children to complete photocopiable page 133. Support less confident learners in the written work.
- Go to page 6 of the Notebook file. Press the thumbnail image to open the ITP *Measuring cylinder*. Revise how liquids are measured. Talk about the scale and measurements. Ask questions such as: *Is '100' more likely to refer to 100 litres or 100 millilitres?*

Independent work
- Ask the children to copy the table on page 7 of the Notebook file onto a piece of paper or into their books.
- Give each group of four children a measuring jug and a set of measuring containers.
- The children should measure out 300ml of four different materials and record their observations in the table.
- They should then transfer one of the liquids from one measuring cylinder to another that is a different shape. Is the measurement the same? Ask them to test this again with another liquid.
- They should observe closely what the material looks like when it is poured. Are there any similarities or differences in the way the materials behave?
- Extra adult support will be helpful to monitor the groups as they measure out the materials. Support less confident learners in reading the measurements.

Plenary
- Discuss the children's results and make notes on page 8 of the Notebook file. Ask: *Did the materials all behave in the same way? What happened when a liquid was poured from one container into another of a different shape?*
- Lead the children to understand that, although liquids change shape when they are poured into a different container, their volume will stay the same. Some solids consisting of particles (or very small pieces), such as salt and sand, will behave in a similar way to a liquid.

Science Lesson 13

Mixing solids and liquids

Learning objectives
QCA Unit 4D 'Solids, liquids and how they can be separated'
- To understand that changes occur when some solids are added to water.
- To make careful observations, recording results in tables, and make comparisons.

Resources
'Mixing solids and liquids' Notebook file; a selection of transparent containers; water; a range of different soluble and insoluble solids, such as sand, coffee granules, and marbles; tea; sugar; full kettle; individual whiteboards and pens; exercise books and pens.

Links to other subjects
Art and design
PoS (2b) Pupils should be taught to apply their experience of materials and processes.
- Follow up this work by experimenting with mixing different quantities of powder paint with the same amounts of water. What kind of effects does this produce when the paint is applied to paper?

Starter
Divide the children into small groups and press the image on page 2 of the Notebook file to start the quiz. The children should decide on the correct answer as a group and write it on their individual whiteboards, to show after the count of five. According to the majority vote, press the appropriate button on the screen to check whether the children's answer is correct.

Whole-class shared work
- Make a cup of tea in front of the class, adding a spoonful of sugar and stirring.
- Ask: *What has happened to the sugar? Can you still see it?* Note the children's responses on page 3.
- Compare the state of the sugar before it goes in your tea, and after. Ensure that the children understand that the sugar is solid.

Independent work
- Provide each group with a selection of transparent containers, water and a mixture of different solids. Go to page 4 and discuss what the children think will happen to the solids when they are added to water. Change the names of the solids on the board or add more if necessary. Write the children's predictions on the board. Tell them they are going to carry out an investigation to find out if these predictions are correct.
- Tell the children to copy the table on page 5 to record their results and observations.
- Explain that they should measure out 500ml of water into each container. They should then add two teaspoons of one of the solids to the water in each container. Ask: *What happens when you mix the materials? What does the mixture look like after it has had time to settle?*
- Ask the children why they think the amount of water and solid have to be kept the same. Remind them of the importance of a fair test.
- Less confident learners may need help in making sure the same measurements are used each time.
- Challenge more confident learners to investigate what happens if they have the same amount of water but double the amount of solid.

Plenary
- Encourage the children to look carefully at their results. Ask: *What do you notice about your results? Were your predictions correct? What happened when you added one of the solids to the water? Did everyone get the same result? Did the same thing happen when you added marbles to the water?*
- Make a note of the children's conclusions on page 6 of the Notebook file (changing the names of the materials or adding more if necessary). Press the red box at the top of the screen to bring up a list of key words.

Whiteboard tools
Use the On-screen Keyboard to amend, delete or add text.

- Pen tray
- Select tool
- On-screen Keyboard

Science Lesson 14

Sieving and filtering solids

Learning objectives
QCA Unit 4D 'Solids, liquids and how they can be separated'
- To understand that when solids do not dissolve or react with the water they can be separated by filtering.
- To choose apparatus to separate an undissolved solid from a liquid.

Resources
Two clear containers, one with sand and water and one with glass beads or marbles and water; sieve with large holes; loose tea leaves; fine sieve; tea strainer; filter teapot (optional); tea bag; materials to filter tea leaves (net, muslin, tissue paper, foil with pinpricks); jug of water, bowl and clear measuring container for each group; exercise books and pens; a data-handling application such as Microsoft Excel.

Links to other subjects
ICT
QCA Unit 4D 'Collecting and presenting information'
- Ask children to use a data-handling package to create a bar chart and use this to interpret their results.

Whiteboard tools
Use the On-screen Keyboard to enter data into the spreadsheet.

- Pen tray
- Select tool
- On-screen Keyboard

Starter
Show the children the marbles and water and the sieve. Ask them to predict what will happen when you pour the marbles and water through. Carry out the experiment to confirm their prediction. Repeat for the sand and water. They should predict that the sand and water will fall through the holes in the sieve and the mixture will not separate easily. Ask: *What could you use to separate the sand?* Make a note of their responses.

Whole-class shared work
- Show the children some loose tea leaves and tell them that, when you make a cup of tea with it, tiny parts float around on the top. Ask: *What could I use to prevent this?* They may suggest a sieve, tea strainer, or filter teapot. Show these items, if available.
- Show the children a tea bag. Gently pull it apart so that they can see the loose tea inside. Allow them to handle the material of the tea bag. Establish that it has tiny holes that let the water through but that the bag keeps the tea leaves inside it. Explain that the bag is a filter and separates the tiny particles from the water.

Independent work
- Give each group of four children a selection of different filtering materials, a container of loose tea leaves, a jug of water, a bowl and a measuring container.
- Explain that you want them to test the materials to find out which is the best filter to make a cup of tea.
- On a blank Notebook page, write down what they will change and what they will keep the same each time, to ensure a fair test. They could investigate which filter lasts the longest, which filter is the fastest or which filter lets the most water through without letting tea through.
- Open a data-handling application, such as Microsoft Excel, and together create a suitable table to record results. The children should copy this onto paper.
- Ask: *Which material do you predict will be the best filter? Why?* Note the children's responses on the whiteboard.
- Allow sufficient time for each group to complete their investigation.
- Support less confident learners by helping them to analyse the properties of the different materials.
- Challenge more confident learners by adding a timed element to the task. Will the best filter also be the fastest filter?

Plenary
- Invite the children to report their findings to the rest of the class. Ask: *Which material was the best filter? Why? Which was the poorest? Why? What was it about the structure of that material that made it the worst?*
- Compare the children's findings with their prediction. Did they predict correctly?

Science ▪ Lesson 15

Dissolving solids

Learning objectives
QCA Unit 4D 'Solids, liquids and how they can be separated'
- To understand that some solids dissolve in water to form solutions and that although the solid cannot be seen it is still present.
- To predict whether sugar can be separated from a solution by filtering and to test the prediction.
- To decide what apparatus to use.
- To know when it is safe to taste things to test them.

Resources
Kettle; mug; instant hot chocolate; clean cold water; recently boiled water; sachets of sugar; clean teaspoons, bowls, sieves and jugs; clean materials for filtering (filter paper, different sieves, kitchen towel, foil with pinpricks); digital images of solids, liquids, and the processes of filtering, dissolving, melting and sieving (copyright permitting).

Links to other subjects
PSHE
PoS (3a) To consider what makes a healthy lifestyle.
- Explain that although we can't always see the salt and sugar in our foods, that does not mean that they are not present. Remind the children of the disadvantages of too much salt and sugar in a diet and discuss how we can find out about, and reduce, the amount of sugar and salt that we consume.

Whiteboard tools
Upload scanned images by selecting Insert, then Picture File, and browsing to where you have saved the image.

- Pen tray
- Select tool
- Gallery

Starter
Make a cup of hot chocolate and ask: *What has happened to the instant hot chocolate granules? What has happened to the water?* (The granules, a solid, have dissolved in the water, a liquid). Write *dissolve* on a new Notebook page.

Whole-class shared work
- Dissolve sugar in a mug of hot water. Add cold water to cool it. Ask: *Can you see the sugar?* (No.) *Does that mean it has disappeared? How could you test that the sugar is still in the water?* (By tasting the solution.)
- Ask the children to predict whether the sugar can be separated from the water by filtering, and the reasons for their prediction. Discuss how they could investigate this prediction.
- Remind the children that it is only safe to taste the solution because they are using clean water and clean teaspoons and cups, and because they know exactly what they are putting in it. The sugar is from sachets, so it has not been contaminated. Stress the importance of never tasting anything in experiments unless they know that clean equipment and non-toxic ingredients have been used.
- Impeccable hygiene must be observed for all activities that require tasting. Ensure that all equipment and surfaces are clean and washed with antibacterial spray. Ask the children to wash their hands thoroughly before the activity.

Independent work
- Give each group a jug of warm water, a bowl, a teaspoon, a sugar sachet, a sieve and a filtering material.
- Ask each group to predict whether their material will filter the sugar from the water. They should then make up the sugar solution in the jug, line the sieve with the filtering material, place it over the bowl and carefully pour the solution through it. Warn them not to pour too fast. They can then taste the filtered solution to see whether or not the filter has worked.
- Compare results, and ask the children to explain why filtering cannot separate the dissolved sugar. (The holes in the filters are big enough for the sugar to get through because the sugar has dissolved into tiny particles.)
- Explain that some solids dissolve in water and that the mixture is called a solution. Although the solid cannot be seen, it is still present.

Plenary
- On a blank Notebook page, place digital pictures of everyday examples of solids and liquids, as well as the processes of filtering, dissolving, melting and sieving.
- On the same page place the words *filtering, dissolving, melting* and *sieving*.
- Ask the children to sort the pictures into the different processes. Encourage them to explain their decisions.

Science Lesson 16

In a spin

Learning objectives
QCA Unit 4E 'Friction'
- To know that air resistance is a force that slows objects moving through air.
- To plan a fair test saying what to change, what to keep the same and what to measure.
- To make measurements of time.
- To identify a pattern in the results and to explain it in terms of air resistance.

Resources
Ten sheets of large sugar paper; two large tissues (one screwed up into a ball and one flat piece); photocopiable page 134 'Spinners' for each child; stopwatches, one per pair; data-handling program, such as Microsoft Excel; paper clips, pencils and scissors.

Links to other subjects
ICT
QCA Unit 4D 'Collecting and presenting information'
- Use a bar chart created in a data-handling package to interpret the children's results.

Starter
Take the children outside and ask them to run from one end of the playground to the other. What can they feel on their faces? (Air.) Provide each pair of children with a large sheet of sugar paper and ask them to run again with the paper held in front of them. What can they feel this time? Explain that what they are feeling is air *resistance*: air pushing against them.

Whole-class shared work
- Throw a flat piece of tissue up into the air. What do the children notice? (It falls slowly.)
- Now throw a screwed-up piece of tissue up into the air. What do they notice? (It falls much faster.) Explain that the flat tissue has a bigger surface area than the screwed-up tissue. The air cannot get round it so easily. Therefore, the air acts as a brake on the tissue, slowing it down.
- Demonstrate how to make a spinner, using photocopiable page 134. Tell the children they are going to find out whether the size of the spinner affects how fast it falls.
- Open a blank Notebook page and plan the investigation, using headings such as *Prediction, Method, Equipment* and so on.
- Ask: *How will you make the test fair?* (Dropping spinners from the same height; measuring the time in the same way for each spinner.)

Independent work
- Provide the children with a stopwatch, a copy of photocopiable page 134, pencils, paper clips and scissors. Ask them to make the spinners and carry out the experiment, using the stopwatches to make their time measurements. The times can be recorded on the back of each spinner.
- Less confident learners may need support in taking careful measurements of time.
- Extend the experiment for more confident learners by asking them to make another set of spinners and see what happens if the wings are made narrower or wider.

Plenary
- Use a data-handling program such as Microsoft Excel to collect the children's results. Use the Sort function to arrange the data in order, beginning with the spinners that took the longest time to reach the ground.
- Look at the spinners that have the longest times, and then at those that have the shortest times. Can the children see a pattern emerging? (The larger spinners take longer to fall.)
- Ask the children why they think the large spinners take longer to fall. Link their explanations to the idea of air resistance. Write their ideas on a Notebook page.
- Children who extended the experiment could explain their findings, relating them to the concept of air resistance.

Whiteboard tools
Enter data into the spreadsheet with the On-screen Keyboard.

- Pen tray
- Select tool
- On-screen Keyboard

Science ▫ Lesson 17

Complete circuits

Learning objectives
QCA Unit 4F 'Circuits and conductors'
● To learn that a circuit needs a power source.
● To learn that a complete circuit is needed for a device to work.

Resources
'Circuits' Notebook file; sets of crocodile wires, bulbs and batteries (one set for each group); photocopiable page 135 'Making circuits work'.

Links to other subjects
PE
PoS (4b) To warm up and prepare appropriately.
● As a warm-up exercise, get the children to link hands in a circle. Then ask them to jump up and down, or run on the spot. If someone breaks the circuit by letting go, they all have to stand still.

Starter
Tell the children that in this lesson they will be looking at electricity. Invite them to look at the pictures on page 2 of the Notebook file and sort them into two groups: those that need electricity to make them work, and those that do not. Ask: *How do you know that these objects need electricity? How does the torch light up even though it is not plugged into the mains?* Explain to the children that all objects that use electricity need a circuit to make them work.

Whole-class shared work
● Show the children the picture of a simple circuit on page 3. Use a Pen from the Pen tray to label the wires and battery.
● Ask the children to point out the component that provides the power to the circuit. (The battery.)
● Can they explain what will happen if a bulb is added to the circuit? Invite a volunteer to add a bulb to the circuit.
● Challenge the children to explain in their own words what a circuit needs to make something work. For example, it needs a battery, and the wires need to connect to both ends of the battery.
● Show the children the pictures of different circuits on page 4. Ask them to predict if each circuit will light up the bulb or not, encouraging them to give reasons for their predictions. Ask: *Why do you think the bulb will not light up? What component is missing?*
● After the children have made their predictions, press each image to hear a a cheer or an 'aahh' noise to show whether they were correct or not.

Independent work
● Organise the children into groups of three or four. Provide each group with a set of wires, a bulb, a battery and a copy of photocopiable page 135.
● Ask the children to make each circuit and then complete the table at the bottom of the sheet. They will need to explain why the circuit did or did not work.
● Mixed-ability groups should provide support to less confident learners in making the circuits.
● Challenge more confident learners to consider how they could change the incomplete circuits to make them work.

Plenary
● Ask the children to tell you which circuits did and did not work, and to explain their results. Review the predictions they made on page 4 of the Notebook file. Address misconceptions, if any of the predictions were incorrect. Ensure that the children understand why a circuit is incomplete.
● Show the pictures of two circuits on page 5 and ask the children to explain if these circuits would work. Voting methods (for example, by asking the children to write 'a' or 'b' on their individual whiteboards) could be used to gather yes or no responses for each circuit.
● Challenge the children to explain what could be done to make the circuits work. After they have made their predictions, press each image on the Notebook page to hear whether they were correct or not.

Whiteboard tools
Use the Select tool to move the bulb on page 3.

▫ Pen tray
▫ Select tool

Science ◼ Lesson 18

Circuits and switches

Learning objectives
QCA Unit 4F 'Circuits and conductors'
● To understand that a circuit needs a power source.
● To know that a complete circuit is needed for a device to work.
● To know that a switch can be used to make or break a circuit to turn things on or off (using batteries or mains).

Resources 💿
'Circuits' Notebook file; *Crocodile Clips Elementary* (available on the CD-ROM *Learning and teaching using ICT: Example materials* DfES 0315 2004G, or download from **www.crocodile-clips.com**); mains and battery-operated devices with switches (mains appliances must have had an electrical supply check); crocodile wires, bulbs and batteries (one set for each group); materials to use as a switch (paper clip, tin foil, drawing pins, card).

Links to other subjects
Design and technology
QCA Unit 4E 'Lighting it up'
● The work in this lesson links well with this unit, as children need to understand how to make a bulb light up in a simple electric circuit and how switches work.

Whiteboard tools
🖥 Pen tray
🖱 Select tool

Starter
Revise the children's previous knowledge about circuits. Open page 6 of the Notebook file. Tell the children that you are going to use the *Crocodile Clips* program to draw a simple circuit.
   Start the *Crocodile Clips* program. Discuss what is needed to make a circuit work. Ask: *What would happen if I put a bulb into my circuit? What would happen if I put a bulb and a buzzer into my circuit?* Create a circuit that includes a bulb and a buzzer. Use the bigger 9V battery rather than the 1.5V battery, as these components will need more power.

Whole-class shared work
● Return to the Notebook file and go to page 7.
● Show the children a selection of devices that use switches and demonstrate how each one works.
● In pairs, the children should discuss what the devices have in common, and how each device works. Start the Timer to allow three minutes for this.
● Ask the children to name the devices and write the names as headings on page 7. Ask what the devices have in common, and write responses on the same page.
● Ask how each device works. Make notes on the board.
● Explain that in each circuit there is a component (or part) called a switch. Go to page 8 and look at the different ways to make switches.
● Invite the children to use the *Crocodile Clips* program to make a circuit with a switch and a bulb.
● Turn the switch on and off and ask what is happening in the circuit. Emphasise that a complete circuit is needed to make the item work. When the switch is off, it means that there is a break in the circuit.

Independent work
● Provide each group with a set of wires, a bulb, a battery and a selection of resources to make a switch. (Safety note: This activity must not be carried out using mains electricity!)
● The children should construct a circuit with a switch and make a diagram of it.
● Monitor the groups to ensure that they understand how to use a switch to break or complete a circuit. On page 9, compile an electricity word bank to support the children in their drawing of their circuits.
● Give the children 15 to 20 minutes to make and draw their circuits.
● Encourage discussion in mixed-ability groups to provide support for less confident learners.
● Challenge more confident learners to think of a different way of making a circuit.

Plenary
● Go to page 10 of the Notebook file. Ask groups in turn to demonstrate how their switch works. Ask: *What type of material did you use to make your switch work?*
● Write or draw diagrams on the board to illustrate the different ways in which the groups devised and used switches. Alternatively, take digital pictures and insert them into a Notebook file to keep as a record of the children's work.

Science ▫ Lesson 19

Using switches

Learning objectives
QCA Unit 4F 'Circuits and conductors'
- To know that a circuit needs a power source and needs to be complete for a device to work.
- To understand that a switch can be used to make or break a circuit to turn things on or off.
- To construct a circuit with a switch.

Resources
'Circuits' Notebook file; the Hasbro board game *Operation*, if available; photocopiable pages 136 'Sounding it out' and 137 'What's the answer?', enlarged to A3 and copied onto card; blank cards, crocodile clips, bulbs, buzzers, batteries, tin foil and large paper clips to make switches and dice (one set per group).

Links to other subjects
English
Creating and shaping texts
- Write instructions to explain how the board game works.

Word structure and spelling
- Use the sound cards to practise reading and spelling words through identifying phonemes.

Design and technology
PoS (5c) Design and make assignments using a range of materials.
- Ask the children to create their own board game using a circuit with different components.

Whiteboard tools
Use a Pen from the Pen tray to annotate the gameboards on pages 12 and 13 to show how the children built their circuits.

- Pen tray
- Select tool

Starter
Display page 11 of the Notebook file. Discuss how the Hasbro game *Operation* works and how it uses the idea of circuits and switches. (The tweezers are attached by wire to the gameboard. When the tweezers touch the metal sides of the cavities, this completes a circuit and the buzzer and light are activated.) Make a note of the children's ideas.

Whole-class shared work
- Show page 12 of the Notebook file. Explain that the children will be making a game, using switches, called 'Sounding it out'. Players from two teams will take turns to turn over a letter card and a word or picture card (which they are going to make). If the cards match, the players press a switch to sound the buzzer. The quickest player has to say the letter and word out loud. If correct, their team gets a point. If incorrect, the other team gets a point. The players then swap places with another team member.
- The children have to:
  - write the alphabet around the edge of the gameboard;
  - cut out the holes for the switch and buzzer;
  - cut out the blank cards and draw pictures or write words on them to match the letters;
  - build a circuit to place underneath the gameboard, the switch and buzzer positioned in the cut-out holes.
- Provide groups with copies of the photocopiable pages as appropriate (see independent work, below). Each group will need extra cards.
- Show page 13 of the Notebook file. One child has to be quizmaster. Two others compete to be the first to answer a question. One player presses a switch to light a bulb; the other presses a switch to sound a buzzer.
- The children have to:
  - cut out the holes in the gameboard as indicated;
  - cut out the cards and devise questions and answers based on a subject of their choice (they can swap quiz cards with another group so that the game is fairer);
  - build one circuit with a switch and a bulb, and another with a switch and a buzzer, to place beneath the gameboard.

Independent work
- Provide groups with the necessary materials (see Resources) and get them to make and then play their board games.
- Photocopiable page 136 is more suitable for less confident learners, while more confident learners should find photocopiable page 137 more challenging.

Plenary
- Choose one group and ask the children to explain how they used circuits and switches in their board game.
- On the appropriate page, ask the children to draw where they placed the components for their circuit and explain what materials they used, and why.
- Use page 14 of the Notebook file to summarise what the children have learned.

Science Lesson 20

How bright?

Learning objectives
QCA Unit 4F 'Circuits and conductors'
- To make predictions about the effect of including additional batteries in a circuit, and check whether results support the prediction made.
- To understand that bulbs can burn out if components in a circuit are changed.
- To know how to change the brightness of bulbs in a circuit.
- To plan to change one factor and keep others constant.

Resources
Crocodile Clips Elementary (see Resources for Lesson 18); sets of bulbs, crocodile clips, wires, batteries (one set per group); sheets of A4 paper.

Links to other subjects
Design and technology
QCA Unit 4E 'Lighting it up'
- Ask the children to design circuits with lights for different purposes – for example, a night light for a small child, or a light to dazzle burglars.

Whiteboard tools
- Pen tray
- Select tool

Starter
Review the children's knowledge on electricity. Ask: *Can anyone tell me what I need to make a complete simple circuit? Where does the bulb get its power from? What would happen if I replaced the bulb with a buzzer or motor?*

Ask the children to draw a circuit on paper, showing how to make a bulb light up.

Whole-class shared work
- Using the *Crocodile Clips* program, draw the simple circuits shown below and ask the children to decide whether each device will work.

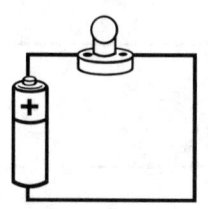

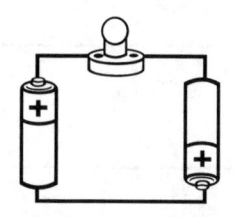

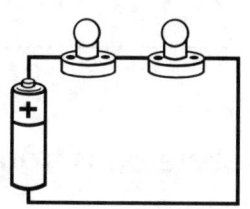

- Ask: *Why is one bulb brighter than the other? Why are some bulbs unlit? Is it because the circuit is not complete?*
- Challenge the children to predict what would happen if an extra battery were added to each circuit and to explain their reason. Write their responses on a blank Notebook page.
- Add an extra battery to each circuit to check the predictions.
- The children are not expected to know the term *voltage* but should understand that the battery is a source of power and that more batteries will produce more power. They also should understand that bulbs on the same circuit share the power.
- Explain that if too much power were supplied to the light bulb it would explode. Tell them that you cannot show them this because it is dangerous.

Independent work
- Provide each group of three or four children with crocodile clips, wires, bulbs and batteries (9V and 1.5V).
- Set a context for the investigation. For example, a lighthouse's light has become too dim and it needs to be made brighter.
- Ask: *How could you change the brightness of the bulb?* (Change the number of bulbs in the circuit, the type of bulb, the number of batteries used to make the circuit, the voltage of the battery.)
- Ask the children to plan and draw the way in which they would make the bulb burn brightly. What type of circuit will they use? How will they set up their circuit?
- How can the children ensure a fair test? Help them to recognise the importance of changing only one thing at a time.
- Allow the children time to make and test their circuits.

Plenary
- Encourage the children to explain their results, saying which circuits helped to make the bulb burn brightly.
- Place some incorrect and correct concluding statements on the right-hand side of the Notebook page and ask the children to drag the statements that are correct to form a sound scientific conclusion. For example:
  - The bulbs burned brightly when the number of batteries was the same as the number of bulbs.
  - The bulbs burned brightly when there were more batteries than bulbs.

SCIENCE LESSON 1   Name _____

Similar skeletons?

■ Look carefully at the two pictures of skeletons that your teacher has given to you. What animals are they from?

Picture 1
This skeleton is from _____
I can tell because _____
_____

Picture 2
This skeleton is from _____
I can tell because _____
_____

■ Use the word bank below to label the parts of the skeleton.

  ☐ Are any parts the same?

  ☐ Are any parts different?

These parts of the skeletons are similar:

These parts of the skeletons are different:

Word bank			
skull	rib cage	knee bone	arm bone
shoulder bone	teeth	spine (backbone)	pelvis
foot	toes	hand	fingers
hard	fragile	brittle	curved

128 ■ PHOTOCOPIABLE
100 SMART Board™ LESSONS • YEAR 4

■ SCHOLASTIC
www.scholastic.co.uk

SCIENCE LESSONS 2, 10 & 11   Name _____

Investigation report 1

◾ **Aim**

Our aim was to find out _____

_____

◾ **Method**

First we _____

_____

Then we _____

_____

Finally, we _____

_____

◾ **Equipment**

◾ **Making the investigation fair**

We made the test fair by _____

_____

_____

◾ **Predictions**

We thought the end result would be _____

_____

We thought this because _____

_____

_____

SCHOLASTIC
www.scholastic.co.uk

PHOTOCOPIABLE 129
100 SMART Board™ LESSONS • YEAR 4

SCIENCE LESSONS 2, 10 & 11   Name _____

Investigation report 2

◼ **Results**

These are the results from our investigation:

Our results show that _____
_____
_____

◼ **Conclusion**

Our investigation showed that
_____
_____
_____

◼ **Evaluation**

We could have improved our test by _____
_____
_____

SCIENCE LESSON 5   Name _____

Organisms cards

Wasp	 Spider	 Woodlouse	 Hummingbird
 Snail	 Squirrel	 Dog	 Fly
 Tiger	 Sunflower	 Jellyfish	 Crab
 Shark	 Sparrow	 Killer whale	 Conifer
 Duck	 Frog	 Daffodil	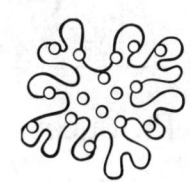 Seaweed
 Ladybird	 Zebra	 Mouse	 Starfish

PHOTOCOPIABLE 131

SCIENCE ▪ LESSON 6   Name _____

Food chains

 Grass	 Ferns	 Lettuce	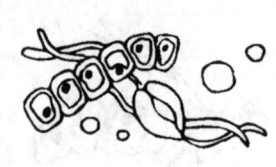 Algae
 Eagle	 Seal	 Carrots	 Frog
 Shark	 Rat	 Cat	 Seeds
 Sparrow	 Worm	 Slug	 Fish
 Fly	 Zebra	 Mouse	 Lion
Producer	Consumer	Predator	Prey
Producer	Consumer	Predator	Prey

132 ▪ PHOTOCOPIABLE
100 SMART Board™ LESSONS • YEAR 4

SCHOLASTIC
www.scholastic.co.uk

Illustrations © William Gray, except seeds © Jim Peacock / Beehive Illustration

SCIENCE LESSON 12   Name _____

Flowing materials

■ Draw a picture of a solid and a liquid in these boxes:

[   ]   [   ]

This is a picture of   This is a picture of
_____   _____

■ Complete these explanations.

A solid is:

A liquid is:

Can you explain how solids and liquids are different?
_____
_____
_____

SCHOLASTIC   PHOTOCOPIABLE 133
www.scholastic.co.uk   100 SMART Board™ LESSONS • YEAR 4

SCIENCE LESSON 16 Name _____

Spinners

■ Cut out these spinners. Clip the tail end together with a paper clip.

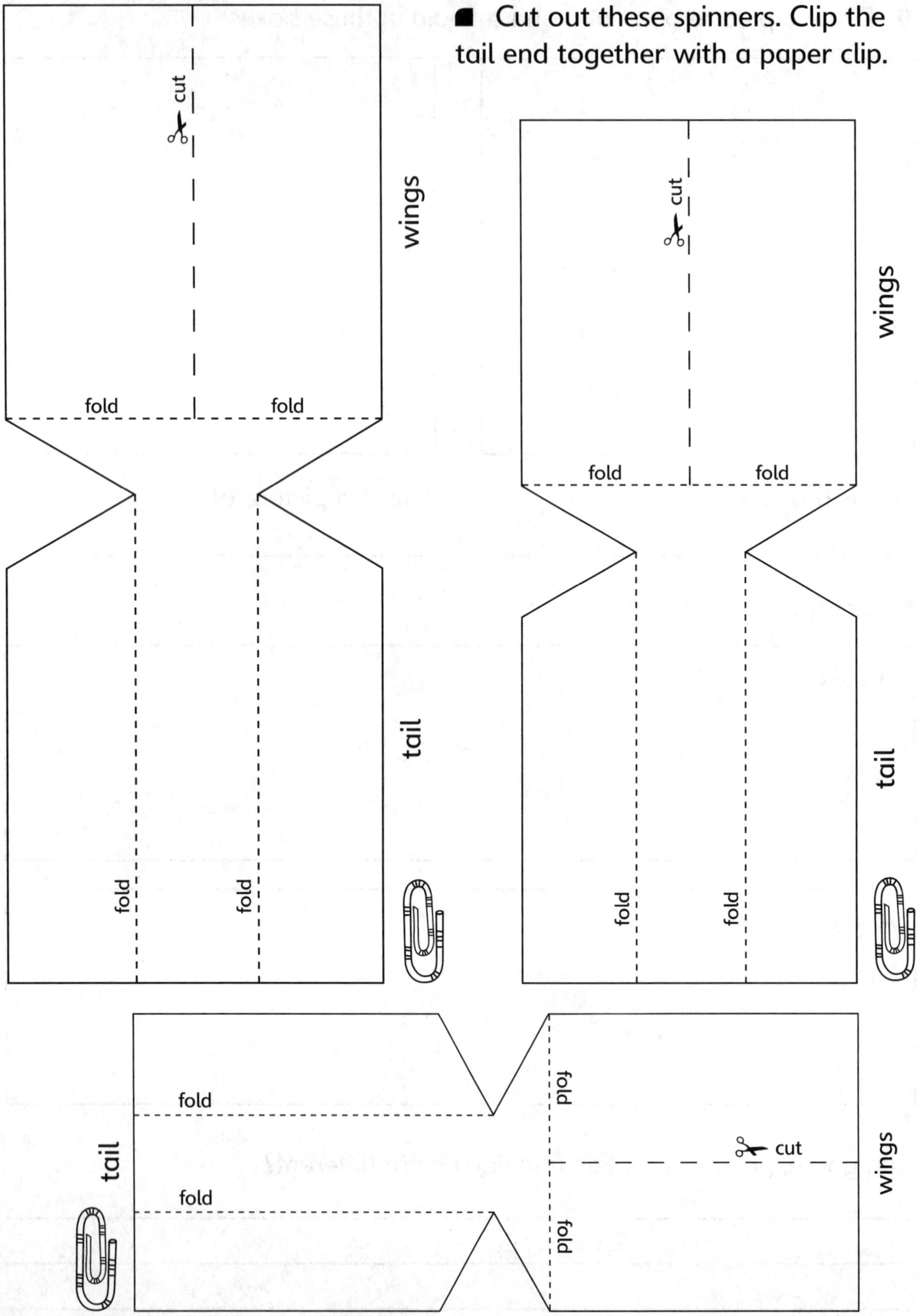

134 PHOTOCOPIABLE
100 SMART Board™ LESSONS · YEAR 4

SCHOLASTIC
www.scholastic.co.uk

SCIENCE LESSON 17   Name _____

Making circuits work

- Make each of the circuits below with your group, and find out if they work.
- Record what you find out in the table.
- Can you explain why some of the circuits work and some do not?

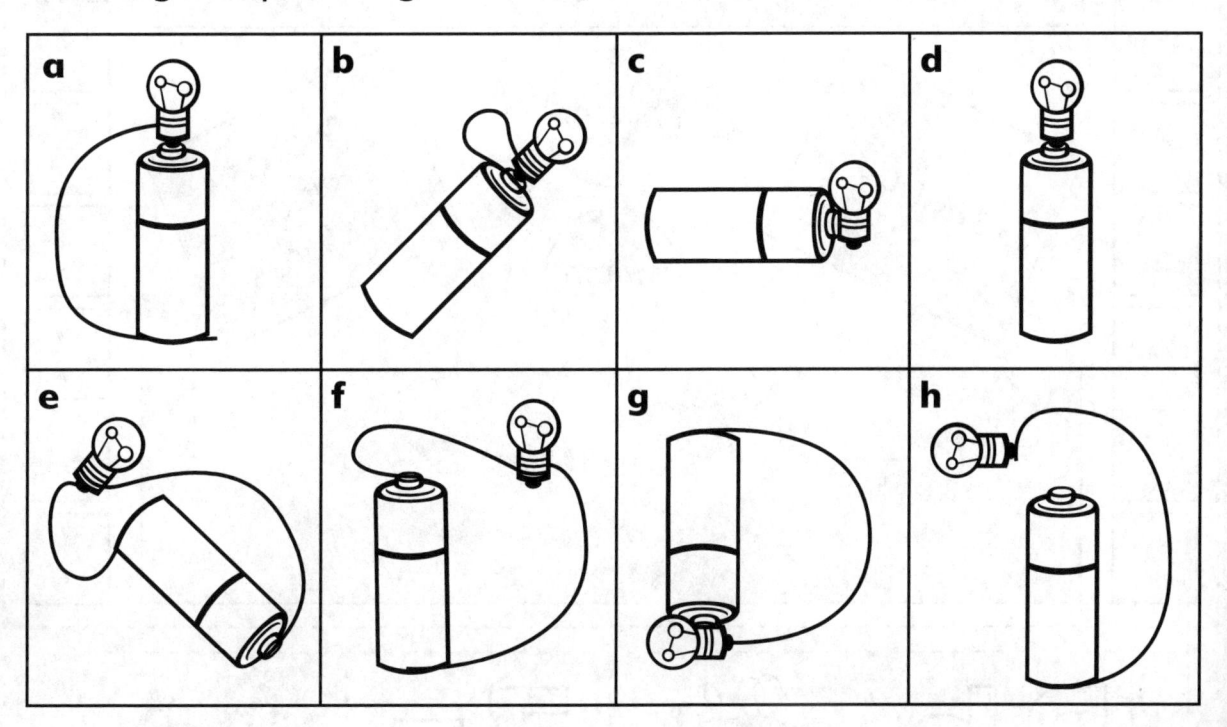

Circuit	Does the circuit work? (Yes/No)	Why?	Circuit	Does the circuit work? (Yes/No)	Why?
a			e		
b			f		
c			g		
d			h		

SCHOLASTIC
www.scholastic.co.uk

PHOTOCOPIABLE 135
100 SMART Board™ LESSONS • YEAR 4

SCIENCE LESSON 19   Name _____

Sounding it out

✂ cut

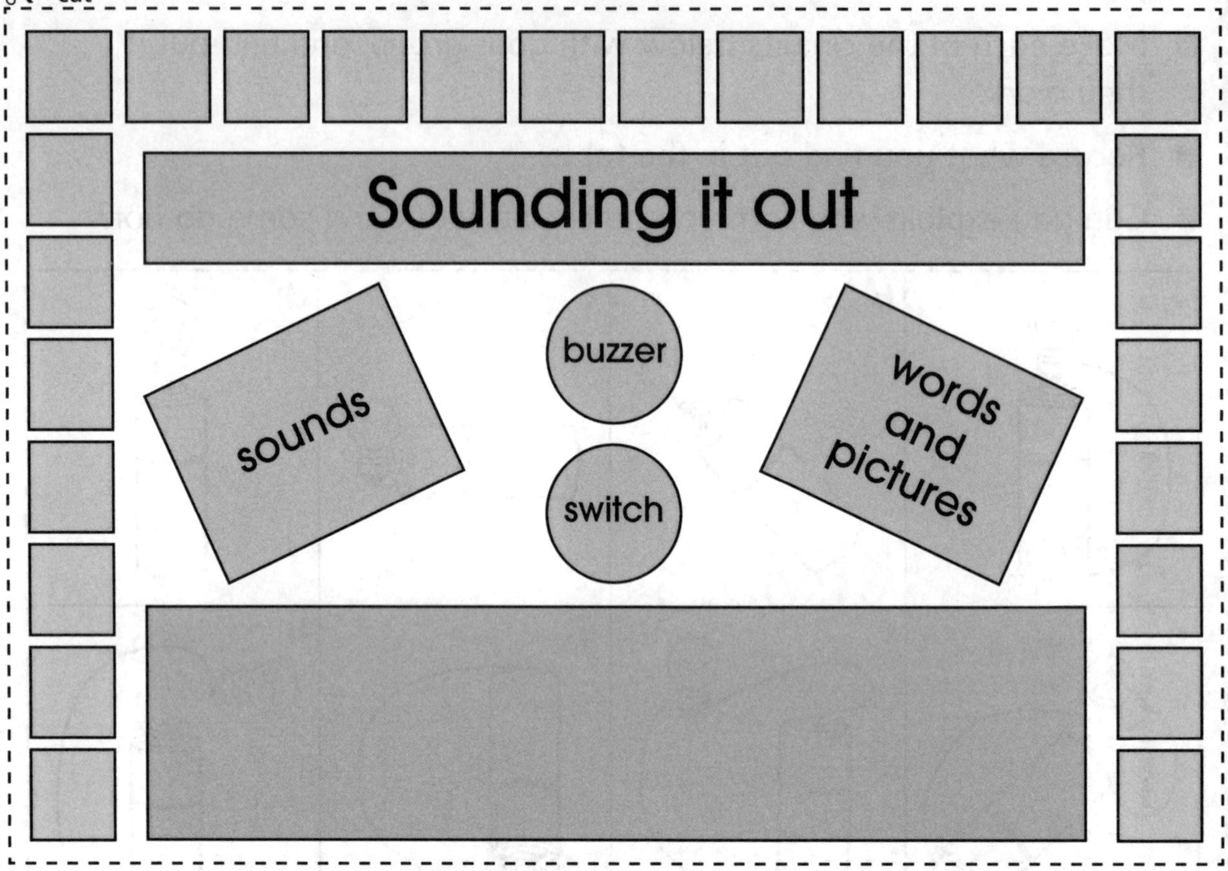

Sounding it out

sounds

buzzer

switch

words and pictures

Bb 🐝 Zz 🦓

136 PHOTOCOPIABLE
100 SMART Board™ LESSONS • YEAR 4

SCHOLASTIC
www.scholastic.co.uk

Illustrations © Jim Peacock / Beehive Illustration

SCIENCE LESSON 19   Name _____

What's the answer?

✂ cut

What's the answer

new questions

buzzer

light

used questions

The Scores

Q _____	Q _____	Q _____	Q _____
A _____	A _____	A _____	A _____
Q _____	Q _____	Q _____	Q _____
A _____	A _____	A _____	A _____
Q _____	Q _____	Q _____	Q _____
A _____	A _____	A _____	A _____
Q _____	Q _____	Q _____	Q _____
A _____	A _____	A _____	A _____

■ SCHOLASTIC
www.scholastic.co.uk

PHOTOCOPIABLE 137
100 SMART Board™ LESSONS • YEAR 4

Foundation Chapter 4

Foundation subjects

The following lessons offer ways to use an interactive whiteboard to teach the foundation subjects, using different whiteboard tools to target different learning styles.

Using an interactive whiteboard gives teachers and children a unique opportunity to project, annotate and save large-scale images. The children will be able to study and focus on details of historical artefacts, maps and aerial photographs, as well as audio and video resources. This in turn facilitates group discussion. In practical lessons, such art and design, and design and technology, you can film techniques and processes with a digital camera or take pictures of children's work, and then display the results on an interactive whiteboard. This allows you to annotate the images and it provides a great opportunity for assessment, as well as a way to record the children's progress and achievements throughout the year.

Lesson title	Objectives	Expected prior knowledge	Cross-curricular links
History			
Lesson 1: Rich or poor?	QCA Unit 8 'What were the differences between the lives of rich and poor people in Tudor times?' • To use inventories to identify characteristic features of different types of people in Tudor times. • To draw conclusions about life in Tudor times from different sources of information. • To learn that there are different ways of interpreting the same information.	• That there are a range of sources of evidence, including written and pictorial sources and artefacts. • Know about the lives of people in other societies and periods.	**Mathematics** Using and applying mathematics: Solve one-step and two-step problems involving money.
Lesson 2: In short supply	QCA Unit 9 'What was it like for children in the Second World War?' • To learn why rationing was necessary. • To learn about the impact of rationing on the way of life of people living in England during the Second World War.	• Know what life was like when their parents/carers and grandparents were children. • When the Second World War occurred and some of the effects on people living in Britain.	**Mathematics** Calculating: Develop and use written methods to record, support and explain multiplication. **Science** PoS Sc2 (2b) To understand the importance of diet. **PSHE** PoS (3a) To understand what makes a healthy lifestyle.
Lesson 3: Preparing for the afterlife	QCA Unit 10 'What can we find out about Ancient Egypt from what has survived?' • To learn about Egyptian tombs, pyramids and burial sites. • To learn that what we know about the past is dependent on what has survived.	• The way of life of people who lived a long time ago.	**English** Creating and shaping texts **Geography** QCA Unit 24 'Passport to the world'
Lesson 4: Living here in the past	QCA Unit 18 'What was it like to live here in the past?' • To learn that the area has changed at different times in the past. • To learn to use maps to help describe some of the characteristic features of the past.	• They should have worked with sources such as pictures and artefacts. • They should have studied, photographed and classified local buildings according to age.	**Geography** QCA Unit 9 'Village settlers' **Geography** PoS (2c) To use maps and plans at a range of scales. **Mathematics** Handling data: Answer a question by identifying what data to collect; organise, present, analyse and interpret the data in tables, diagrams, tally charts and bar charts.
Geography			
Lesson 5: Too much rubbish	QCA Unit 8 'Improving the environment' • To explore how people improve the environment or damage it. • To ask and respond to geographical questions. • To collect and record evidence to answer questions.	• Know that data can be represented in a pictogram for easier analysis. • Know that materials can be recycled.	**Mathematics** Handling data: Answer a question by identifying what data to collect; organise, present, analyse and interpret the data in tables, diagrams, tally charts and bar charts. **ICT** PoS (1b) To prepare information for development using ICT. **Science** QCA Unit 4B 'Habitats'

Foundation Chapter 4

Lesson title	Objectives	Expected prior knowledge	Cross-curricular links
Lesson 6: Virtual village	QCA Unit 9 'Village settlers' • To recognise that settlements have specific features and are located in response to physical features and human choice. • To draw a map of the layout of a settlement.	• Know that maps have various features that are represented by symbols. • They should understand how to drag items from the Gallery in the Notebook file.	History PoS (7) Local history study
Lesson 7: What did we do?	QCA Unit 19 'How and where do we spend our time?' • To be able to analyse and communicate findings. • To understand that collecting and storing information in an organised way helps to find answers to questions. • To interpret and analyse information in graphs.	• Know that data can be represented in tables and graphed by a computer.	ICT PoS (1c) To interpret information. English Presentation
Lesson 8: Where on Earth is it?	QCA Unit 24 'Passport to the world' • To investigate places. • To analyse evidence. • To use secondary sources of information.	• Know that there are features of places that can be memorised.	English Understanding and interpreting texts ICT QCA Unit 4A 'Writing for different audiences'

Design and technology

Lesson title	Objectives	Expected prior knowledge	Cross-curricular links
Lesson 9: What makes a good bridge?	• To understand and analyse how bridges are constructed. • To recognise the features of a strong bridge. • To develop ideas and explain them clearly.	• Know that bridges connect areas of land together and need to be strong to support the weight of vehicles.	Mathematics Understanding shape: Visualise 3D objects from 2D drawings and make nets of common solids. Geography QCA Unit 24 'Passport to the world' Speaking and listening Objective 37: To use and reflect on some ground rules for dialogue.
Lesson 10: Designing a bridge	• To generate suitable and realistic ideas to build a bridge. • To communicate personal ideas clearly when working in a group.	• Know how to analyse the features of good bridges. • Know how to work together to achieve a common goal.	Speaking and listening Objective 43: To use time, resources and group members efficiently by distributing tasks, checking progress, and making back-up plans.
Lesson 11: Building bridges	• To display effective teamwork skills when constructing their group bridge. • To select appropriate tools, materials and techniques for making their bridge. • To assemble, join and combine components and materials accurately. • To reflect on the progress of their work and identify ways they could improve their work.	• Be able to work as a team. • Know how to appraise and evaluate their own work.	Mathematics Using and applying mathematics: Solve word problems involving money. English Creating and shaping texts Science PoS Sc1 (2d) To make a fair test or comparison.

Art and design

Lesson title	Objectives	Expected prior knowledge	Cross-curricular links
Lesson 12: Viewpoints	QCA Unit 4A 'Viewpoints' • To collect information about viewpoints. • To explore ideas about dreams.	• Be able to empathise with another's situation. • Know how to work with plans.	PSHE PoS (2e) Reflect on spiritual, moral, social and cultural issues, using imagination to understand other people's experiences.

Foundation — Chapter 4

Lesson title	Objectives	Expected prior knowledge	Cross-curricular links
Lesson 13: Take a seat	QCA Unit 4B 'Take a seat' • To identify different types of chairs, their parts, uses and materials from which they are made.	• Know how to look at photographs and pictures from past and present, identifying key features.	**History** PoS (2) Knowledge and understanding of events, people and changes in the past **ICT** QCA Unit 4B 'Developing images using repeating patterns' **English** Creating and shaping texts
Lesson 14: Journeys	QCA Unit 4C 'Journeys' • To describe personal journeys that are made. • To design symbols/pictures that show aspects of their journey.	• Map-reading skills and how to identify key features. • Road signs and their meanings. • Symbols that convey instructions, warnings and information.	**Religious education** Non-statutory national framework (3i) To think about symbols and religious expression. **Geography** PoS (2e) To draw plans and maps at a range of scales. **Mathematics** Understanding shape: Describe and identify the position of a square on a grid of squares.
Lesson 15: Making mosaics	• To understand how mosaics are made.	• Know that mosaic artwork was used to provide decoration during Roman times. • Know that mosaics were created using clay tiles and pieces of broken crockery.	**History** QCA Unit 6A 'Why have people invaded and settled in Britain in the past? A Roman case study' **Mathematics** Understanding shape: Draw polygons and classify them by identifying their properties, including their line symmetry. **ICT** QCA Unit 4B 'Developing images using repeating patterns'

Music

Lesson title	Objectives	Expected prior knowledge	Cross-curricular links
Lesson 16: Rhythmic patterns	QCA Unit 10 'Play it again - Exploring rhythmic patterns' • To recognise repeated rhythmic patterns. • To listen carefully and repeat a rhythmic pattern. • To combine two different rhythms with a steady pulse.	• Know that music has a pulse and often is made of layers of sound. • Children should have experience of playing one line of music against another.	**Art and design** PoS (4a) To learn about visual elements, including colour, pattern and texture, line and tone, shape, form and space. **English** Creating and shaping texts
Lesson 17: Painting with sound	QCA Unit 13 'Painting with sound - Exploring sound colours' • To identify descriptive features in art and music. • To analyse and comment on how sounds are used to create different moods.	• Know that music can make us feel different emotions, and that art can have a similar effect.	**Art and design** PoS (5d) Investigate art, craft and design in a variety of genres, styles and traditions.
Lesson 18: What's the weather like today?	QCA Unit 6 'What's the score?' • To understand how symbols can represent sounds. • To be able to follow a sequence of sounds and play as an ensemble.	• Know that weather can be represented using symbols.	**Geography** QCA Unit 16 'What's in the news?' **English** Creating and shaping texts

Religious education

Lesson title	Objectives	Expected prior knowledge	Cross-curricular links
Lesson 19: What is God like?	• To think carefully about what God means to them. • To recognise and respect how different people seek comfort in God. • To develop a sense of awe and wonder in terms of God as an entity.	• Be aware that people have different ideas about God.	**English** Creating and shaping texts
Lesson 20: Visions of light	• To think about light and dark as symbols.	• Know that light and dark are used in various religious festivals.	**PSHE** PoS (2e) Reflect on spiritual, moral, social and cultural issues, using imagination to understand other people's experiences.

History — Lesson 1

Rich or poor?

Learning objectives
QCA Unit 8 'What were the differences between the lives of rich and poor people in Tudor times?'
- To use inventories to identify characteristic features of different types of people in Tudor times.
- To draw conclusions about life in Tudor times from different sources of information.
- To learn that there are different ways of interpreting the same information.

Resources
Prepared Notebook file showing pictures of rich and poor Tudor people, and rich and poor Tudor homes (check copyright); photocopiable page 161 'Rich or poor?' for each pair; computers with internet access; writing materials; PDF of 'Rich or poor?' (provided on the CD-ROM).

Links to other subjects
Mathematics
Using and applying mathematics: Solve one-step and two-step problems involving money.
- Set up a spreadsheet to convert £.s.d values to £.p and ask the children to work out modern-day values of the goods in the inventory (£1 = 20s; 1s = 12d; £1 = 240d).

Whiteboard tools
View the website and PDF and use the Floating tools to annotate and highlight the screen.

- Pen tray
- Spotlight tool
- Select tool
- Floating tools

Starter
Display the two Tudor people in your prepared Notebook file (see Resources). Ask: *Which do you think is richer? What is the evidence for this?* Annotate the pictures with the children's observations.

Whole-class shared work
- Ask the children if they think the people would have had the same kind of home.
- Focus on the images of rich and poor homes. Ask: *Who lives in this house? Why do you think that?* Invite a volunteer to the whiteboard to put each person in front of the correct house.
- Do the children think the contents of each house would have been the same?
- Ask: *How do we know what people owned?* Explain that when a person died a list was made of all their property and this was called an inventory.
- Open the site www.windowsonwarwickshire.org.uk/spotlights/rich_or_poor/tedder_inventory.htm (last accessed 10/7/07) and read through the inventory for David Tedder with the children.
- Challenge the children to decide whether David Tedder was rich or poor, and to give their reasons. Highlight any words that are indicative of wealth.

Independent work
- Give each pair of children a copy of photocopiable page 161. It shows part of an inventory made in 1596.
- Ask the children to transcribe the inventory into their exercise books or on a separate piece of paper, using the glossary to help them. They need to decide whether the person was rich or poor and explain their reasons.
- The children should start by reading the inventory out loud in pairs or as a class. Remind them that Roman numerals have been used.
- More confident learners could use all the material from the lesson to construct an inventory for a person in a different social class.
- Give less confident pupils a simplified version of the inventory.

Plenary
- Display the PDF of the photocopiable sheet and read through it together. Ask if there were any sections the children did not understand and work through these together.
- Challenge the children to tell you whether they think the owner was rich or poor and to justify their answers. Highlight the text in the inventory that is evidence of wealth. Discuss any differences of opinion, helping the children to understand that evidence can be interpreted in different ways.

History — Lesson 2

In short supply

Learning objectives
QCA Unit 9 'What was it like for children in the Second World War?'
- To learn why rationing was necessary.
- To learn about the impact of rationing on the way of life of people living in England during the Second World War.

Resources
'Rationing' Notebook file; pictures of ration books; pictures of people shopping in wartime Britain; examples of quantities of rationed food to help the children visualise the quantities; printed copies of page 9 of the Notebook file for each child; pencils.

Links to other subjects
Mathematics
Calculating: Develop and use written methods to record, support and explain multiplication.
- Use mathematical strategies to work out the family ration.

Science
PoS Sc2 (2b) To understand the importance of diet.

PSHE
PoS (3a) To understand what makes a healthy lifestyle.
- Look at what foods make up a healthy diet.

Whiteboard tools
The Calculator, accessed through the SMART Board tools menu, can be used to check answers to the sums in the independent work.

- Pen tray
- Select tool
- Calculator

Starter
List what the children already know about the Second World War on page 2 of the Notebook file. Ask: *Why were British docks targeted for bombing raids? What would the effects have been?* (Destruction of shipping, destruction of goods stored.) Tell the children that German submarines attacked the Merchant Navy ships that brought supplies to Britain. Do they know why rationing became essential? Note their suggestions on page 3 of the Notebook file.

Whole-class shared work
- Explain that before the war most of Britain's food was imported. Scarcity usually results in price rises and the government didn't want this to happen, so some foods were rationed.
- Write the children's thoughts on rationing on page 4 of the Notebook file. Ask why rationing was fair.
- Display the picture of the ration book on page 5 of the Notebook file and explain how such books were used. Rations for a household were combined. Ask: *Would it be better to be part of a large or a small household? Why?*
- Display the leaflets on page 6. The Ministry of Food produced many leaflets to help people make the most of their rationed foods. With the children, look at and discuss how the leaflets would have been helpful.
- Go to page 7 of the Notebook file. Explain that not all foods were rationed at the same time. Ask the children why they think that was, and what foods were not rationed. (Food was only rationed if the government could guarantee a regular supply; some foods were never available.) Move the shapes to reveal the foods that were rationed in each of the years shown.
- Go to page 8 and show the children how rations varied in different years of the war. Ask them to guess which items you could get less or more of in 1942, compared with 1940. Move the shape to reveal the answers.
- Show the children the examples of rationed food and compare these quantities to what they may eat in a day or a week.
- Explain that some people supplemented their ration by, for example, bartering goods grown or produced at home.

Independent work
- Give out copies of page 9 of the Notebook file for the children to complete in pairs.
- Less confident learners could work with you on the whiteboard version.
- Challenge more confident learners to work out a food ration for a different family.

Plenary
- Do the multiple-choice quiz on page 10 of the Notebook file with the children. Use this as an opportunity to assess and clarify misconceptions.
- Ask: *Would you have enjoyed wartime food? What would you have missed most? Do you think the diet was healthy? Why/why not?*
- Page 11 offers an opportunity for the children to think more about the effects of rationing. The question asks them to consider the alternatives for sugar. (Answer: Potatoes were not used to sweeten cakes.) This could be used as a stimulus for a subsequent lesson to look at what people used instead of the rationed foods.

History Lesson 3

Preparing for the afterlife

Learning objectives
QCA Unit 10 'What can we find out about Ancient Egypt from what has survived?'
- To learn about Egyptian tombs, pyramids and burial sites.
- To learn that what we know about the past is dependent on what has survived.

Resources
'Ancient Egypt' Notebook file; computer with internet access; sheets of plain paper; pencils; printouts of completed page 5 of the Notebook file; scissors; glue.

Links to other subjects
English
Creating and shaping texts
- Ask the children to write clear instructions for mummifying a body.

Geography
QCA Unit 24 'Passport to the world'
- Use the internet and reference books to find out what it was like to live in Ancient Egypt, and compare this to life in Egypt today.

Whiteboard tools
Add annotations using a Pen from the Pen tray.

- Pen tray
- Select tool
- Fill Colour tool

Starter
Recap what the children already know about Ancient Egypt, making notes on page 2 of the Notebook file. Explain that they are going to learn how the dead were prepared for the afterlife.
Record what the children know about funeral customs in Ancient Egypt on page 3.

Whole-class shared work
- Display page 4 and press the link to open the British Museum's Ancient Egypt website at **www.ancientegypt.co.uk/mummies/home.html** (last accessed 10/7/07).
- Once you have opened up the website, press *Story* on the left-hand side of the page. Begin with the embalming process and then go on to the wrapping and burial of the body (pressing underlined text opens a glossary).
- Ask: *Why do you think it was important to the Ancient Egyptians that the body was preserved?*
- Discuss the differences between the rich and poor. Were their bodies prepared for burial in exactly the same way? In what way were they different?
- Ask questions about the mummification process. For example: *Why was the heart left inside the body? Why was it important to fill the body with dry materials?*
- Discuss the ritual involved: *Why was the opening of the mouth an important ritual? What would happen if it wasn't performed?*
- Complete the activity on page 5 of the Notebook file, putting the instructions for mummifying a body in the correct order.

Independent work
- Hand out sheets of plain paper. Tell the children to pretend to be master embalmers, and write a manual explaining how to prepare a body for burial.
- Encourage the use of annotated illustrations and diagrams (neither the embalmers nor their apprentices would have been able to read or write).
- Give less confident learners copies of completed page 5 of the Notebook file, as prompts for the instructions.

Plenary
- Write any interesting facts that the children have learned on page 6 of the Notebook file.
- Address any misconceptions that may have arisen. (For example, if the master embalmers could not write, how do we know about the embalming process?)
- Discuss the sources of evidence that tell us about the Egyptian belief in life after death. Remind the children of artefacts from the story, such as the canopic jars and amulets.
- Question the children about the reasons for each of the processes. For example: *Why were amulets wrapped with the bandages?* Use page 6 to note down questions to research in a subsequent session.
- Page 7 offers an opportunity to assess the children's understanding of what they have learned. The children can use voting methods to answer the question. (Answer: The heart.)

History — Lesson 4

Living here in the past

Learning objectives
QCA Unit 18 'What was it like to live here in the past?'
- To learn that the area has changed at different times in the past.
- To use maps to help describe some of the characteristic features of the past.

Resources
Internet access; prepared Notebook file showing plan of area, with digital pictures of old and modern buildings (copyright permitting) and hyperlink to www.old-maps.co.uk (last accessed 10 July 2007). Modern, large-scale map of same area, showing individual buildings (include in Notebook file, copyright permitting); one copy of both maps for each child (copyright permitting); paper and pencils; PDF of photocopiable page 162 'Streets past and present' (provided on the CD-ROM).

Links to other subjects
Geography
QCA Unit 9 'Village settlers'
- Consider why the area in the old and new maps has changed.
PoS (2c) To use maps and plans at a range of scales.
- Consolidate and apply map skills learned in geography.

Mathematics
Handling data: Answer a question by identifying what data to collect; organise, present, analyse and interpret the data in tables, diagrams, tally charts and bar charts.
- Make a Venn diagram to sort the information into *Past*, *Present* and *Past and present*.

Whiteboard tools
Use the Spotlight tool to focus on your locality when you visit the website.

- Pen tray
- Lines tool
- Spotlight tool
- On-screen Keyboard

Starter
Revise with the children any earlier work regarding study of the local area, reminding them of the locations of older and newer buildings in the region. Mark these on the simple plan of the local area in the Notebook file. Remind the children of some of the features of older properties.

Whole-class shared work
- Ask the children to imagine what the area might have looked like in the past. Can they suggest familiar buildings or features that would not have existed?
- Explain that the children are going to look at an old map of the area. Open the hyperlink (www.old-maps.co.uk). Locate your town, centre the map on your locality and focus on it using the Spotlight tool.
- Point out the date of the map and ask the children to tell you how long ago that was. Encourage them to relate this date to other periods in history that they have studied.
- Ask the children if they can identify any features on the map.
- Look at the names of any old buildings. Ask: *Are the names familiar? Are these used in modern features, such as roads or housing estates?*
- Draw attention to the modern map and ask the children to say briefly how the locality has changed: perhaps there was a railway in the past that isn't there now, for example. Annotate this map to show the changes.

Independent work
- Tell the children that they are going to pretend to be time travellers. Using the old and new maps of the area as a starting point, they will describe in detail walks between two familiar points in the past and the present.
- Discuss with the children the sorts of information they could include (such as the styles and functions of the buildings).
- Encourage the children to describe other things that they might have seen or heard, such as transport or clothing.
- Less confident learners could be given more supportive writing frames.
- Encourage more confident learners to summarise the changes.

Plenary
- In this session the children will sort the names of objects into those from the past and those from the present.
- Display the PDF of 'Streets past and present' (photocopiable page 162) on the CD-ROM.
- Read through the list of items together. Ask children to come up to the whiteboard and use the Lines tool to draw arrows from the words to the correct heading.
- Discuss the things that can go under both headings. How have these things changed over time?
- Discuss and clarify any misconceptions as they arise.
- Type other words suggested by the children onto the Notebook file. Can the children classify these words too?

Geography — Lesson 5

Too much rubbish

Learning objectives
QCA Unit 8 'Improving the environment'
- To explore how people improve the environment or damage it.
- To ask and respond to geographical questions.
- To collect and record evidence to answer questions.

Resources
'Litter survey' Notebook file; data collected from the survey.

Links to other subjects
Mathematics
Handling data: Answer a question by identifying what data to collect; organise, present, analyse and interpret the data in tables, diagrams, tally charts and bar charts.
ICT
PoS (1b) To prepare information for development using ICT.
- This lesson links well to the above objectives.
Science
QCA Unit 4B 'Habitats'
- Make a recycling poster to recognise ways in which living things and the environment need protection.

Whiteboard tools
Use the Area Capture tool to add images of the finished pictograms onto a Notebook page via the Page Sorter. They can be printed out later for a display or used in maths work.

- Pen tray
- Select tool
- Area Capture tool
- Page Sorter

Starter
Organise a survey of the rubbish thrown away in the classroom every day for a week. Put a tally sheet by the bin for people to fill in when they throw something away. Use the categories on the pictogram on page 3 of the Notebook file. Decide on sensible units of measurement for each item (a certain number of sheets could constitute one bundle of paper). Put up a sign reminding people to use the tally chart. At the end of the week, total each day's rubbish.

At the start of this lesson, go to page 2 of the Notebook file. Recap on what the survey was about, fill in the dates and discuss the children's predictions about results.

Whole-class shared work
- Go to page 3 and press the image to open the pictogram. Ask one child to read out the survey results for the first day and drag the relevant quantities of each symbol onto the pictogram.
- Use the Area Capture tool to take a snapshot of the day, reduce it to fit, and paste it into the relevant box on page 3 of the Notebook file. Repeat the process for the other days of the week.
- Discuss the results. Ask what the items made of the different materials might have been. Use mathematical vocabulary to compare quantities of different materials.
- Go to page 4. Discuss what materials can be recycled and make notes. Drag and drop the items to the correct recycling box.
- Display page 5 and discuss which materials in the children's survey will have been recycled. Complete the spider diagram.
- Go to page 6. Ask whether there were any items that could have been recycled, and weren't. What items would have been hard to recycle?

Independent work
- Return to page 4, about recycling different materials. Ask the children to draw a series of pictures, using arrows, to show how a recyclable material can be continually reused (for example, aluminium). Talk about the vocabulary they will need and write the words for them to copy.
- Provide children who need more guidance with an information sheet on a particular aspect of recycling.
- Ask more confident learners to add a title and persuasive text to their diagram.

Plenary
- Look at page 7 of the Notebook file. Press the link to see a contract to try to recycle more, to help save resources and energy. Discuss the statements. Do the children all agree that this is a good thing to do? Invite them to sign the contract and print out copies to display, or to stick in their books.
- Ask the children to find out more about recycling and its good effects as part of their homework.

Geography — Lesson 6

Virtual village

Learning objectives
QCA Unit 9 'Village settlers'
- To recognise that settlements have specific features and are located in response to physical features and human choice.
- To draw a map of the layout of a settlement.

Resources
'Build your own' file; photocopiable page 163 'Virtual village' for each child; computer with internet connection; URL for Ordnance Survey Get-a-map (www.ordnancesurvey.co.uk/oswebsite/getamap).

Links to other subjects
History
PoS (7) Local history study
- Use this technique to study or develop a map of a particular period in time. Decide on the features to include or exclude.

Whiteboard tools
Use the map symbols from the Foundation folder under My Content in the 'Build your own' file to add features and compass points. Create buildings using the Shapes tool.

- Pen tray
- Select tool
- Shapes tool
- Gallery

Starter
Bring up the Ordnance Survey *Get-a-map* site (see Resources). Start with the map of the British Isles. Choose a location, and gradually zoom in by pressing the map. Ask the children what is changing as you do this. They should be able to see details of roads, rivers, buildings and land use. Alternatively, start zoomed in on a known place, and zoom out.

Whole-class shared work
- Open the 'Build your own' file, which consists of a blank Notebook page and a ready-made Gallery collection of resources saved under My Content. Tell the children that they are going to create a map for an imaginary village in the countryside. Ask: *What colour should the background be? What is the main colour in the countryside?* Select Format, then Background Colour, to set the background colour as requested by the children. Put a compass rose on the screen and explain its purpose.
- Ask the children: *What features in the village would be very hard to move or remove, even with a bulldozer or crane?* (Lakes, hills, and so on.) Invite a volunteer to draw a river running across the screen, using a sensible colour and thickness of line. Ask: *Why do many settlements have rivers?*
- Ask: *What features of a settlement often cross a river?* Draw a couple of roads and/or a railway on the Notebook page.
- Add appropriate mapping symbols and ask the children to justify the sites of the features.
- Finally, use the Shapes tool to add buildings to the map.

Independent work
- Save the map and leave it on display for reference. Tell the children that they are going to design their own village. They will need to think about all the points discussed as a class.
- Hand out copies of photocopiable page 163. Point out the compass rose, key, the space for a village name and the space for the map. Ask the children to design their village to include a river and a hill. Tell them that colour will play an important part in their maps.
- Adapt the sheet for less confident learners, providing a framework of river and roads to start them off.
- More confident learners could look at an Ordnance Survey map to see how the background is shaded in different colours, depending on what it is used for.

Plenary
- Ask the children to work in pairs to discuss their maps. Challenge each child to describe a route though their partner's village, commenting on what is seen on the journey.
- Invite pairs of children to describe a walk through the village on the interactive whiteboard. Ask them to relate to the key when they describe what they see.
- Tell the children that they will now be able to look at maps of real places and know what it is like there.

Geography — Lesson 7

What did we do?

Learning objectives
QCA Unit 19 'How and where do we spend our time?'
- To be able to analyse and communicate findings.
- To understand that collecting and storing information in an organised way helps to find answers to questions.
- To interpret and analyse information in graphs.

Resources
'What did we do?' Notebook file. Prior to the lesson, insert digital photographs of places in the local area (eg shops, the park) onto page 2 of the Notebook file. Complete the spreadsheet on page 3 showing how children spent their time during the week. Re-link the spreadsheet and save the Notebook file for this lesson. (Microsoft Excel is required to view the embedded spreadsheet in the Notebook file.)

Links to other subjects
ICT
PoS (1c) To interpret information.
- Change one item of data to illustrate how a typing error would affect the graph.

English
Presentation
- Design a poster for a leisure activity.

Whiteboard tools
Use the On-screen Keyboard to enter data, and the Pen, Highlighter and Eraser tools to annotate the charts. Use the Area Capture tool to paste the data and charts to a new Notebook page, for saving or printing.

- Pen tray
- Select tool
- Area Capture tool
- On-screen Keyboard

Starter
In the week preceding this lesson, ask the children to record how they spent their time every day for a week. Use the spreadsheet on page 3 of the Notebook file for the criteria. Collate the data and enter it into the spreadsheet prior to this lesson. Re-link the file to the button on page 3 of the Notebook file and save the Notebook file.

Look at the series of photographs of places in the local area that you have placed on page 2 of the Notebook file. Ask the children to arrange them in the Carroll diagram, according to the criteria of *work, leisure, near,* and *far.* Use this to remind the children of the data they collected. Ask: *Do we visit places less if they are far away? Why?*

Whole-class shared work
- Press the link on page 3 to display the completed spreadsheet. Make sure that the percentage row is not visible.
- Look at the data. Which activity has the largest amount of time? Use mathematics skills to try to work this out. Scroll down to reveal the percentage row. Point out that a computer can do the calculations for us, so that we can spend longer on thinking about what the results mean.
- Identify highest and lowest hours spent on any of the activities.
- Ask questions about the data, relating to largest/smallest number of hours, and make annotations.
- Scroll down to the chart. Ask: *How does the bar chart help us to understand the data? Which things are easy to see and which are difficult? Does the bar chart help to spot any obvious errors in the data?* (The chart doesn't show the hours each child spent on each activity, but it is easier to see which activity takes up the most and least time.) Annotate with the children's observations.
- Save the annotated screen to the Notebook file using the Area Capture tool.

Independent work
- Ask the children to make a poster to advertise one of the leisure activities. The posters might include information about the locality of the activity, its benefits and when it can be used. The posters could be displayed around the school.
- Print out several copies of the annotated data that has been saved to the Notebook file. Distribute the printouts to the children to provide data and vocabulary.
- Provide a few relevant phrases for those children who need them.
- Encourage more confident learners to include a witty slogan, including alliteration or a pun, as part of their poster.

Plenary
- Go back to the chart of activities. Discuss possible explanations for the different amounts of time spent on the various activities. Draw out the idea that some activities can only be done once in a while. Perhaps they just did not occur in this particular week. Travelling distance might be a factor, as might the weather.
- Discuss how the data collected could be improved. Make a note of the children's responses on page 4 of the Notebook file.
- Ask: *What would the effect be of taking a sample over four weeks?*
- Discuss whether the data would be different for adults.

Geography Lesson 8

Where on Earth is it?

Learning objectives
QCA Unit 24 'Passport to the world'
- To investigate places.
- To analyse evidence.
- To use secondary sources of information.

Resources
'Investigating Europe' Notebook file; photocopiable page 164 'Where on Earth is it?' for each child; facts about the places to be investigated; photographs of the places if available; internet access; computers with desktop publishing package (optional).

Links to other subjects
English
Understanding and interpreting texts
- The children can practise note-making skills when they research the different countries.

ICT
QCA Unit 4A 'Writing for different audiences'
- Encourage the children to think about their audience if they are putting together a multimedia presentation.

Whiteboard tools
Use the Screen Shade to reveal the mystery countries.

- Pen tray
- Select tool
- Screen Shade

Starter
Do this activity over a few days, for about 15 minutes each day. The final session will include the independent work.

Press the URL on page 2 of the Notebook file to go the European Union website (**http://europe.eu.int**). Enter the portal through the English link (en). Select *The EU at a glance* in the left-hand menu, then *Countries*, and *Maps of Europe*. Invite the children to select countries and explore the maps, commenting on what they see.

Whole-class shared work
- Return to the Notebook file and go to page 3. Use the Screen Shade to gradually reveal the page from the top, asking the children if they can guess the name of the mystery country as you do so.
- Once you have revealed the entire page, discuss the outline map of the country and emphasise which parts of it border other countries and which border the sea. Check the children's predictions by using the Eraser from the Pen tray to rub out the right-hand side of the yellow strip to reveal the name of the mystery country.
- Repeat this each day, using pages 4 to 10. Make associations to help the children remember the shape of a country (for example, *Italy is shaped like a boot*). The children should be able to predict the items on each page when they have seen them a few times. They can record information about each country on photocopiable page 164.

Independent work
- On the final day, group the children into pairs. Allocate one country to each pair.
- Ask each pair to produce a booklet about the country. Encourage them to use their photocopiable sheets as a source of information.
- If necessary, provide a template document for the children to build on. This could include key headings that match the data in the Notebook file.
- Pages 11 and 12 summarise all the information given on the preceding pages. Printouts of these two pages can be used to support less confident learners.
- More confident learners could produce a simple multimedia presentation instead of a booklet. They could use a desktop publishing package to insert text, clipart, maps, photographs and numerical data.
- Ask those children who are more competent in using the internet, to include a couple of words (vocabulary) from their country's language in their booklet or presentation.

Plenary
- Visit the EU online website again (see page 2 of the Notebook file). Press *The EU at a glance* and then *The symbols of the EU* to look at the flag and listen to the anthem.
- Use the list of member states (*The EU at a glance > Countries*) to investigate other countries that form part of the European Union. Ask the children to open up the ones that interest them by pressing on their names on the screen.
- Allow the children to share their booklets on the various countries. Write any interesting facts on page 13 of the Notebook file. If possible, display the booklets in the classroom, or show them at a special assembly.

Design and technology — Lesson 9

What makes a good bridge?

Learning objectives
- To understand and analyse how bridges are constructed.
- To recognise the features of a strong bridge.
- To develop ideas and explain them clearly.

Resources
'The bridge competition' Notebook file; photocopiable page 165 'What makes a strong bridge?' for each child.

Links to other subjects
Mathematics
Understanding shape: Visualise 3D objects from 2D drawings and make nets of common solids.
- Encourage the children to use correct shape vocabulary when describing the bridges.

Geography
QCA Unit 24 'Passport to the world'
- Use the internet and reference books to find out about famous bridges.

Speaking and listening
Objective 37: To use and reflect on some ground rules for dialogue.
- The children should make structured contributions, speak audibly and listen to others when discussing the images.

Starter
Begin by posing the following problem to the class:
You are standing beside a river and you want to cross to the other side. The river is too deep to walk through or drive through. How could you get across to the other side without getting wet?
Discuss the children's ideas, which will probably include building a bridge, and list them on page 2 of the Notebook file. Explain to the children that over the next few lessons, they will be looking at different types of bridges and how they are built. They will then design and build a bridge of their own. In this lesson, they will be looking carefully at what is needed to build a strong bridge.

Whole-class shared work
- Tell the children they are going to look at some pictures of bridges. Go to page 3 of the Notebook file and draw their attention to the questions. Ask: *What makes each bridge different? What do you notice about the base of each bridge? What kind of material has been used? Why?* Use the Spotlight tool to focus on aspects of the bridges.
- Write up the children's suggestions in the area around the pictures. Press *Extend Page* (at the foot of the screen) to provide additional writing space below the pictures if necessary.
- Reset the page scale to 100% or *Best fit* (whichever is your preferred setting). Read the explanations of three different types of bridge on pages 4, 5 and 6. Ask the children to discuss, in pairs, real-life examples of these types of bridges.
- Look at pages 7 to 10. Discuss with the children the types of bridges that are being shown. Focus on particular features and annotate the children's ideas around the photographs.

Independent work
- Show the children page 11 and hand out copies of photocopiable page 165. Ask them to choose the bridge they like best, to draw it on the sheet and label the features that make it a really strong bridge.
- Half way through the lesson, ask the children to complete their drawings.
- Go to page 12 of the Notebook file and tell the children that, in the next two lessons, they will work in groups to design and build a bridge for the competition, using art straws.
- Ask the children to try designing a bridge for the competition on the second half of the photocopiable sheet.
- Less confident learners may need further explanation of the task. Consider working with them as a group.
- Encourage more confident learners to use what they have learned about what makes a good bridge to inform their own designs.

Plenary
- Ask the children to share their ideas for the bridge competition. Display good examples to share with the class.
- Tell the children that they will be using these designs in the next lesson.

Whiteboard tools
Use the Spotlight tool to focus on particular areas of the images on page 3.

- Pen tray
- Spotlight tool

Design and technology Lesson 10

Learning objectives
- To generate suitable and realistic ideas to build a bridge.
- To communicate personal ideas clearly when working in a group.

Resources
'The bridge competition' Notebook file; photocopiable page 166 'Designing a bridge' for each child; art straws; paper clips; sticky tape; sticky tack; string; examples of children's bridge designs from Lesson 9.

Links to other subjects
Speaking and listening
Objective 43: To use time, resources and group members efficiently by distributing tasks, checking progress, and making back-up plans.
- Monitor the group work to ensure that the children are working together as a team, and are supporting less confident learners in making a contribution.

Designing a bridge

Starter
Remind the children of the previous lesson. Display some of their bridge designs and discuss them. Encourage them to describe the features they particularly like.

Tell the children that they will be working in groups to design a bridge for a competition. Their individual ideas will be important in the design process, but each group must come to an agreement about the final design.

Whole-class shared work
- Spend a few minutes discussing pages 12 and 13 of the Notebook file. Explain the task to the children.
- Ask the children what they know about the word *force*. Give them a few minutes to think about their replies. Explain that it means *pressure*.
- Use the Lines tool to draw a picture of a beam bridge across the river on page 12. Draw an arrow in the middle of the bridge. Ask: *What will happen if weights are placed in the middle of the bridge?*
- After discussion, ask: *How can we protect the bridge against that pressure?* Explain that for each force applied directly, there is an indirect force acting against it.
- Explain that the children will be competing to win a prize. The winner will be the group with the strongest bridge and the most money left.
- Go to page 14, which shows the materials the children can use, and discuss. Show them page 15, and explain that they must use this to keep a tally of the materials that they use.

Independent work
- The children should work in mixed-ability groups of five, using their bridge designs from the previous lesson.
- Encourage the groups to think creatively of different ways of constructing the beam across the two bases. They should consider ways in which their materials could be strengthened.
- Allow the groups to spend five to ten minutes looking at the individual designs. They should look for a good idea from each sheet.
- Tell the groups that they have the remainder of the lesson to design their bridges.
- Each group should use plain paper to sketch and note down their ideas for a group design. The final design should be drawn on photocopiable page 166.
- Provide each group with a few art straws for reference. As they work, encourage them to think about the different types of bridges that you have looked at.
- Ensure that each group's members work as a team, supporting those who are less confident and allowing them the opportunity to contribute.

Plenary
- Encourage the different groups to share their ideas for their bridge.

Whiteboard tools
Use the Lines tool to draw a beam bridge on page 12.

- Pen tray
- Lines tool

Design and technology — Lesson 11

Building bridges

Learning objectives
- To display effective teamwork skills when constructing their group bridge.
- To select appropriate tools, materials and techniques for making their bridge.
- To assemble, join and combine components and materials accurately.
- To reflect on the progress of their work and identify ways they could improve their work.

Resources
'The bridge competition' Notebook file; 40 art straws and a pair of scissors for each group; £1.50 in plastic money for each group (50 pence pieces and sufficient 5p and 10p coins for change); digital camera; 10g weights to test the bridge; two boxes to represent the villages; blue paper to represent the river that the bridges have to span.

Links to other subjects
Mathematics
Using and applying mathematics: Solve problems involving money.
- Calculate change, keep to budget and compare how much each group spent.

English
Creating and shaping texts
- Use a report format when writing up the project.

Science
PoS Sc1 (2d) To make a fair test or comparison.
- Discuss how to keep the competition fair.

Whiteboard tools
Use a Pen from the Pen tray to annotate and complete the charts. Upload digital images by selecting Insert, then Picture File, and browsing to where you have saved the images.

- Pen tray

Starter
This lesson will take more than the hour allocation. It can be extended at your discretion, depending on the detail required of the written work.

Ask the groups to show their bridge designs from the previous session (Lesson 10). Go through the previous pages of the Notebook file to review the task and remind the children of the equipment they can use.

Whole-class shared work
- Go to page 16 of the Notebook file. Discuss the idea that teamwork is essential when designing and building any structure. Ask the children what skills they will need as they work in their groups, and make a note of their suggestions.
- Move on to page 17 and discuss how the class can make sure this will be a fair test (for example, the length that the bridge has to span must be established at the start). Note down the children's ideas.

Independent work
- Within their groups, allow the children sufficient time to build their bridges.
- Set up the shop next to the whiteboard. Use the table on page 15 to keep a tally of the resources that each group purchases.
- Monitor the children as they work. Discuss their different techniques for joining the straws, and the ways in which they use the available resources.
- Take digital pictures as the children work. If possible, use a digital camcorder to film children as they demonstrate and explain their techniques and bridge designs. (Remember to obtain permission from parents before filming the children.)
- Ensure that the 10g weights are available for the children to test their bridges as they build them.
- Again, ensure that more confident learners support those who are less confident, and allow them to contribute.

Plenary
- Display the chart on page 18 of the Notebook file. Ask each group to record how much money it has left.
- Test each bridge to see how strong it is. Add 10g weights until the bridge collapses. Record the final load in the chart on page 18.
- Use a digital camera to take a picture of each group's bridge before, during and after the test. Insert these photos on page 19 of the Notebook file.
- Discuss which bridge is the winner. The bridge must be strong, but also must not have cost too much to make. Discuss what made the bridge strong.
- Encourage the children to evaluate their models in a positive light using the *two stars and a wish* approach: name two things about making your bridge or working in a group that you really liked; then name one thing you would change or improve.
- Use pages 20 to 23 to talk through the process of producing a written report and evaluation of the project. (This can be done in a subsequent lesson.)

Art and design — Lesson 12

Viewpoints

Learning objectives
QCA Unit 4A 'Viewpoints'
● To collect information about viewpoints.
● To explore ideas about dreams.

Resources
Prepared Notebook page showing digital photographs (copyright permitting) of the following:
● a bird's eye view (aerial) or oblique view (taken from the top window in building, for example);
● a worm's eye view (taken from the ground looking upwards);
● a view from a normal perspective.
Viewfinders, one for each child; paper; pencils; crayons.

Links to other subjects
PSHE
PoS (2e) Reflect on spiritual, moral, social and cultural issues, using imagination to understand other people's experiences.
● Encourage the children to empathise with the characters. Discuss with the children moments when they have felt small or big.

Whiteboard tools
Use the Gallery to select suitable images.

- Pen tray
- Select tool
- Gallery

Starter
Display the prepared Notebook page (see Resources) showing photographs taken from bird's eye/oblique, worm's eye and regular perspectives. Ask the children what they notice about these photographs. Ask: *How are they different?* Lead them to think about the notion of viewpoints: these could be scenes viewed by a bird or a giant, a worm or insect, and a person.

Whole-class shared work
● Open the Gallery and browse to English and Language Arts and then Storytelling. Select two contrasting characters (for example, a boy and a witch, or a child and an animal), and paste them onto a new Notebook page. Make sure the characters are the same size.
● Ask the children to describe what the characters may be thinking. Ask: *What might be happening in this situation?* Write up their ideas.
● Increase the size of one character and ask the children if the character's viewpoints have changed. *How have they changed? Why?* Write their comments, using a different-coloured pen from the Pen tray.
● Think about the characters in isolation. Ask the children to look at the big character: *What would the world look like from this viewpoint? Would you feel really powerful if you were this big?*
● Think about the small character. Ask questions such as: *What does everything look like from this viewpoint? How would it feel to be the size of an insect? Would you feel scared, or would you feel safe because you could hide in lots of small places?*

Independent work
● Tell the children to think about their classroom. Ask: *What would everything look like to a person as tall as the ceiling/no taller than a ruler?* Encourage the children to pick up objects and to look at them from different perspectives.
● Give out sheets of paper, pencils and crayons. Ask the children to draw a particular object from a bird's eye (or worm's eye) point of view.
● Next, ask them to draw their own pictures, imagining that they are looking at a scene from a bird's eye or worm's eye viewpoint. This can be a real-life scene, such as the classroom or playground, or it can be a fantasy scene (from the viewpoint of a giant, for example).
● Remind the children that they need to think about their viewpoints. *How do things look if you are really big or small? Does everything look frightening? Do you feel safe? Do things get in the way?*

Plenary
● Invite some of the children to share their work.
● Ask the class to guess from which viewpoint the picture has been drawn.
● Encourage the children to describe what they have drawn. How did the different viewpoint make them feel about the things in the picture?

Art and design Lesson 13

Take a seat

Learning objective
QCA Unit 4B 'Take a seat'
● To identify different types of chairs, their parts, uses and materials from which they are made.

Resources
'Take a seat' Notebook file; photocopiable page 167 'Take a seat' for each pair; drawing materials; coloured pencils.

Links to other subjects
History
PoS (2) Knowledge and understanding of events, people and changes in the past.
● Study furniture and how it has been used in different periods of time.
ICT
QCA Unit 4B 'Developing images using repeating patterns'
● Design a repetitive pattern for the back and seat panel.
English
Creating and shaping texts
● Use new vocabulary to write a short story based on the drawings.

Starter
Start by telling the children that in this lesson they will be looking at different types of chair, and designing a chair of their own. Go to page 2 of the Notebook file. Ask the children where they use chairs in their daily life, and what they use them for. Write up their suggestions.

Whole-class shared work
- Show the children the photographs of the different chairs on page 3 and ask: *What do we use chairs for? What are they made from?* Ask the children to compare the chairs and to tell you what is similar about each chair and how they differ. Group the chairs according to their similarities.
- Use the Spotlight tool to focus on particular chairs or to focus on special details. For example, the high chair is very different to the wicker chair, although they are both made for sitting.
- Focusing on individual chairs, ask: *How is this chair used? What is it used for? What material has the chair been constructed from? Why do you think that material has been chosen? Is the chair meant to be portable?*
- Go to page 4 of the Notebook file. Discuss why we use chairs. Add the children's suggestions to the list.
- Display page 5. Ask for volunteers to drag the labels to the correct features of the chair. Once they have done this, invite them to answer the questions on the tabs. Discuss the different ways in which chairs are made.

Independent work
- Group the children into pairs. Provide each pair with a copy of photocopiable page 167.
- Talk through the task, explaining the terms *front view, back view, side view* and *plan view*.
- Encourage the children to spend some time thinking before they begin designing. They should consider the purpose of the chair. Is it for a special occasion, or a particular person?
- Go to page 6 of the Notebook file and draw attention to the Character box. Invite the children to pick a character for whom to design a chair. You can also use this page to note down ideas for different purposes of chairs, to stimulate thinking.
- If groups finish early, encourage them to think of patterns that could be used for the seat and back panels of their chairs. They could draw and colour these in their sketchbooks.

Plenary
- After completing their drawings, ask the children to show their chair designs to the rest of the class. Invite each child to point out the features they particularly like.
- Ask questions such as: *What type of occasion could* (for example) *Eve's chair be used for? How do you know this chair is fit for a king?* Write any interesting findings on page 7 of the Notebook file.

Whiteboard tools
Use the Spotlight tool to focus on particular chairs. Annotate the children's suggestions with a Pen from the Pen tray.

- Pen tray
- Select tool
- Spotlight tool

Art and design — Lesson 14

Journeys

Learning objectives
QCA Unit 4C 'Journeys'
- To describe personal journeys that are made.
- To design symbols/pictures that show aspects of their journey.

Resources
'Build your own' file; internet map site, such as Multimap (www.multimap.com) or the AA (www.theaa.com); digital photographs of different landmarks from the local area (copyright permitting); selection of road traffic signs from the Gallery; sketchbooks; selection of collage materials; digital camera.

Links to other subjects
Religious education
Non-statutory national framework (3i) To think about symbols and religious expression.
- Look at how symbols are used by different religions.
Geography
PoS (2e) To draw plans and maps at a range of scales.
Mathematics
Understanding shape: Describe and identify the position of a square on a grid of squares.
- Lay a grid over a digital area photograph and number the axes. Use for work on coordinates. For example: *Who can show me where the shopping centre is?*

Whiteboard tools
Use the Shapes tool to help in building symbols. Use the Spotlight tool to focus on aspects of the photographs.

- Pen tray
- Select tool
- Gallery
- Shapes tool
- Spotlight tool

Starter
Ask the children to explain what a journey is. (The way you get from one place to another.) Ask them to spend a few minutes thinking about a journey that they often make – for example, from home to school, from home to town, or from home to a grandparent's house.

Display a map of the local area (copyright permitting) and ask volunteers to describe their journeys. Encourage them to describe in detail the places of interest they notice on the way. Ask: *Why do you notice that house more than the others? Describe what the entrance to the church looks like. Do you like that sculpture that is in the park? Can you explain why?*

Whole-class shared work
- Open the 'Build your own' file, which consists of a blank Notebook page and a ready-made Gallery collection of images saved under My Content. On the first page of the file, write the phrase *Every picture tells a story*. Discuss what the phrase means.
- Display the selection of road symbols provided in the Foundation folder uner My Content in Gallery, and ask the children to tell you what each symbol means. Record their suggestions.
- Return to the map and focus on a small section by the school. Ask the children to point out the road signs they pass each day and to explain what the signs show.
- Display a few photographs of landmarks on the map, such as the church, shopping centre, theatre or playground. Ask the children how these things could be shown using a symbol.
- Use the Spotlight tool to focus on particular aspects of the photographs. Encourage the children to think carefully about the shapes that they see and recognise in the landmarks.
- To support less confident learners, insert actual shapes by the landmarks. Which shape would the children choose for a background?

Independent work
- Encourage the children to look carefully at the photographs on the board and to choose two aspects of their particular journey that always catch their eye.
- Using their sketchbooks, ask the children to think of as many different ways of showing that landmark in pictures. For example, if they pass a church, they could draw a dove or a stained-glass window.
- Encourage them not to draw the obvious representations but to think creatively about different ways to represent the landmark. They should consider how this landmark makes them feel when they see it.
- Once they are happy with their designs, invite the children to create a collage of the symbols using different materials.

Plenary
- Take digital pictures of some of the children's work and display them on the whiteboard.
- Challenge the rest of the class to guess what the symbols depict.
- Invite some of the children to explain why they chose to represent the landmark in this way, and to explain their choice of materials.

Art and design — Lesson 15

Making mosaics

Learning objective
- To understand how mosaics are made.

Resources
'Mosaics' Notebook file; computer with internet access; examples of mosaics (printed resources as well as digital, copyright permitting); photocopiable page 168 'Making mosaics' for each child; coloured sticky paper or a selection of magazines; coloured pencils; scissors.

Links to other subjects
History
QCA Unit 6A 'Why have people invaded and settled in Britain in the past? A Roman case study'
- Investigate Roman mosaics.

Mathematics
Understanding shape: Draw polygons and classify them by identifying their properties, including their line symmetry.
- Create shape mosaics of tiles cut into that shape (for example, use triangular tiles to create a triangular pattern).

ICT
QCA Unit 4B 'Developing images using repeating patterns'
- Use a computer graphics package to create a simple mosaic pattern.

Starter
Display page 2 of the Notebook file. Ask the children to explain what they know already about mosaics and write up suggestions on the board. Show the examples of mosaics on page 3 to 7. Share other examples, using your printed resources (for example, postcards, photos or books), or examples from the internet, copyright permitting - for example, the Roman Mosaics page from the BBC website **www.bbc.co.uk/history/ancient/romans/mosaics_gallery.shtml** (last accessed 10/7/07). Explain to the children that in this lesson they will be making their own alphabet mosaic.

Whole-class shared work
- Use the Spotlight tool to look in detail at the mosaic examples. Encourage the children to identify the features they notice. Ask: *How have these mosaics been created? How have the colours been used? What shapes can you see?*
- Display page 8, which shows letters made out of mosaic tiles. Discuss the image and invite the children to build up their own letter using the grid on page 9, and the Fill Colour tool.
- Once they have completed their letter, use the Undo button to start again.

Independent work
- Give each child a copy of photocopiable page 168 and some sheets of scrap paper. Ask them to design their initials using the mosaic grid.
- Explain that they need to think about the colours that they want to use and whether they would like to include other elements, such as a patterned border.
- Encourage the children to mix different types of media to add interest to their mosaics. They can cut up coloured paper or pages from colour magazines to use as mosaic tiles.
- Suggest that they plan out the shape of their mosaic pattern before sticking everything down.
- Less confident learners may find it easier to concentrate on the initial letter of their first name only.
- Extend more confident learners by encouraging them to fill the entire grid with colour, ensuring that their letters are clearly visible.

Plenary
- Encourage the children to show their work, inviting them to draw attention to any elements of their mosaics that they particularly like. Ask them to explain why they chose different types of materials.
- Write any points of interest on page 10 of the Notebook file.

Whiteboard tools
Use the Spotlight tool to focus on aspects of the photographs on pages 3-7 of the Notebook file.

- Pen tray
- Spotlight tool
- Fill Colour tool
- Select tool
- Undo button

Music — Lesson 16

Learning objectives
QCA Unit 10 'Play it again - Exploring rhythmic patterns'
- To recognise repeated rhythmic patterns.
- To listen carefully and repeat a rhythmic pattern.
- To combine two different rhythms with a steady pulse.

Resources
Prepared Notebook file, each page showing a different four-beat rhythm, for example:

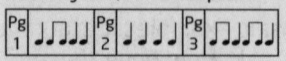

Pg1 ♪♪♪♪ Pg2 ♩♩♩♩ Pg3 ♪♪♪♩

Also in the prepared file, include a page with the words to *Polly Put The Kettle On*, followed by a page showing the same rhyme with musical notes showing the rhythm under each line; a selection of percussion instruments.

Links to other subjects
Art and design
PoS (4a) To learn about visual elements, including colour, pattern and texture, line and tone, shape, form and space.
- Ask the children to identify how artists evoke different moods through their paintings.

English
Creating and shaping texts
- Use the children's work as a stimulus to create a setting for a story. Encourage them to think about the moods and scenes that music can evoke.

Whiteboard tools
Use the music symbols from the Gallery to create rhythm patterns. Use the Lines tool to divide the screen to separate the rhythms that groups play.

- Pen tray
- Gallery
- Select tool
- Lines tool
- Highlighter pen

Rhythmic patterns

Starter
Play 'Switch' with the children. Ask them to tap out a four-beat pulse on their knees. Encourage them to keep the pulse steady and not to rush. Then call out *Switch* and show the first page of the prepared Notebook file (see Resources). The children have to change to this rhythm. After repeating this rhythm a couple of times, tell the children to return back to the four-beat pulse. Repeat for the other rhythms.

Whole-class shared work
- Show the prepared Notebook page with *Polly Put The Kettle On*. Ask: *How many lines/phrases are there in each verse?* (Four.) Say the rhyme out loud with the children.
- Go to the following page of your prepared Notebook file, and show the musical notes under each line.
- Practise clapping the rhythm with the children. Point out that the same rhythmic phrase repeats itself several times. Tell the children that this is called an *ostinato*.
- Go to a blank Notebook page and divide it into two parts using the Lines tool. In the top part, draw four crotchets. Explain that this is the pulse of the rhythm. Ask the children to clap out the pulse.
- When the pulse is steady, clap the rhythm of the song *Polly Put The Kettle On* over it. Ask: *What is the difference between your rhythm and mine?* (Theirs is quicker.)
- Duplicate the pulse rhythm five times across the board.
- In the next line, duplicate the rhythm of the whole song under the last four pulse patterns, leaving the first part blank.

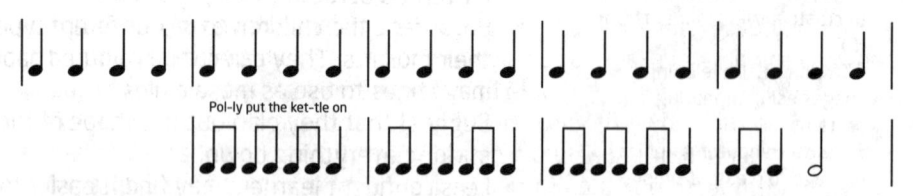

♩ ♩ ♩ ♩	♩ ♩ ♩ ♩	♩ ♩ ♩ ♩	♩ ♩ ♩ ♩	♩ ♩ ♩ ♩
	Pol-ly put the ket-tle on			
	♪♪♪♪♪♪	♪♪♪♪♪♪	♪♪♪♪♪♪	♪♪ ♩

- Divide the class into two. Explain that one half will clap the first line and the other half the second line. Ask the class to perform both parts together a few times.

Independent work
- Ask the children to select an instrument and get into small groups of about six. Label each child in the group A or B. Ask the A children to play the steady pulse on their instruments and the B children to play the rhythm of *Polly Put The Kettle On*.
- Stop the children half way through and listen to some of the groups.
- Next, ask them to devise their own repeated rhythmic pattern. When they practise the pattern, half the group should maintain the steady pulse while the other half performs the rhythmic pattern. They should then swap roles.

Plenary
- Listen carefully to each group as it performs its rhythmic pattern.
- Add the children's patterns to a new Notebook page. Build up a set of rhythmic patterns and ask groups to try to play each other's patterns.

Music Lesson 17

Painting with sound

Learning objectives
QCA Unit 13 'Painting with sound - Exploring sound colours'
- To identify descriptive features in art and music.
- To analyse and comment on how sounds are used to create different moods.

Resources
Digital pictures of an elephant, a tortoise, a swan and a lion (copyright permitting); recording of Saint-Saëns' *Carnival of the Animals*; print of Van Gogh's *Starry Night* and an example of music to accompany it (for example, Beethoven's *Moonlight Sonata*); digital and printed versions of paintings that evoke a sense of mood and allow scope for aural interpretation (copyright permitting); large pieces of sugar paper; selection of tuned and untuned musical instruments.

Links to other subjects
Art and design
PoS (5d) Investigate art, craft and design in a variety of genres, styles and traditions.
- Ask the children to identify how artists have created impressions/effects in their paintings.

Whiteboard tools
If a microphone is available, use Windows® Sound Recorder (accessed through Start>Programs>Accessories>Entertainment) to record the children's compositions. Then open your Notebook file and attach the sound files by selecting Insert, then Sound, and browsing to where you have saved the sound files.

- Pen tray
- Select tool

Starter
Paste pictures of an elephant, a tortoise, a swan and a lion onto a blank Notebook page. Play the appropriate pieces from Saint-Saëns' *Carnival of the Animals*, and ask the children which animal is being described. What is it about the music that makes them think of that animal? Encourage words that describe the music, such as *loud, soft, fast, slow, high, low* and so on. Tell them about the music, and that Saint-Saëns wanted to 'paint' a picture of each animal in sound.

Whole-class shared work
- Display the picture of Van Gogh's *Starry Night*. Ask the children what it shows, what effect it creates and how it makes them feel.
- Invite the children to describe what sounds they would hear if they were in the picture, or what sounds the picture make them think of. Write up their suggestions.
- Play a recording of Beethoven's *Moonlight Sonata*. Ask: *Does this music go with the picture? What kind of sounds would you choose to use?* Add the children's ideas to the board.
- Look at other paintings. Discuss how each picture makes the children feel and what kind of music they think could accompany it.

Independent work
- Divide the class into small groups. Provide each group with a large piece of sugar paper.
- Explain that each group is going to create a piece of music to accompany one of the pictures.
- Ask each group to select a picture. Give the group the printed version of its chosen picture to place in the middle of the piece of sugar paper.
- Tell the groups to annotate the features they would particularly like to illustrate in their composition (for example, the stars, or the hustle and bustle of the town).
- After completing this, encourage each group to think about the instruments they will use.
- Provide a selection of tuned and untuned musical instruments for the children to choose from. Ask each child to select an instrument to help them with their composition (children could use their own instruments if appropriate).
- Ask: *What instruments, or combinations of instruments, will you use at different points to give different effects?*
- Give the children sufficient time to complete their group compositions.

Plenary
- Invite each group to perform their composition for the rest of the class. If a microphone is available, use Windows® Sound Recorder to record the children's compositions.
- Display the pictures on the whiteboard. Ask: *Can you guess which painting this group's composition is for? What helped you to guess? How did the group create the feeling of stars high up in the sky?* Encourage the children to use musical terminology when they give their answers.
- If possible, add the children's music to the Notebook file containing the images. The music can then be played as the pictures are viewed.

Music · Lesson 18

What's the weather like today?

Learning objectives
QCA Unit 6 'What's the score?'
- To understand how symbols can represent sounds.
- To be able to follow a sequence of sounds and play as an ensemble.

Resources
'What's the weather like today?' Notebook file; extracts from Debussy's *La Mer*, or another orchestral piece about the sea; printouts of page 4, one for each group; selection of musical instruments; writing materials.

Links to other subjects
Geography
QCA Unit 16 'What's in the news?'
- Study weather conditions in different parts of the world and compose a range of weather scores to reflect the varying conditions.

English
Creating and shaping texts
- Ask the children to write short descriptive pieces that reflect the weather scores.

Whiteboard tools
If a microphone is available, use Windows® Sound Recorder to record the children's scores. Use the Timer's count-up option to keep time.

- Pen tray
- Select tool

Starter
Begin the lesson by playing Debussy's *La Mer*. Ask the children what the music makes them think of. Tell them the title of the piece and what it means. (The sea.) Explain that Debussy's piece is written for an orchestra, which is a large group of different instruments. Debussy used different combinations of instruments to get different effects.
  Tell the children that in this lesson they will be using symbols to create a piece of music about the weather.

Whole-class shared work
- Go to page 2 of the Notebook file and ask the children to look at the symbols displayed on the screen. Suggest that these symbols could be used to represent different kinds of sounds. Press each symbol to hear a linked sound.
- Ask the children to think of different sounds they could make for each of the symbols. Make a note of the instruments that they suggest, and any sound-related vocabulary, such as *loud* and *soft*.
- Go to page 3 and explain that this is a graphic score: it gives instructions for playing a piece of music.
- Discuss the symbols and the timeline. Explain that the symbols stand for different kinds of sounds, and that the timeline keeps everyone in step and shows them when they have to make their sound.
- Discuss the wavy line. Explain that this tells the players how loud or soft to play. Ask the children how they would do this. For example, for a loud sound, ask: *Do you need a big sound from one instrument, or do you need to add more instruments at this point?*
- Seat the children in a circle and place the instruments in the middle. Ask them to name the instruments and describe how they are played.
- Discuss and agree upon a sound for each of the weather symbols in the graphic score. Divide the children into groups and assign each group a weather symbol and sound.
- Give the groups a few minutes to practise their sounds.
- Keep page 3 of the Notebook file on display and perform the score as a class. Use the Timer's count-up function to keep time and move the vertical line across the board to show when each group must perform their sound.

Independent work
- Distribute the printouts of page 4 of the Notebook file and ask the groups to compose their own weather score. They can use the symbols on the sheet or create new ones of their own.
- Give less confident learners a limited range of symbols and sounds.
- Encourage more confident learners to consider different combinations of sounds to achieve particular effects.
- Invite one of the groups to recreate its graphic score on the whiteboard, using page 4 of the Notebook file. Duplicate the symbols as required.

Plenary
- Invite the class to perform the score on page 4.
- If there is time, allow all the groups to perform their score for the rest of the class. Discuss which scores the class liked the best and what they enjoyed the most about this lesson. Write the children's responses on page 5 of the Notebook file.

Religious education Lesson 19

What is God like?

Learning objectives
- To think carefully about what God means to them.
- To recognise and respect how different people seek comfort in God.
- To develop a sense of awe and wonder in terms of God as an entity.

Resources
Photocopiable page 169 'What is God?' for each child; prepared Notebook page showing a variety of contrasting scenes, from different cultures and countries (for example, a peaceful rural landscape, a busy market scene in a different country, a majestic mountain range, a busy city street); some meditative music; a candle.

Links to other subjects
English
Creating and shaping texts
- Link this to the work in this lesson by providing existing poems as models on which the children can base their own poems.

Starter
Display the prepared Notebook page of contrasting scenes. Above the images, write the questions *Where is God?* and *What is God like?* Tell the children you would like them to think about these questions quietly for a short time. Play the meditative music to them while they look at the Notebook page.

Whole-class shared work
- Ask the children to share their thoughts about the questions on the board. Ask: *How do you imagine God? Where do you think He is?* Make notes of their suggestions.
- Display an enlarged copy of photocopiable page 169, which shows some of the names given to God by three different religions.
- Discuss the names, and what they tell us about God. Annotate a blank Notebook page with the children's ideas.
- Point out that in Islam, Muslims learn the 99 names of God (Allah), of which only three are given on the photocopiable sheet. The many names relate to different attributes of God.
- Talk about other names that could be given to God, relating these to different aspects of Him. These could include forgiveness, protection, justice and so on.

Independent work
- Give each child a copy of photocopiable page 169. Ask the children to answer the questions on the sheet. The last question requires them to make notes about what God means to them, what they think He is like and where they think He can be found. They should then use these notes to write a poem entitled 'What is God?'
- Work with less confident learners in a group, to help them organise their ideas and to write a collaborative poem.
- Challenge more confident learners to use interesting similes and imagery in their poems.

Plenary
- Gather the children on the floor with their poems. Darken the room and light a candle.
- Ask the children to look quietly at the stillness of the candle.
- Explain that you will ask them to read their poems to the class. Tell them that you will tap their shoulders to show when they should read out their poem.
- Invite one child to begin. When that child has finished, tap a different child on the shoulder to signal that he/she should read his/her poem to the class.
- Continue until all the children have read their poem aloud.

Whiteboard tools
- Pen tray
- Highlighter pen
- Select tool
- Gallery

Religious education — Lesson 20

Visions of light

Learning objective
- To think about light and dark as symbols.

Resources
'Visions of light' Notebook file; calm music; candles.

Links to other subjects
PSHE
PoS (2e) Reflect on spiritual, moral, social and cultural issues, using imagination to understand other people's experiences.
- Encourage the children to listen to and respect each other's ideas.

Starter
Before the lesson begins, open the Notebook file, read the instructions on page 2 and then go to page 3. Turn off the lights and play the children some calm music. Gradually reveal the two questions on the screen by slowly pulling the Screen Shade down from the top of the page.
Give the children a few minutes to think carefully about each question.

Whole-class shared work
- Discuss the children's responses to the questions on page 3. Write their ideas on the board. Encourage them to think about the actual use of light as well as the feelings that light brings.
- Go to page 4. There is a picture on the page, hidden in darkness. Slowly reveal the picture by repeatedly pressing the box in the bottom right-hand corner. (The final image is revealed on page 10 of the Notebook file.)
- Explain to the children that when we are in the dark, we use lights to find our way around. Relate this to experiences of power cuts or camping at night.
- Tell the children that the words *light* and *dark* do not always refer to the presence or absence of a light source. Go to page 11 and discuss the phrase *to keep someone in the dark*. Ask: *Does this mean to put someone in a dark room?*
- Use the Delete button to delete the objects covering the other three words and phrases on page 11. Talk about what they mean. Lead the children to think about *light* and *dark* in terms of knowledge or truth.
- Drag the different proverbs out of the box at the bottom of the page and discuss their meanings. Are they literal sayings?
- Use the Highlighter pen to draw attention to the occurrences of the word *light*.
- Bring the children to the understanding that light can mean knowledge, truth and joy. Light is also used in many celebrations, such as Divali, Advent and Hanukkah, to represent happiness.

Independent work
- Ask the children to think carefully about the meanings of *light* and *dark*.
- Challenge them to write new proverbs and/or sentences that relate to light and dark. For example: *I feel full of light when I'm happy.*
- Focus less confident learners on the feelings that lightness and darkness can evoke.
- More confident learners may be able to think more about *light* and *dark* in terms of religion.

Plenary
- Invite volunteers to add their proverbs or sentences to page 12.
- End the lesson by lighting a few candles and turning off the lights. Play some calm music and invite volunteers to read out their sentences in turn.

Whiteboard tools
Move the Screen Shade to reveal the text on page 3.

- Pen tray
- Screen Shade
- Delete button
- Select tool
- Highlighter pen

HISTORY — LESSON 1   Name _____

Rich or poor?

■ This is part of an inventory taken in 1596.

In the Hall there.-In primis, three tables, foure fourmes, sixtene holbeardes, and one paire of tables, praised at iij^{li}. xii^{js}. iii^{jd}.

In the Parlor.-Itm, iij greene carpetts, ij greene clothe cheyres, one blacke wrought velvet cheyre laide wth silver and golde lace, iij long cussins of redde sattyn laide wth golde lace, preised at xj^{li}.

In the Warthrope.-Itm, one litle table wth a frame, one playne presse of elme, j iron-bound cheast, two playne cheasts, j cofer, ij paire of olde virginalls, preised at [torn]

In Sr Henrie Unton's Studie.-Itm, vij hanginges of gilded lether, one table there, shelves, wth many bookes of diverse sortes, to the number of ccxx, and one cheast, praised at xx^{li}.

In the Drawing Chamber.-Itm, one fielde bedstede wth a cover of yelowe sattyn layde wth silver lace, and five riche taffitie curtyns layde wth silver lace, one fetherbedde, j bolster, j paire of pillowes, j paire of blankettes, i yelowe rugge, j matterys of flockes preised at xl^{li}.

Glossary

bolster .... long pillow	gilded .... decorated with gold or silver
cheast .... chest	holbearde .... long shafted axe used as a weapon
cheyres .... chairs	In primis .... firstly
cofer .... coffer, chest	Itm .... item
curtyns .... curtains	matterys of flockes .... a mattress stuffed with wool
cussins .... cushions	
diverse .... different	playne .... plain
fetherbedde .... mattress stuffed with feathers	praised/preised at .... priced at
	presse of elme .... elm cupboard
fielde bedstede .... bed with curtains hanging from a central point	sattyn .... satin, an expensive shiny material
forme or fourme .... bench decorated with gold or silver	taffitie .... taffeta, a glossy silk fabric
	virginals .... keyboard instruments like pianos

Inventory extracts from The Unton inventories printed for the Berkshire Ashmolean Society in 1841.

HISTORY LESSON 4   Name _____

Streets past and present

- Which things would you only have seen a long time ago, and which things would you only see today? Draw an arrow to link each thing to the right column.

- Underline with a coloured pencil the things that you could have seen long ago and today. Would they have looked the same? How would they have been different?

A long time ago	Today
Cars	
Bicycles	
Horse and cart	
Railway station	
Burglar alarms	
Telephone boxes	
uPVC windows	
skateboards	
Traffic lights	
Blocks of flats	
Mobile phone masts	
Terraced houses	
Gas mantles	

GEOGRAPHY LESSON 6   Name _____

Virtual village

- Design your own village!
    - Create a map and give it a name and a key.
    - Remember to include a hill and a river.
    - Give your village a name.
    - Make a key, showing the symbols you have used and what they stand for.

- Find a partner. Ask them to describe a route through your village. What do they see on the way?

Name of village:

_____

Key

GEOGRAPHY ▸ LESSON 8   Name _____

Where on Earth is it?

■ Find out about these European countries. Record your information in the table below. If you have time, add more countries of your own choice.

Country	Capital	Language	Famous sight	Area in square km	Physical feature
Ireland					
United Kingdom					
France					
Spain					
Germany					
Italy					
Netherlands					
Switzerland					

DESIGN AND TECHNOLOGY LESSON 9   Name _____

What makes a strong bridge?

- Look at the bridges on the whiteboard.
- Draw the bridge you like best on the whiteboard screen. Use a ruler to draw the straight lines.
- Give your picture a heading saying what kind of bridge it is.
- Label the features that make the bridge strong.

My favourite bridge. It is a _____ bridge.

- Read about the bridge competition on the whiteboard. Imagine you are going to enter it.
- Draw what your bridge would look like. Remember, you will only have art straws to build your bridge.

My bridge design. It is a _____ bridge.

DESIGN AND TECHNOLOGY LESSON 10   Name _____

Designing a bridge

◾ What type of bridge will your group make?

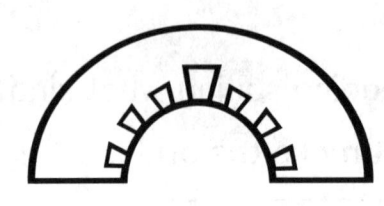

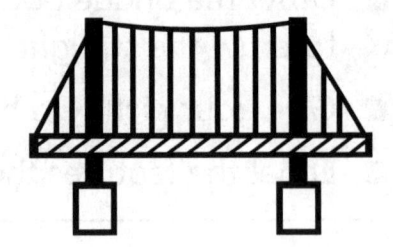

A beam bridge   An arch bridge   A suspension bridge

◾ Or something new?

Remember! You can use:
- 40 art straws
- A pair of scissors

You have £1.50 to spend in the shop on:
- Paper clips – 20p each
- Sticky tape – 20p for 2cm strip
- Sticky tack – 25p for 1cm square
- String – 25p for 30cm

◾ Draw your group's design here:

◾ The people in my group are: _____

ART AND DESIGN LESSON 13   Name _____

Take a seat

- Use this sheet to help you design a chair.
- What purpose (or use) is your chair going to have?

My chair is designed for: _____

- What special features does your chair have?

The special features of my chair are: _____

_____

_____

- Draw a picture of your chair:

Side view	Front view
Back view	Plan view

ART AND DESIGN ▬ LESSON 15   Name _____

Making mosaics

- Use the grid to help you make your own mosaic.
- Think about the colours you want to use. Cut the tiles from coloured paper or pages from magazines.

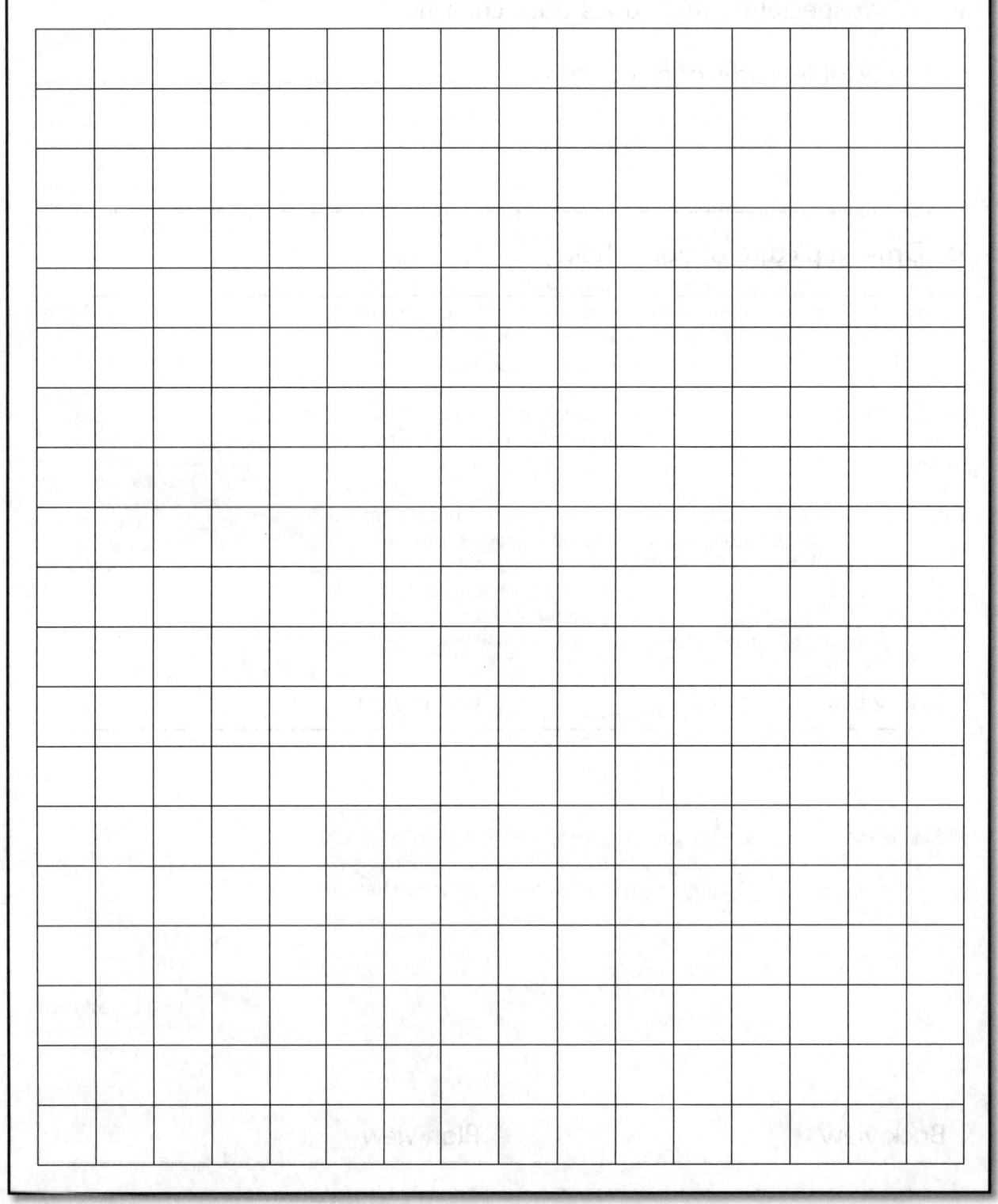

Illustrations © Jim Peacock / Beehive Illustration

RELIGIOUS EDUCATION LESSON 19   Name _____

What is God?

- Many religions have different names for God. The different names reflect the many aspects of God. Here are some examples:

Judaism
Jehovah-Jireh (The Lord our Provider)
Jehovah-Ropheka (The Lord our Healer)
Jehovah-Shalom (The Lord our Peace)

Christianity
The rock
The shepherd
The creator

Islam
Al-Ghafur (The All-Forgiving)
Al-Wadud (The Loving)
Al-Hakeem (The Wise)

- What do these names tell you about God? _____
  _____

- What names would you give God? _____
  _____

- On the back of this sheet, draw or write down a few notes about what you think God is like, what God means to you, and where you think God can be found. Use the notes to write a poem entitled 'What is God?'

Whiteboard diary

Teacher's name: _____

Date	Subject/Objective	How was the whiteboard used?	Evaluation

Whiteboard resources library

Teacher's name: _____

Name of resource and file location	Description of resource	How resource was used	Date resource was used

SMART BOARD™

Using your SMART Board™ interactive whiteboard

This brief guide to using your SMART Board interactive whiteboard and Notebook software is based on the training manual *SMART Board Interactive Whiteboard Masters Learner Workbook* © SMART Technologies Inc.

Your finger is your mouse

You can control applications on your computer from the interactive whiteboard. A press with your finger on a SMART Board interactive whiteboard is the same as a click with your mouse. To open an application on your computer through the interactive whiteboard, double-press the icon with your finger in the same way that you would use a mouse to double-click on your desktop computer.

The SMART Pen tray

The SMART Pen tray consists of four colour-coded slots for Pens (black, red, green and blue) and one slot for the Eraser. Each slot has a sensor to identify when the Pens or the Eraser have been picked up. You can write with the Pens, or with your finger, as long as the pen slot is empty. Likewise, if you remove the Eraser from the slot you can use either it or your hand to erase your digital ink.

The Pen tray has at least two buttons. One button is used to launch the On-screen Keyboard and the second button is used to make your next touch on the interactive whiteboard a right-click. Some interactive whiteboards have a third button, which is used to access the Help Centre quickly.

The On-screen Keyboard

The On-screen Keyboard allows you to type or edit text in any application without leaving the interactive whiteboard. It can be accessed either by pressing the appropriate button in the Pen tray, or through the SMART Board tools menu (see page 173).

A dropdown menu allows you to select which keyboard you would like to use. The default Classic setting is a standard 'qwerty' keyboard. Select the Simple setting to arrange the keyboard in alphabetical order, as a useful facility for supporting younger or less confident learners. A Number pad is also available through the On-screen Keyboard.

The Fonts toolbar appears while you are typing or after you double-press a text object. Use it to format properties such as font size and colour.

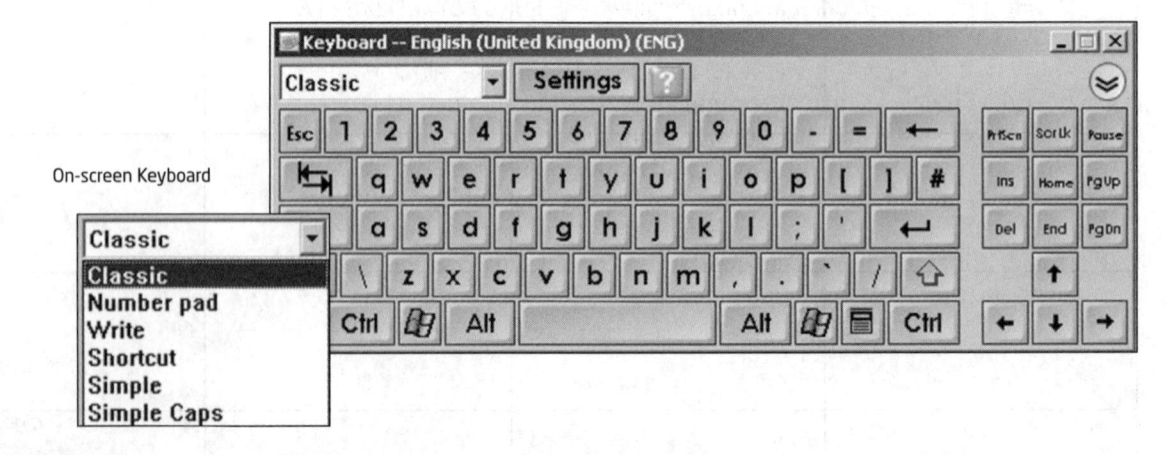

On-screen Keyboard

SMART BOARD™

Floating tools toolbar

The Transparency layer

When you remove a Pen from the Pen tray, a border appears around your desktop and the Floating tools toolbar launches. The border indicates that the 'transparency layer' is in place and you can write on the desktop just as you would write on a transparent sheet, annotating websites, or any images you display. The transparency layer remains in place until all the Pens and the Eraser have been returned to the Pen tray. Your first touch of the board thereafter will remove the border and any notes or drawings you have made.

Ink Aware applications

When software is Ink Aware, you can write and draw directly into the active file. For example, if you write or draw something while using Microsoft Word, you can save your Word file and your notes will be visible the next time you open it. Ink Aware software includes the Microsoft applications Word, Excel, PowerPoint; graphic applications such as Microsoft Paint and Imaging; and other applications such as Adobe Acrobat. Ensure that the SMART Aware toolbar is activated by selecting View, then toolbars, and checking that the SMART Aware toolbar option is ticked.

Aware tools

When you are using Microsoft Word or Excel, you will now notice three new buttons that will be either integrated into your current toolbar (as shown on the left), or separated as a floating toolbar. Press the first button to insert your drawing or writing as an image directly into your document or spreadsheet. The second button converts writing to typed text and insert it directly into your document or spreadsheet. Press the third button to save a screen capture in Notebook software.

SlideShow toolbar

When you are using Microsoft PowerPoint on an interactive whiteboard, the SlideShow toolbar appears automatically. Use the left- and right-hand buttons on the SlideShow toolbar to navigate your presentation. Press the centre button to launch the Command menu for additional options, including access to the SMART Floating tools (see page 175), and the facility to save notes directly into your presentation.

SMART Board tools

The SMART Board tools include functions that help you to operate the interactive whiteboard more effectively. Press the SMART Board icon at the bottom right of your screen to access the menu.

- SMART Recorder: Use this facility to make a video file of anything you do on the interactive whiteboard. You can then play the recording on any computer with SMART Video player or Windows® Media Player.
- Floating tools: The features you use most are included in the Floating toolbar. It can also be customised to incorporate any tools. Press the More button at the bottom-right of the toolbar and select Customise Floating Tools from the menu. Select a tool from the Available Tools menu and press Add to include it.
- Start Centre: This convenient toolbar gives you access to the most commonly used SMART Board interactive whiteboard tools.
- Control Panel: Use the Control Panel to configure a variety of software and hardware options for your SMART Board and software.

See page 175 for a visual guide to the SMART Board tools.

NOTEBOOK™ SOFTWARE

Using SMART Notebook™ software

Notebook software is SMART's whiteboard software. It can be used as a paper notebook to capture notes and drawings, and also enables you to insert multimedia elements like images and interactive resources.

Side tabs
There are three tabs on the right-hand side of the Notebook interface:

Page Sorter: The Page Sorter tab allows you to see a thumbnail image of each page in your Notebook file. The active page is indicated by a dropdown menu and a blue border around the thumbnail image. Select the dropdown menu for options including Delete page, Insert blank page, Clone page and Rename page. To change the page order, select a thumbnail and drag it to a new location within the order.

Gallery: The Gallery contains thousands of resources to help you quickly develop and deliver lessons in rich detail. Objects from the Gallery can be useful visual prompts; for example, searching for 'people' in an English lesson will bring up images that could help build pupils' ideas for verbs and so on. Objects you have created yourself can also be saved into the Gallery for future use, by dragging them into the My Content folder.

The Search facility in the Gallery usually recognises words in their singular, rather than plural, form. Type 'interactive' or 'flash' into the Gallery to bring up a bank of interactive resources for use across a variety of subjects including mathematics, science, music and design and technology.

Attachments: The Attachments tab allows you to link to supporting documents and webpages directly from your Notebook file. To insert a file, press the Insert button at the bottom of the tab and browse to the file location, or enter the internet address.

Objects in Notebook software
Anything you select inside the work area of a Notebook page is an object. This includes text, drawing or writing, shapes created with the drawing tools, or content from the Gallery, your computer, or the internet.

Manipulating objects: To resize an object, select it and drag the white handle (i). Use the green handle (ii) to rotate an object. To adjust the properties of a selected object, use the dropdown menu.
- Locking: This sub-menu includes options to 'Lock in place', which means that the object cannot be moved or altered in any way. Alternatively you can choose to 'Allow Move' or 'Allow Move and Rotate', which mean that your object cannot be resized.
- Grouping: Select two or more objects by pressing and dragging your finger diagonally so that the objects are surrounded by a selection box. Press the dropdown menu and choose Grouping > Group. If you want to separate the objects, choose Grouping > Ungroup.
- Order: Change the order in which objects are layered by selecting 'Bring forward' or 'Send backward' using this option.
- Infinite Cloner: Select 'Infinite Cloner' to reproduce an object an unlimited number of times.
- Properties: Use this option to change the colour, line properties and transparency of an object.
- Handwriting recognition: If you have written something with a Pen tool, you can convert it to text by selecting it and choosing the Recognise option from the dropdown menu.

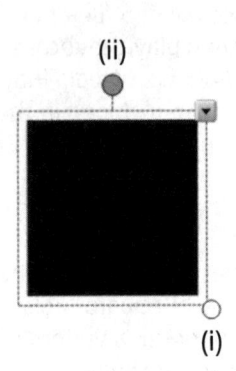

TOOLS GLOSSARY

Tools glossary

Notebook tools
Hints and tips
- Move the toolbar to the bottom of the screen to make it more accessible for children.
- Gradually reveal information to your class with the Screen Shade.
- Press the Full screen button to view everything on an extended Notebook page.
- Use the Capture tool to take a screenshot of work in progress, or completed work, to another page and print this out.
- Type directly into a shape created with the Shapes tool by double-pressing it and using the On-screen Keyboard.

Icon	Tool	Icon	Tool
	Pen tray		Lines tool
	Next page		Shapes tool
	Previous page		Text tool
	Blank Page button		Fill Colour tool
	Open		Transparency tool
	Save		Line properties
	Paste		Move toolbar to the top
	Undo button		
	Redo button		Capture tool
	Delete button		Area Capture tool
	Screen Shade		Area Capture 2
	Full screen		Area Capture 3
	Select tool		Area Capture (freehand) tool
	Pen tool		
	Highlighter pen		Page Sorter
	Creative pen		Gallery
	Eraser tool		Attachments

SMART Board tools
Hints and tips
- Use the SMART recorder to capture workings and methods, and play them back to the class for discussion in the Plenary.
- Adjust the shape and transparency of the Spotlight tool when focusing on elements of an image.
- Customise the Floating tools to incorporate any tools that you regularly use. Press the More button at the bottom right of the toolbar and select Customise Floating Tools from the menu.

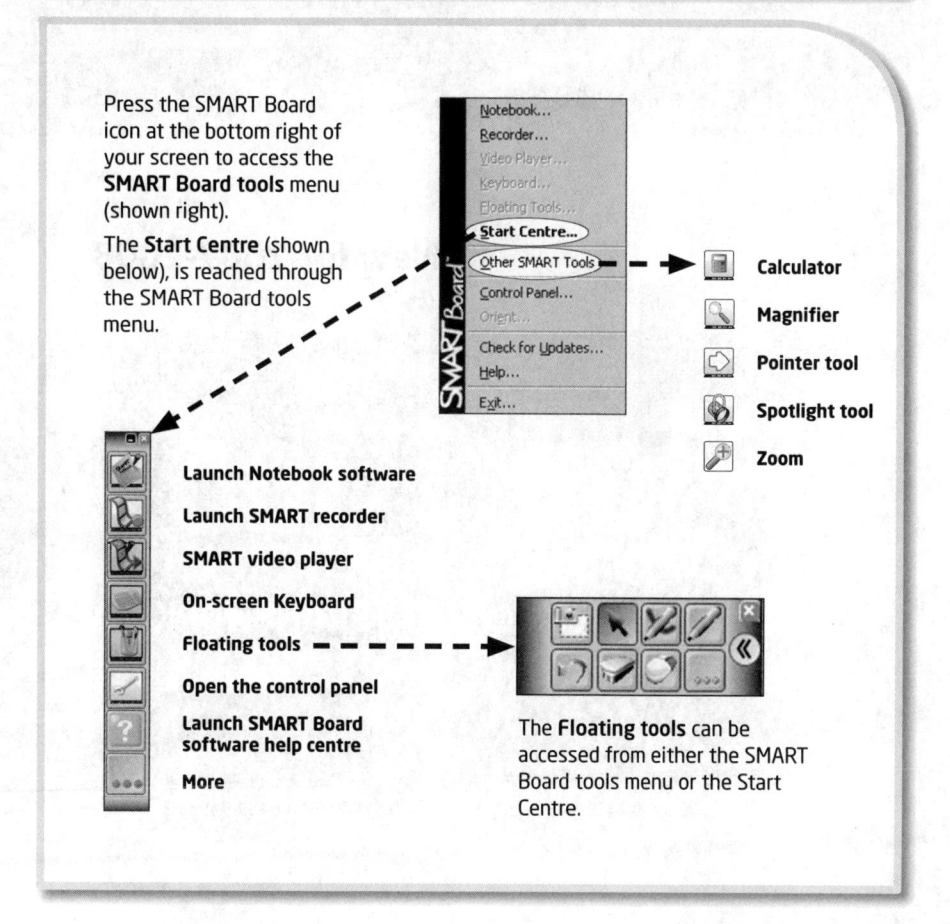

Press the SMART Board icon at the bottom right of your screen to access the **SMART Board tools** menu (shown right).

The **Start Centre** (shown below), is reached through the SMART Board tools menu.

- Launch Notebook software
- Launch SMART recorder
- SMART video player
- On-screen Keyboard
- Floating tools
- Open the control panel
- Launch SMART Board software help centre
- More

- Calculator
- Magnifier
- Pointer tool
- Spotlight tool
- Zoom

The **Floating tools** can be accessed from either the SMART Board tools menu or the Start Centre.

175

100 SMART Board™ LESSONS • YEAR 4

SCHOLASTIC

Also available in this series:

ISBN 978-0439-94536-3 — Year R

ISBN 978-0439-94537-0 — Year 1

ISBN 978-0439-94538-7 — Year 2

ISBN 978-0439-94539-4 — Year 3

ISBN 978-0439-94540-0 — Year 4

ISBN 978-0439-94541-7 — Year 5

ISBN 978-0439-94542-4 — Year 6

New for 2007-2008

ISBN 978-0439-94546-2

ISBN 978-0439-94523-3

ISBN 978-0439-94508-0

To find out more, call: 0845 603 9091
or visit our website www.scholastic.co.uk